SNAKES
A Natural History

SNAKES
A Natural History

Edited by
Roland Bauchot

Sterling Publishing Co., Inc. New York

UNDER THE DIRECTION OF
Roland Bauchot
&
Hervé Chaumeton
EDITORIAL & PICTURE RESEARCH:
S. Castaing, T. Curren
Assisted by:
L. Borot
Drawings by A. Guillemain & J. Theillard
Translated from the French by Catherine Berthier
English translation edited by Keith L. Schiffman

Acknowledgments
The authors and the editorial team would like to thank
the following for their gracious collaboration and their advice:
Jean-Pierre Baron, Rudy Fourmy, Latoxan Laboratory

The Library of Congress has cataloged the trade edition of this book as follows:

Serpents. English.
    Snakes : a natural history / Roland Bauchot, ed.
      p.   cm.
    Includes bibliographical references and index.
    ISBN 0-8069-0654-5
    1. Snakes. I. Bauchot, Roland. II. Title.
QL666.06S392513   1994
597.96—dc20   93-43892
                          CIP

Jacket: A newborn tree boa (*Corallus enydris*)
Page 1: *Bothrops bilineata*, comes from northern South America (Guyana, northern Brazil, Venezuela)
Page 2: This black-and-white cobra (*Naja melanoleuca*) rises in a typical defensive position.
Page 3: Scales of a young emerald tree boa (*Corallus caninus*)
Page 5: The fer-de-lance (*Bothrops lanceolatus*) is the only venomous snake in Martinique, where it is greatly feared. Mongooses were even introduced to the island to prey on it, without much success. The individual pictured is remarkable for its color, which is different from the color usual for this species—grey with two black marks on each side of the head.
Page 7: Slough of a colubrid
Page 8: An Indian snake charmer (from the Madras region) and a cobra (*Naja haje*). In this tourist play, the flute only charms the audience, since the snake is deaf. The snake is defanged. The charmer gestures with his hand to make the snake lunge.
Page 11: *Leptophis ahaetulla*, a tree snake from Guyana
Pages 12–13: Face-off between a suricate (*Suricata suricata*) and a Kalahari cobra (*Botswana*). Viveridae (of which suricates and mongooses are part) defend themselves well against snakes. The cobra, in an intimidation posture, risks losing the battle.
Pages 48–49: Jameson's green mamba (*Dendroaspis jamesoni*) is a diurnal tree snake from Africa (southeastern Cameroon), where it has a rather bad reputation. Males can be aggressive during mating season.
Pages 122–123: This rattlesnake from the northern Pacific (*Crotalus viridis oreganus*), a subspecies of Crotalus viridis, lives in the U.S., from northern California to Oregon. Disturbed while it basked on rocks, here it assumes a classic defensive posture, shaking its rattle, all senses alert.
Pages 182–183: The Indian python (*Python molurus*) which ranges from India into Thailand, is a large snake that can reach 23 ft. (7 m) long. It is protected by the Washington Convention.

10 9 8 7 6 5 4 3 2 1

First paperback edition published in 1997 by
Sterling Publishing Company, Inc.
387 Park Avenue South, New York, N.Y. 10016
Originally published 1994 by Bordas, Paris, under the title *Les Serpents*
Created and © 1994 by A.T.P., ZA Les Vignettes, Chamalières, 63400, France
English translation © 1994 by Sterling Publishing Co., Inc.
Distributed in Canada by Sterling Publishing
%o Canadian Manda Group, One Atlantic Avenue, Suite 105
Toronto, Ontario, Canada M6K 3E7
Distributed in Great Britain and Europe by Cassell PLC
Wellington House, 125 Strand, London WC2R 0BB, England
Distributed in Australia By Capricorn Link (Australia) Pty Ltd.
P.O. Box 6651, Baulkham Hills, Business Centre, NSW 2153, Australia
Printed and bound in Spain
All rights reserved

Sterling ISBN 0-8069-0653-7

THE AUTHORS

Roland Bauchot
Former student of the Ecole Normale Supérieure, agrégé of the University, professor emeritus, Université Paris 7

Cassian Bon
Doctor of Science, research director of the National Center for Scientific Research, head of the laboratory at the Institut Pasteur

Patrick David
Member of the Herpetological Society of France

Patricia Fourcade
Ethnologist, Doctor of Social Anthropology and Comparative Sociology at Université Paris 5, freelancer at the laboratory of ethnobiology-biogeography of the National Museum of Natural History

Jean-Pierre Gasc
Doctor of Science, under-director of the National Museum of Natural History, vice president of the Societas Europaea Herpetologica

Laurence Gravier
Veterinarian

Daniel Heuclin
Wildlife photographer, member of the Herpetological Society of France

Jean Lescure
President of the Herpetological Society of France, researcher at the National Center for Scientific Research

Gilbert Matz
Professor of Biology at the University of Angers

Guy Naulleau
Researcher at the National Center for Scientific Research

Roland Platel
Doctor of Science, Conference Director at Université Paris 7

Jean-Claude Rage
Director of Research at the National Center for Scientific Research

Hubert Saint-Girons
Director of Research at the National Center for Scientific Research

Marie-Charlotte Saint-Girons
Former Director of Research at the National Center for Scientific Research

Yannick Vasse
D.E.A. in Zoology at Université Paris 7

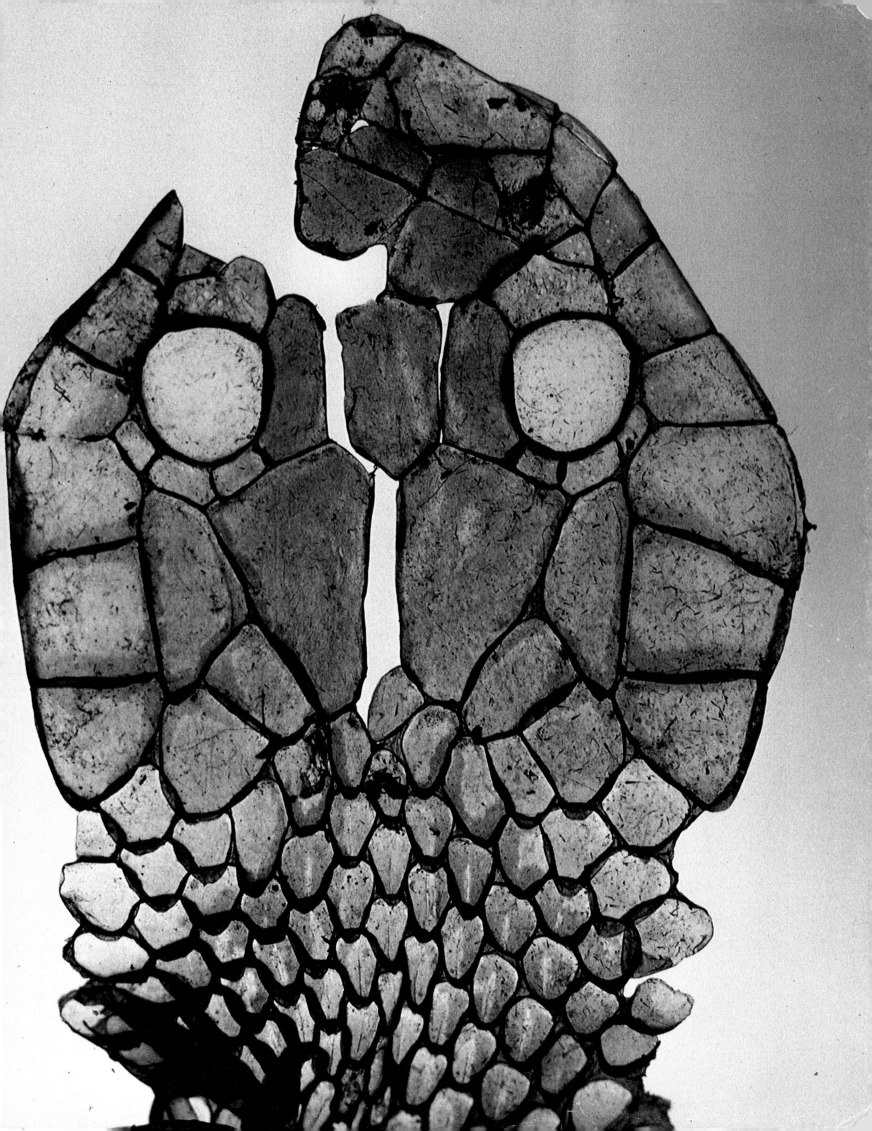

CONTENTS

FOREWORD

The snake: For most of us, it is a cold animal with slimy skin that slides towards its victim and injects it with its mortal poison with lightning speed. Does any name in the animal world give rise to so many legends and fears, so much repulsion, terror, or mortal fascination?

Beyond these images—which are common to so many civilizations—the 2700 or so present-day snake species constitute a homogeneous and yet diversified group within the reptile class. They are homogeneous by their anatomical peculiarities (lack of limbs and eyelids, forked tongues, etc.). However, even at first glance, there are many commonalities between a 35-ft. (10 m) reticulated python living in rain forests, and a 10-in. (25 cm) long colubrid living in Mexican deserts, or between the huge Gaboon viper, found in the rain forests, and the frail Orsini's viper, with its European habitat of steppes and prairies.

During their long evolution, snakes have lived under most climates, except polar and subpolar, and every biotope, from sandy deserts to flooded forests and mountain streams. These animals constitute an important link in the ecological chain.

This book presents contemporary knowledge of these vertebrates in a clear, precise, and accessible manner. It is divided into seventeen richly illustrated chapters, each written by one or more specialists discussing snakes' origins, classification, diversity, morphology and biology. The various relationships between man and snake are also discussed.

Although snakes do cause serious injuries throughout the world, man is their greatest enemy. Snakes are victimized by direct destruction and by the eradication of their biotopes through deforestation and overdevelopment. They also suffer, albeit more subtly, from a bad image, which is kept alive by publicity-hungry "explorers." On the other hand, snakes have become "pets," and the animal trade takes a heavy toll.

We hope that snakes will become better known thanks to this book. Despite numerous and pointed studies, many aspects of their biology remain mysterious—what subjects for future zoologists to explore! But above all, we hope to contribute to these maligned but fascinating animals' rehabilitation—and thus to their protection.

SNAKES IN THE ANIMAL KINGDOM

A PORTRAIT OF SNAKES

Roland Bauchot

The general public only sees snakes as cold-blooded, footless, and often poisonous animals, but those who know them are fascinated by their diversity and peculiarities. Snakes, or Ophidians, are reptiles whose main characteristics include a considerably elongated body and the absence of any limbs. These so-called "cold-blooded" animals differ from apodal lizards, like the blind worm; lizards have movable eyelids, snakes' eyelids are fused and transparent. Body length greatly influences shape, and sometimes the quantity of most viscera, and the absence of limbs, has led to a certain uniformity of the numerous vertebrae and ribs along the entire body. Snakes are predators, and thus have a zoophagous diet. A number of families have a venom apparatus.

SNAKE SKIN

Contrary to popular belief, snake skin is not clammy, but smooth, due to the configuration of the corneal scales that cover it.

The epidermis is composed of a superficial layer or cuticle, which is often covered with spikes or microscopic crests that diffract the light, giving snakes some of their coloration. Four layers of cells are superimposed: at the surface, a keratin-rich layer that is eliminated with each molting (see p. 18), a thick and more flexible corneal layer, an intermediary zone, and the deeper basal layer.

The dermis is composed of a collagen-rich, irrigated and nerve-laden conjunctive tissue, where most of the pigmentation cells are found.

As in other vertebrates, the hypodermis can store fat, particularly in the caudal area, but these fatty stocks are often found in the tissues of the abdominal area. The unattached posterior edge of one scale generally covers the next. Scutellum, large and heavy scales with contiguous sides, are found only on the back of the head and neck. Certain Ophidian families (Scolecophidia, Acrochordidae, and many marine Elapidae) are like lizards, in that they have many small ventral scales per segment (vertebrae), whereas more "evolved" families have only one scale per segment.

In each species, some scales have a lighter-colored center, which is due to a thinning of the cuticle and indicates the presence of a sensory organ. Spines and apical pits differ by their size; there can be tens of the former on a single scale, while the latter are larger and rarely exceed twelve per scale. Species can be identified by the differences in the arrangement, number and shape of scales, ornamentation, or the number of sensory organs. One can easily tell the difference between a Western European colubrid, its head covered with large scutella, and a viper of the same region, with its many scales (see Illus. 1).

Unlike most other reptiles, snakes have no osteoderms, dermal ossifications by which scales are implanted into the underlying dermis. The fossorial Scolecophidians have a large and thickened scale by their mouth, and *Ahaetulla* (arboreal colubrids) have scaly appendages. Another specialized tegumentary formation is the rattle, which is found on the tail of some members of the *Crotalus* family. This organ is composed of trilobal corneal segments which fit together loosely and make a rattlelike sound when the animal shakes it. Male *Anilius scytale* have small corneal tips which cover their vestigial femurs. This kind of sexual dimorphism is rare in snakes.

Other examples include the male in the Latin American harlequin snake (*Chironius carinatus*), which has ridged scales, as opposed to the smooth

▽ *ILLUS. 1: Arrangement of scales on the head of a colubrid, and on the head of a viper. While the viper has only small uniform scales on the top of its head, the colubrid has large overlapping scales in the same place. The most characteristic of these scales are named below.*

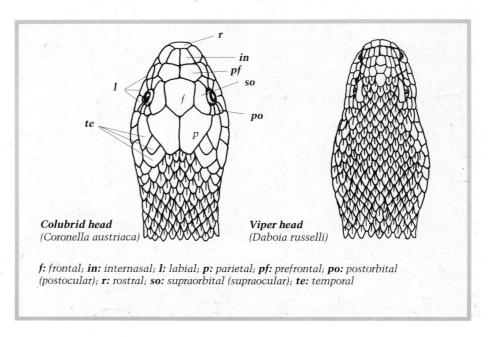

Colubrid head
(*Coronella austriaca*)

Viper head
(*Daboia russelli*)

*f: frontal; **in**: internasal; **l**: labial; **p**: parietal; **pf**: prefrontal; **po**: postorbital (postocular); **r**: rostral; **so**: supraorbital (supraocular); **te**: temporal*

scales of the female. Male long-nosed Madagascar snakes (*Langaha*), have flexible, thin and triangular snouts, while those of the females are large and foliaceous.

The skin has numerous bare nervous fibres which penetrate the epidermis and go either to the spines or pits beneath the corneal layer. Only the latter are composed of nonkeratinized epidermic cells which are unaffected by molting; they are generally found only in the anterior half of the body. In Acrochordidae they are found between disjointed scales and are covered with many short "hairs." Arboreal species have few spines, while pits are more commonly found in burrowing snakes.

Although these sensory organs' functions and sensitivity are not well known, it is believed that spines are tactile organs while apical pits are heat detectors.

Snake pigmentation is the result of the interaction of pigment-charged cells in the dermis, the chromatophores, and of the colors obtained through the corneal layer's light refraction (see the table on pages 16–17).

Depending on the species, various types of chromatophores are found, giving the following general colors:

—melanophors (pigment: melanin): brown shades;
—melanophors + guanophors (pigment: guanin): grey shades;
—melanophors + guanophors + lipophors: yellow-green shades;
—melanophors + guanophors + allophors: pale red shades.

Again, sexual dimorphism is not very pronounced. The female common viper (*Vipera berus*) is a reddish color, while the male is grey, with more pronounced designs. A melanic female viper never gives birth to black young; they acquire their definitive color as they grow. In some species, the young are a different color from the adults. In the American snake, *Coluber constrictor*, the young are grey with brown dorsal markings, while the adults are uniformly black, cobalt blue, and brown. The mussurana (*Clelia clelia*), which is black as an adult, has a red body and a black head in its youth. Young *Tropidolaemus wagleri* are bright green with a few transverse red bands on their backs, while adults are mottled in black, green, and yellow. In the ladder snake (*Elaphe scalaris*), so named because of its designs, the transverse "steps" of the ladder fade with age and often all that is left on adults are two lateral lines on a light background.

Reptile skin, like that of birds, is poor in glands and these glands are holocrine; the glandular cell is expelled along with the substance it has secreted, just as in the sebaceous glands of mammals. These glands are not vascularized. Members of the Typhlopidae family (blind snakes) have glandular thickenings under the scales' covered areas, while the colubrids' nuchal glands may secret an irritating liquid, thus playing a defensive role.

The anal glands, or "anal sacks," which are larger in females than in males, appear to play a role in sexual relations, and they are, alone, common to all species. Snakes lack sudoriferous glands and defend themselves against overheating in high temperatures with appropriate behavior (see the chapter on physiology). Salt glands are located in the marine snakes' (Hydrophiinae's) nasal cavity, allowing them to eliminate the sea salts they ingest with their prey.

A RESTRICTED SKELETON

The absence of limbs restricts snakes' skeletons to a cranium, a spine, and ribs. There is no sternum, and the belts of the primitive snakes (Typhlophidae, Leptophidae, Aniliidae, Loxocemidae, Boidae, and Tropidophiidae) are composed of a vestigial pelvis and femurs.

▶ The body's framework: ribs & vertebrae

The zygapophysis of snakes' ribs allows neither vertical movements nor twisting of the spine; however, the very large number of ribs (100 in vipers, over 300 in most colubrids, over 400 in the great pythons, and close to 600 in certain fossils) let the body twist with great flexibility (see the chapter on locomotion). Ventral extensions (hypapo-

▷ RIGHT: *Juvenile mussurana* (Clelia clelia). *This powerful colubrid, which sometimes measures over 7 ft. (2 m), eats rattlesnakes and lives in southern Mexico and Amazonia. Red and black as a juvenile, it turns shiny blue-black as an adult.*

▽ BELOW, LEFT AND RIGHT: *Emerald tree boa* (Corallus canina). *This attractive arboreal boa from South America loses its coral, brick-red, or brown color as a juvenile, before acquiring, as a subadult, a green color, marked with white or yellow.*

PIGMENTS

Roland Bauchot–Yannick Vasse

THE MOST COMMON pigment cells are the melanophores, which contain the brown pigment melanin. Their diverticles branch out to the basal cells of the epidermis. Melanocytes are smaller cells, found in the epidermis, and they also contain melanin. These are the cells responsible for snakes' dark coloring (African house snake, *Lamprophis fulginosis*, the black arboreal snake, *Thrasops jacksoni*, and the gopher snake, *Drymarchon corais couperi*). These cells are also dominant in melanic individuals—all-black specimens of usually lighter species.

Entire melanic populations have sometimes been observed: in the French Jura, at an altitude of 2600 to 3000 ft. (800 to 900 m), 65% of the peliad vipers are melanic. This is believed to be a permanent adaptation, allowing for a better capture of infrared rays in a cold region.

Paler colorations, as well as occasional albino cases, usually described in pythons, are probably the result of an absence of melanin. These indi-

viduals die prematurely in nature. They seem to be more exposed to predators, who see them more easily, and these albinos are generally more fragile.

Albino individuals can be found in captivity (*Elaphe guttata* and *Lampropeltis getulus*, for example).

Red (stripes on coral snakes, both real and false) and yellow tones (*Cerastes*) are due to, respectively, allophore- and lipophore-type cells, which give brown tones when combined with other types of cells (Boidae).

Green and blue pigments do not exist in snakes, but many arboreal species are bright green (some *Ahaetulla*, *Oxybelis*, and *Morelia viridis* species). These colors are due to guanophores, also called iridocytes, colored cells found in the superficial part of the dermis and containing guanin, a semicrystalline substance.

These particles are excellent light reflectors; light is refracted by being divided at the surface of the guanine crystals, through which it moves at a different speed. Light rays are separated by wavelength. By combining with the cells containing melanin, guanophores pro-

△ ABOVE: *The Asian coral snake* (Maticora bivirgata), *is a deep black color, accented by white stripes and a red-brown color.*

▽ BELOW: *An arboreal tree snake from Guyana* (Leptophis ahaetulla), *has a tapered head and a thin body; it is green and yellow.*

△ ABOVE: *This fer-de-lance (*Bothrops lanceolatus*) from Martinique is about 5 ft. (1.5 m) long, and of a uniformly yellow color.*

▽ BELOW: *Rainbow boa (*Epicrates cenchria*) from the Amazon, with magnificent blue color. Its speckled coloration is especially bright as it prepares to shed its skin.*

duce blue, which, in association with the yellow of lipophores, gives rise to green. Guanophores are also responsible for many snakes' iridescence, i.e., the rainbow snake (*Xenopeltis unicolor*), a burrower, by the fracturing of light into the colors of the rainbow. This aspect is the result of the snake's particularly smooth texture, which facilitates burrowing (see the chapter on locomotion).

SHEDDING

Roland Bauchot–Yannick Vasse

SNAKES APPEAR to "change skin" more or less regularly. In fact, they are getting rid of their dead corneal cells. Whereas mammals shed more discretely and permanently, and while lizards lose their old skin in big pieces, snakes' superficial cells are renewed synchronically.

The snake generally does not eat for two weeks before molting. The eye becomes milky, as the scale becomes opaque. The intermediary epidermal zone is full of blood vessels and is separated from the superficial epidermal zone by the introduction of air, while the deeper epidermis becomes more keratinized (see Illus. 2). The molt starts to come off around the mouth. The snake frees its head first and twists out of the sheath by rubbing on the substratum—ground, rocks, branches, whatever the case, to help turn the slough inside out, like the sleeve of a piece of clothing that is taken off by reversing it. This operation takes one to five hours in a healthy asp viper (*Vipera aspis*).

The slough (the old skin) is abandoned by the snake, whose colors now appear brighter. The shed skin is often found on a bush or rock. It is like a mould, showing the scales in relief, and allowing for the identification of the species. The shedding process is the same for all snakes, but its frequency varies according to different species: rattlesnakes shed one to three times a year, asp vipers two to three times, and pythons more often. There is a hypophyseal and thyroidian hyperactivity during molting, but this is not yet understood. The frequency also depends on the snake's age: a young rattlesnake molts approximately seven times a year (the first molt being right after birth), and the intervals between molts grow longer during growth.

△ ABOVE:
Slough of the Montpellier snake (Malpolon monspessulanus). The scales are plainly visible, allowing for proper identification of the species.

◁ LEFT: *A fer-de-lance in the process of shedding. The old skin is quite visible here, gives way to a more brilliant color. The whitish look of the old skin is due to the interposition of a layer of air.*

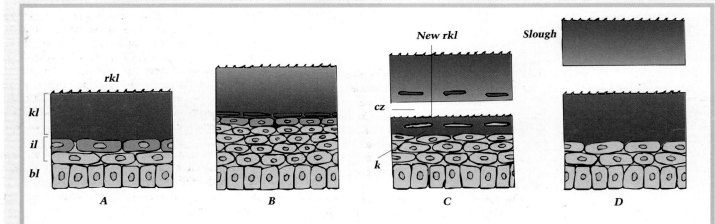

ILLUS. 2. Molting: the four stages: A) rest, B) organization of the future tegument, C) separation of the layer to be molted by interposition of air, and D) rejection of the slough. **rkl:** refractive keratinized layer; **kl:** keratin layer; **il:** intermediary layer in the process of keratinizing; **bl:** basal layer; **cz:** cleavage zone; **k:** keratin.

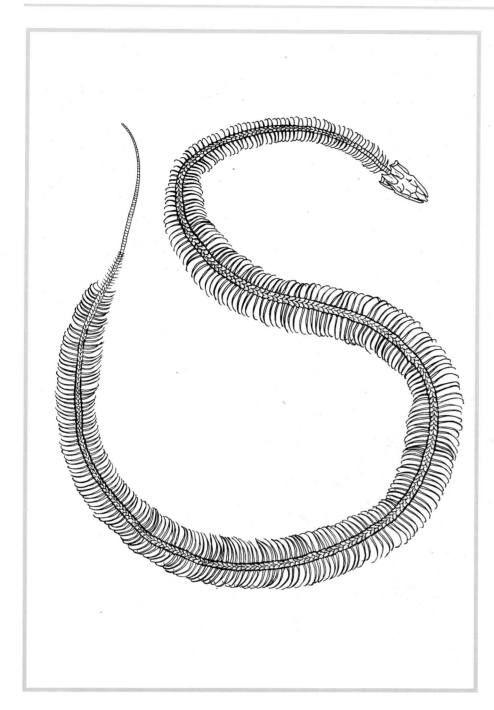

△ ILLUS. 3, ABOVE: Python skeleton. Notice the large number of vertebrae (around 400), and ribs (close to 300), as well as the lack of a pelvic or pectoral belt.

physes), which are found towards the trunk's anterior area, or along all of it in some families, can also be completely absent. These extensions are called hemapophyses when they're near the tail. They form a discontinuous canal, and hold the blood vessels that irrigate this part of the body.

In certain rattlesnakes (*Crotalus* and *Sistrurus*) the last caudal vertebrae are fused and support the rattle.

The ribs are usually sturdy and heavily ossified and are articulated onto the vertebrae by a two-faceted articulation. The lack of a sternum allows for the ingestion of large prey.

▶ *An articulated cranium*

Snakes have a diapsid skull, where two openings,

the temporal windows, lighten the cranium's posterodorsal area (as can be easily seen on a crocodile skull).

In lizards, the lower opening enlarges with the disappearance of the lower temporal bone, whereas in snakes the temporal bone separating the two windows also opens. Another characteristic in many snakes is the great mobility of their jaws (often referred to as cranial kinesis). This region is quite stiff, which allows it to withstand the pressure on the base of the skull when large prey is ingested. In most snakes, the upper jaw is quite loosely attached to the skull and can stretch far enough to jut out beyond its base. The upper skull's jawbones are independent of the quadrate bone (on which the mandible is articulated), ensuring a large oral opening by pivoting to a vertical position, if necessary.

The mandible's suspension mode, the quadrate bone's mobility, and the jaws' positioning with respect to the skull account for a snake's capacity to swallow prey that's larger in diameter than the snake. Scolecophidians, which are burrowers and feed on small prey, are the only snakes whose upper jaw is fused to the rest of the skull, and whose mandibles are linked by a cartilaginous symphysis.

OPHIDIAN MUSCULATURE

Snakes' musculature is relatively uniform due to the absence of limbs. The neck, trunk, and tail are barely distinguishable from each other. Parietal muscles are spread over a large number of vertebrae and joined to the ribs or to the internal muscles' tendons; this deep musculature is covered with superficial muscles—intercostal (between the ribs) and costocutaneous (between the ribs and skin)—and then with a particularly well-developed skin musculature, allowing for mobility of the scales.

THE NERVOUS SYSTEM

The snake's central nervous system is organized much along the same lines as that of other reptiles. The brain has two large cerebral hemispheres, voluminous accessory olfactory bulbs (the center of vomeronasal activity, which is specific to snakes), and a cerebellum, which varies in size according to species and life-style. The very lengthy spinal cord is found in the vertebral canal and can operate a number of motor functions on its own.

Snakes' sensory equipment is particularly specialized. Perceptive senses such as the vomeronasal sense or that of thermic detection have been developed (see the chapter on the nervous system and sensory organs).

CIRCULATORY SYSTEM ADAPTATIONS TO A SPECIFIC MORPHOLOGY

The snake's circulatory system differs little from

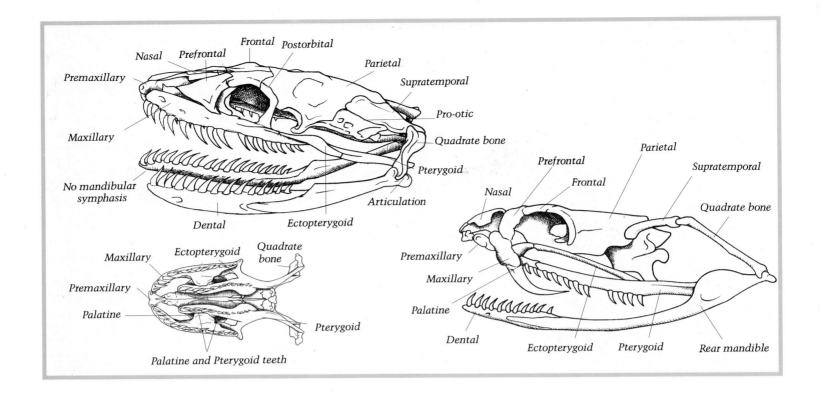

that of other reptiles, and when it does, the difference is mostly due to body length. Reptile hearts have a single ventricle, except for crocodiles, who have two. Snakes' hearts are generally found farther back in the body than those of other reptiles, and their hearts are elongated and asymmetrical. The right auricle is larger than the left and the single ventricle's left wall is thicker than the right wall. The thymus and thyroid are also relatively far back in the body. Cardiac frequencies vary by species and by temperature, ranging from 20 to 70 beats per minute.

Bodily elongation results in a distinct separation between the aortic and carotid arcs and by the presence of large common carotid arteries (two in most snakes, one in colubrids). Visceral arteries are more numerous for the same reason. Lymphatic vessels, which carry blood enriched with nutrients from intestinal irrigation, or blood laden with waste from tissue irrigation, are large in diameter. Due to body length, lymphatic hearts are needed in the cloacal region. These hearts, placed in a sort of bony cage formed by the forked ribs of some vertebrae, are up to ¾″ (2 cm) long in certain pythons.

RESPIRATORY SYSTEM: A SINGLE LUNG

Reptiles' pulmonary volume, that of snakes especially, is usually superior to that of same-sized mammals. Nonetheless, respiratory exchange surfaces are inferior (on the order of 1 to 100) due to poor alveolation. The resulting relatively poor weakness of respiratory gaseous exchange partly explains the snake's slow metabolism. It is with oxygen that the energy contained in various nutrients is liberated. But unlike warm-blooded mammals, snakes expend no energy for the production of heat and maintenance of their internal temperature. The left lung is atrophied or absent in most snakes. Even when this lung is only 1 to 2% of the

size of the right lung, as in *Leptodeira*, it remains functional and receives a branch of the pulmonary artery. The tracheal artery is quite long and opens in the back of the mouth, and the glottis is found on a lingual bulge.

In many species, Viperidae in particular, the epiglottis vibrates when air enters the trachea, and the snake then emits its characteristic hiss.

The lung has an alveolate and vascularized anterior portion in all such species, and a posterior alveolate and vascularized aerial sack which accounts for up to two thirds of the organ's total length. The right lung generally reaches down to the right kidney, and all the way to the cloacal region in aquatic species like the freshwater Acrochordidae or *Pelamis* (marine Elapidae). The lung is thought to play a hydrostatic role comparable to that of the swim bladder in fish through its aerial sack. In other species, the aerial sack acts either as ventilator to the alveolate lung (through its variation in volume when the animal moves), or as a thermic regulator for the male's testicles, which must be maintained at 3.6 to 5.4°F (2 to 3°C) below body temperature for good sperm production.

Snakes' respiratory movements are due to the costal musculature alone. When swallowing large prey that block the musculature's anterior area to some extent, snakes use their aerial sack as a sort of sucking and crushing pump that passes air through the vascularized lungs. Furthermore, the trachea opens towards the front of the buccal cavity, which lets air pass during ingestion.

The vascularized lung is preceded by a tracheal lung in many species. This lung extends along the length of the trachea, ahead of its opening into the normal vascularized lung, with which it joins to some extent.

This lung's structure varies from that of an aerial sack in the Malaysian cobra (*Naja sputatrix*) to many sacks opening independently of each other in the royal cobra's trachea, while it is highly

△ *ILLUS. 4, UPPER LEFT: Python skull. At top, a lateral view; below, a view of the cranial box from the ventral side. The quadrate bone is short and massive, the mandible is small, and the teeth are homogeneous and curve towards the back.*

△ *ILLUS. 5, UPPER RIGHT: Viper skull. The quadrate bone is long, the mandible stretches towards the back, and the teeth (palatine and pterygoidian) are small. The only grooved tooth on the maxillary is the fang.*

▷ *ILLUS. 6, OPPOSITE: general anatomical sketch. Dissection of a female colubrid. The heart and thyroid are placed far back, all of the organs are elongated. The intestine is relatively short (carnivorous diet). The right ovary and kidney are placed farther back than their counterparts.*

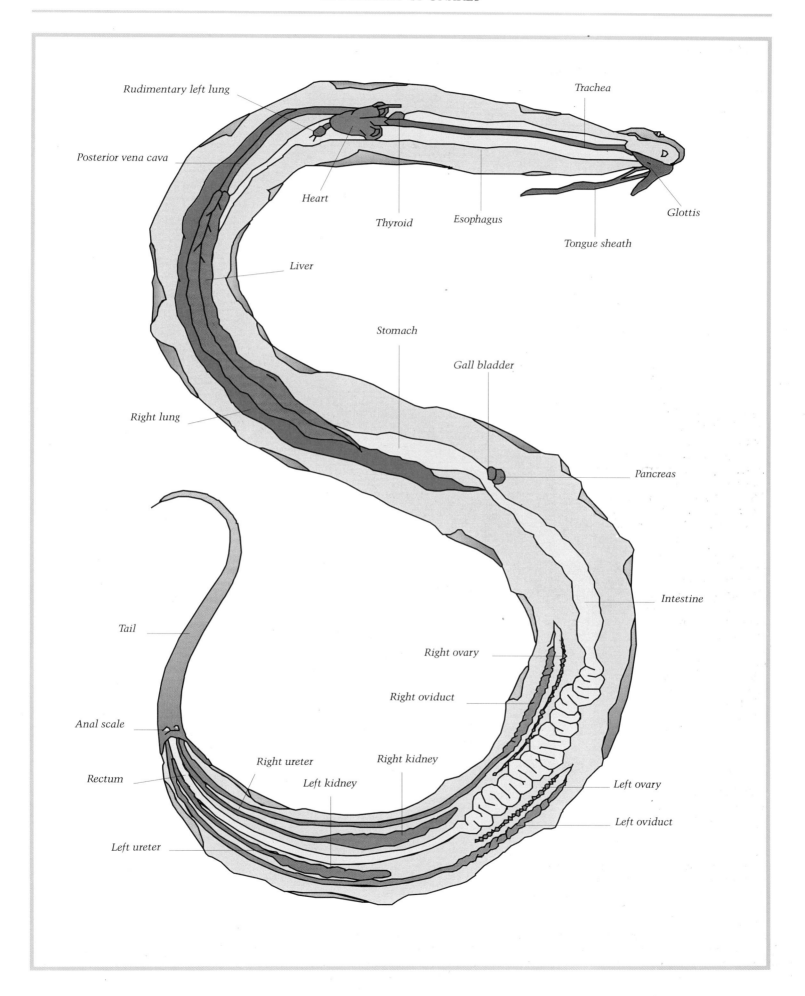

VENOM APPARATUS

Jean-Claude Rage

SNAKES' VENOM apparatus is essentially composed of two glands that synthesize the venom, and of fangs (modified teeth), which inject the venom deep into the prey or aggressor's tissues.

Venom glands evolved from salivary glands. In the Crotalinae, they have derived from some large labial glands, composed of branched-out tubules found in a mass of conjunctive tissue. The tubules' cells secrete the venom.

The collecting system also sports a group of mucous cells near the glands' orifices, which may act as valves. The anatomy of the Elapidae's venom glands is similar, but the separation between the serous (venom-producing) and mucous parts is less clear, so these glands are considered more primitive.

The secreted venom drops into the collecting tubes, where it is kept: there is no specialized storage area. Fangs are larger than other teeth, with a groove that is more or less deep and closed (see below), by which the venom drips and which facilitates its injection during the bite. Maxillary (upper jawbone) teeth are the only ones that can be differentiated by the absence or presence of a groove. These fangs are often separated from the other teeth by a space: the diastema. Snakes are classified into four groups according to their teeth:

Aglyphs have no fangs, and usually no

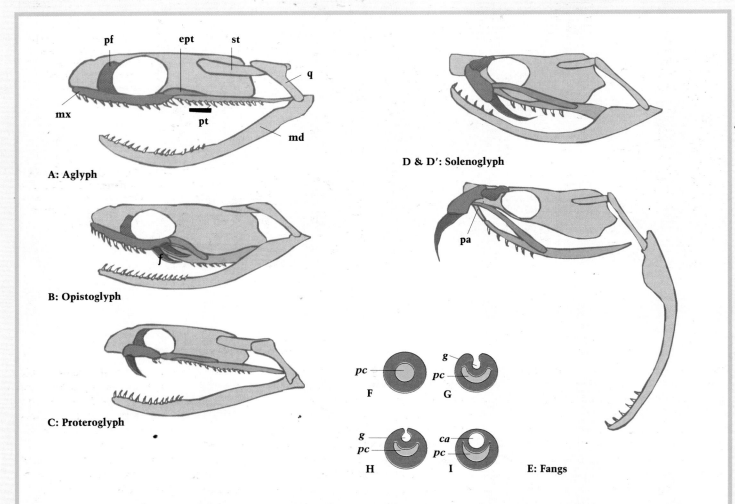

*ILLUS. 7. Venom apparatus. In colubrids, the upper jawbones—except for the premaxillary, the most frontal of these bones, which is not highlighted in this drawing—are loosely affixed to the cranial box. The upper jaw's five bones are the maxillary (**mx**), the pterygoid (**pt**), the ectopterygoid (**ept**), which links the two preceding bones, and the palatine (**pa**), which is often hidden by the maxillary. Two bones link the upper jaw to the cranial box: the prefrontal (**pf**) and the quadrate (**q**), which is itself linked to the cranial box by the supratemporal (**st**). The mandible (**md**) is articulated onto the quadrate. Aglyphous snakes (A) have no venom fangs, but some colubrids do. Three types of venom apparatus are distinguished according to the fangs' (**f**) position on the maxillary: opistoglyph (B), proteroglyph (C), and solenoglyph (D and D'). The maxillary's mobility is extreme in solenoglyphs and varies in the others. At rest (D), the fang is curved towards the back, but can move forward thanks to certain bones (D'). The fangs (E) are teeth: seen in a cross-section (F), they include a pulp cavity (**pc**). Opistoglyphs have a groove (**g**) in the tooth for the venom; this exists in proteroglyphs, but may close (H); in solenoglyphs, the groove becomes a canal (**ca**).*

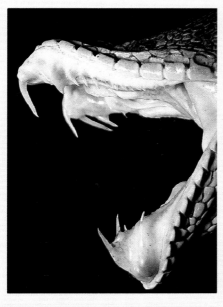

▷ RIGHT: **Corallus canina,** *the emerald tree boa. This nonvenomous species has no fangs, but its front teeth are stronger than its others.*

▽ BELOW: **Dendroaspis angusticeps,** *the green mamba (pteroglyph dentition). This snake's maxillary has only one large fang.*

△ ABOVE: **Psammophis elegans** *(opistoglyphous dentition). The venomous fangs are towards the back of the upper jaw. This snake feeds on lizards in semidesert areas of Africa.*

◁ LEFT: **Ceraste cerastes,** *the desert horned viper. One can easily see the double fang at the front of the maxillary.*

venom glands, although some colubrids secrete a saliva with some toxic properties. Aglyphs are represented by all noncoluboid snakes, and by many colubrids from the genera *Coronella, Coluber,* and *Elaphe.* This is not necessarily the most primitive tooth form: some colubrids may have lost their venomous function secondarily.

In opistoglyphs, one of the back teeth on each side of the upper jaw is usually larger than the others, and it's grooved. The front teeth are small and cone-shaped, sometimes grooved, but never connected to a venom gland.

This type of dentition is often found in colubrids: the Montpellier snake (*Malpolon monspessulanus*), the *Dromophis* genera, and other Boignae.

Species with one or more fangs towards the front of the maxillary bone are pro-

teroglyphs. These fangs correspond to the jaw's most anterior teeth and are sometimes followed by teeth that progressively decrease in size towards the back, as in most Elapidae. The groove may then be closed on part of its length, but the suture remains visible. The groove's opening allows some cobras to spit their venom relatively far (*Hemachatus haemachatus,* the South African spitting cobra, or Ringhal's cobra, and some members of the *Naja* genus). Mambas (*Dendroaspis*) have a single large fang on the maxillary.

Marine Elapidae from the *Emydocephalus* genus, which feed on fish eggs, have, curiously, lost their entire denture except for their venom fangs.

Solenoglyphs have the most elaborate system of venom injection. The fang is a very long tooth, and the injection groove is

closed along its entire length. Furthermore, the maxillary, to which the fang is linked, as well as the replacement tooth, is short and articulated towards the front of the jaw. This allows for a deep injection, and for the folding down of the fangs when at rest.

This type of dentition is characteristic of Viperidae and is also found in Atractaspididae. Some believe that Viperidae evolved from proteroglyphs.

The snakes' venom apparatus, that of the solenoglyphs especially, appears as one of the most perfect in the animal world.

Venom's primary function is obviously the capture of prey, but it also plays an important role in digestion, thanks to some of its constituent enzymes. Certain adaptations, like those of the spitting cobra, also serve as a defense mechanism.

vascularized and the largest part of the functional lung in both snail-eating snakes (*Dipsas indica*) and Viperidae (*Sibon*).

The pulmonary artery gives way to a tracheal branch when entering the lung, which is oriented towards the front. The tracheal branch is sometimes larger than the pulmonary artery itself.

A CARNIVORE'S DIGESTIVE SYSTEM

Snakes are carnivorous predators, and their digestive tube is relatively short. For example, intestines measure only 28% of *Typhlops*' body length and 17.5% of *Pythos*'. Snake intestines are quite short when compared to those of an omnivore like man (450%) or a herbivore like the cow (2000%). Snakes' mouths open quite wide, except for Scolecophidians, which feed on small prey. Like all other nonmammalian vertebrates, snakes have no mobile lips. Their long, thin, and very protractile tongue is protected, when at rest, by a corneal sheath. The oral cavity and tongue's epithelium are covered by numerous glands, salivary and mucoserous.

▶ *Dentition*

Snakes have "fighting" teeth: these are long, pointed, and curved backward, which keeps the prey, always swallowed whole, from escaping. These teeth are implanted in the bone by fusion into the jaw's internal wall. Unlike those of mammals and crocodiles, these teeth lack roots, and some are even mobile. Like other reptiles, snakes have a number of successive dentitions, with each tooth remaining functional for a few months only. Teeth are laterally replaced once the old tooth and its bony base have been reabsorbed. All snakes have one dental arch in the mandible and two in the upper jaw: an external row (maxillary and premaxillary bones), used to capture prey, and an internal row (the palatine and pterygoid bones), which, during ingestion, helps to further the prey's progression towards the esophagus.

Pythons are one of the many species with isomorphous teeth: these teeth are cone-shaped and curve towards the back of the mouth. They differ by size alone, the larger teeth being either at the front (proterodontia) or at the back (opisthodontia). Having teeth on the maxillary bone is a primitive characteristic seen in *Anilius*, *Xenopeltis*, *Loxocemus*, and some pythons. The dental bones in some Leptotyphlopidae sport a few small teeth; they are the only ones to do so. In other species, the teeth found on the palatine and pterygoid bones have kept their simple shape. Certain colubrids only have a few of them.

Atractaspididae have lost all the teeth on the pterygoid.

Maxillary teeth alone may differ by the presence of a groove or canal by which the venom, secreted in a modified labial salivary gland, can flow. These teeth, or fangs, are often separated from the others by a space known as the diastema.

In venomous snakes, ligaments ensure the straightening of the fangs and the venom's expulsion from the mouth. This straightening motion is wide in opistoglyps, with their rear fangs, and maximal in Viperidae (solenoglyphs).

▶ *A digestive tube produces powerful enzymes*

The esophagus is longitudinally pleated and very dilatable, and a large number of very small mucous glands found in the epithelium of the esophagus allow for the prey's progression. The stomach contains highly active enzymes. The liver is elongated and linked to the gall bladder, which is found towards the rear of the body, by a long cystic canal. The massive pancreas is found just behind the spleen and gall bladder.

As in all reptiles, the rear intestine, or rectum, opens into a cloaca, divided into three successive chambers. The rectum has a large cecum in Scolecophidians and Aniliidae. Feces are formed in an anterior position, in an intestinal structure coprodeum.

It is separated by an anal-type sphincter with an intermediary ureodum into which the urethra and genitals open and the urine and feces mix. A posterior proctodeum opens towards the exterior through a transversal cloacal slit (as in lizards).

URINARY TRACT

Snake kidneys are elongated in shape and placed towards the front of the body, the right one always being ahead of the left (except for the genera *Pareas* and *Aplopeltura*, members of the colubrid family). The kidneys contain many small channels, the nephrons, where filtration occurs. Asps (*Vipera aspis*) have 15,000, which is a small amount compared to mammals (200,000 to over a million).

Exchanges between the circulatory system and these filtering tubes occur at one end of the nephron, and its other extremity opens into a urine-collecting tube. This glomerular filtration produces a creamy, off-white urine that is extremely rich in uric acid and which is excreted without any loss of water. The urine ends in the cloaca, where it is mixed with the feces.

GENITAL SYSTEM

Testicles are cylindrical in shape; the right one is always forward of the left, and much bigger (up to twice as big in the peliad viper, *Vipera berus*). Testicle volume varies greatly during the year, and doubles at the time of sexual activity. Ovaries are also elongated, and placed far ahead of the kidneys, the right ahead of the left (see the table on page 25). Odor glands open into the cloaca—their secretions probably play the role of pheromones, allowing for recognition during intercourse.

Males have a pair of copulatory organs, the hemipenes, which retract into a sheath in the tail when at rest.

Both erection outside the cloacal slit and rigidity are ensured by a heavily irrigated tissue and special muscles. Females have a similar hemiclitoris.

ILLUS. 8. Male and female reproductive systems. Snakes have a transversal cloacal orifice, much like lizards. During intercourse, male and female lie next to each other; the male's copulating organ is represented by hemipenes, which are sheathed in the anterior part of the tail and erected by an influx of blood during intercourse. The female hemiclitoris, which is similar to but smaller than the hemipenes, is not shown in this picture.

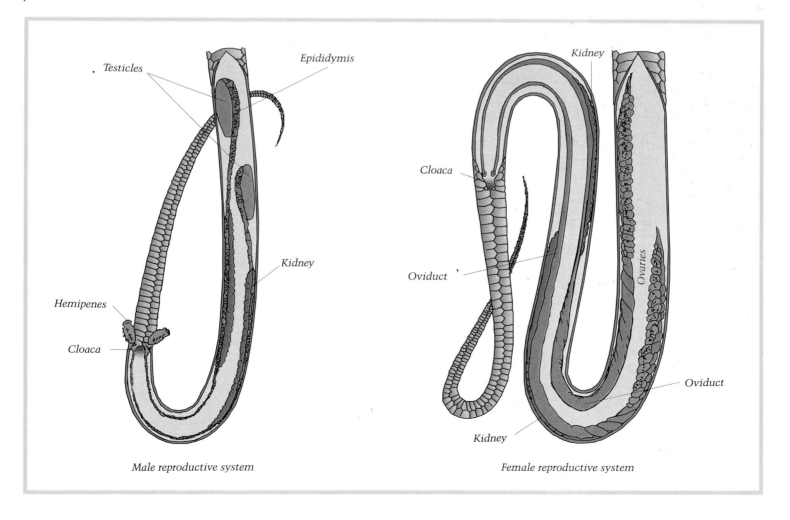

Male reproductive system

Female reproductive system

ORIGIN & EVOLUTION OF SNAKES

Jean-Claude Rage

It is through the history of reptiles that we must search for snakes' origin. This history began towards the end of the Primary Era, approximately 340 million years ago, and developed during the Secondary Era, when a number of groups, like dinosaurs, pterosaurs, and plesiosaurs, died off for still-unknown reasons. Snakes, on the other hand, have not only survived but have been a real success story in evolutionary terms, accounting for around 2600 species today (there are about 20 crocodilian species, and 260 turtle species). Snakes have conquered the various biotopes: deserts, dense forests, and aquatic environments. They are found on every continent but Antarctica. These are highly specialized reptiles, both by their shape and by their locomotive adaptations. But is their evolutionary success due to the loss of their limbs? Apodia could certainly be construed as an advantage, for it allows for movement in a great number of different locations. This is nonetheless a rather unconvincing hypothesis when one considers that other reptiles that have evolved towards apodia, like skinks and the worm lizards, have not been as successful. In any case, snakes have experimented with remarkable forms of apodal locomotion. Is this due to their eating habits? The cranial skeleton's evolution, which allows the snake to swallow large prey, and the development of a venom apparatus do appear to constitute real advantages. Their evolutionary success is probably due to a combination of these factors.

THE ORIGIN OF SNAKES—AN OBVIOUS LINK WITH LIZARDS

The oldest fossil classified as a reptile was found in Scotland, in soil dating from the lower Carboniferous (Primary), about 330 to 340 million years old. It is that of an animal about 8" (20 cm) long with a massive anapsid skull, like that found in turtles. Anapsids have given rise to two major groups characterized by the shape of their skull: Synapsids and Diapsids.

Synapsids have given rise to mammals, and thus we shall only concern ourselves with Diapsids, since it is among them that the snakes' ancestors are found. The oldest Diapsid, *Petrolacosaurus kansenis*, was found in the U.S., in soil dating to the upper Carboniferous, about 300 million years old. It measures 16" (40 cm) and was probably a terrestrial insectivore.

Diapsids quickly separated into 2 major groups: Archosaurs and Lepidosauromorphs. The first group, which included dinosaurs and pterosaurs, is now represented by crocodiles and birds, both descended from certain dinosaurs. Among the fossil groups related to the Lepidosauromorphs, plesiosaurs, ichthyosaurs and placosaurs were marine animals. Lepidosaurians, another group of lepidosauromorphs, include the Sphenodontians (with the only *Sphenodon*, New Zealand's tuatara), lizards, worm lizards, and snakes (see the table on page 33).

Within present-day fauna, lizards and worm lizards are the animals most closely related to snakes. These three groups, all Lepidosaurians, form the squamates (from the Latin *squama*, "scale").

Lizards have varied morphological structures,

▽ *BELOW:* Sphenodon punctatus, *a present-day member of the Sphenodontians, living in New Zealand.*

△ *ABOVE: Amphisbaena alba, a worm lizard, member of the apodal squamates.*

by anatomical criteria (cranial and vertebral osteology, as well as the crystalline and retinal structure). By just looking at the two groups' anatomical characteristics, it would be easy to believe that lizards and snakes evolved from a common ancestor. In fact, it is now commonly believed that snakes originated in the lizard-worm lizard.

IN SEARCH OF AN ANCESTOR

Many different groups of squamates have been considered as closely related to snakes, or even as their ancestors. Since snakes have existed for millions of years, they clearly did not arise from the present-day squamates. Instead, the squamate group most closely associated to snakes must be found, since this is the one which may yield a common fossil ancestor.

Worm lizards are alone among the serpentiform squamates to have been considered as snakes' closest relations. However, this hypothesis is generally refuted by herpetologists for extremely complex anatomical reasons.

Two groups of limbed lizards have also been considered: Varanoids and Scincomorphs. Varanoids include Komodo dragons, Gila monsters (which are the only venomous lizards), and an extremely rare lizard, *Lanthanotus*, from Sarawak (Borneo). These are all plausible relatives, due to the structure of their skull, tongue, and mandible, as well as by the way their teeth are replaced. Furthermore, some of these groups are entirely found as fossil remains. The Mosasauridae, for example, which only lived during the upper Cretaceous (end of the Secondary, 90 to 65 million years ago), were large marine varanoids, some measuring up to 33 ft. (10 m), with limbs transformed into flippers, like those of dolphins. The great American paleontologist, E. D. Cope, has suggested that they may be close to the snakes'

from the "classic" four-legged and long-tailed to the limbless and long-bodied (and thus serpentiform) blindworm. All lizards have lost the ancient skull's inferior temporal arc (see the table on page 32), and both arcs are missing in burrowing species.

Worm lizards, which are sometimes included within lizards, are serpentiform and burrowing animals whose cutaneous grooves give them a ringed aspect and make them look like large worms. Except for one species that has kept very short front legs, they present no trace of limbs, and they have lost both temporal arcs. Snakes have also lost both arcs and have an elongated body. They have no limbs and no movable eyelids. Note that worm lizards and some lizards exhibit these same characteristics.

Snakes differ from worm lizards by their lack of rings, but sometimes the two groups resemble each other so much that they can only be distinguished

▷ *RIGHT: Illus. 1. Snake and lizard skulls: Two types of bone make up the skull. Some (pink) can be differentiated in depth by cartilage (enchondral ossification), while the others (yellow), never go through a cartilaginous stage (dermic ossification). In lizards, the encephalon (grey) is not completely protected by the cranial bones. Except for the anterior and posterior areas, which are surrounded by bone, it is only protected by skin (s). The back of the cranial box carries the occipital condyle (oc), which is articulated onto the spine. Snakes' brains are totally surrounded by bone. Notice the placement of the various cinetisms: mesocinetism (ms) and metacinetism (mt) in lizards, procinetism (pc) in snakes. (a: superior temporal arc).*

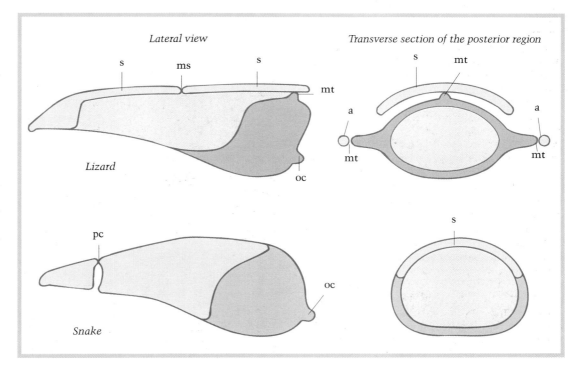

◁ *LEFT: A Gila monster (*Heloderma suspectum*), a present-day varanoid. It is one of two venomous-lizard species.*

original ancestor. Other possibilities have been mentioned, like the Cretaceous marine varanoids Dolichosauridae and Aigialosauridae. All of them exhibited well-developed limbs and differed from snakes, but other serpentiform marine fossils existed during the Cretaceous, such as *Pachyophis* in Bosnia-Herzegovina and *Pachyrhachis* in the Middle East, which are more or less intermediary between Varanoids and snakes. Some specialists even classify these last two among the snakes.

Scincomorphs (Cordylidae, "true" lizards) include a large number of tetrapod lizards and a few serpentiform species. Similarities in the encephalic structures have led some herpetologists to suggest that these animals may share a common ancestor with snakes, but studies on fossils have failed to confirm this hypothesis.

The possibility of a link between snakes and Pygopodidae (Australian lizards, similar to gekkos), with their long bodies lacking forelimbs and with only minimal hind limbs, has also been discredited.

Finally, it is now agreed that snakes evolved from lizards, and the search for their closest relatives is taking place among present-day Varanoids, as the missing common ancestor has not been found among fossils.

TERRESTRIAL, AQUATIC, OR BURROWING ANCESTOR?

How did lizards give rise to snakes? Three hypotheses have been suggested, with snakes descending from terrestrial, aquatic, or burrowing lizards.

The first hypothesis, that of terrestrial origin, has been abandoned for any lack of solid proof. A theory of aquatic origin has been offered by some paleontologists, who have considered mosasaurs, dolichosaurs, and aigialosaurs from the Cretaceous to be close to the snake's source. These were all aquatic (or even marine) Varanoids, and adaptation to an aquatic environment has never led to a significant reduction of limbs in reptiles.

Nonetheless, the aquatic-origin theory has not been completely rejected, for the fossils that seem most closely related to snakes have been found in deposits with a marine origin.

The third hypothesis, that of an origin among burrowers is generally agreed upon. This hypothesis was initially based on the fact that primitive snakes were burrowers and that burrowing lizards are usually serpentiform.

Research done on the retina (see the chapter on the nervous system and sensory organs) has lent further support to this hypothesis.

The strengthening of snakes' skull, the loss of mobility between its various components, and elements such as the temporal arcs all support the notion of a burrowing period, since burrowing lizards exhibit the same modifications.

▽ *BELOW:* Pachyophis woodwardii, *a fossil found in Bosnia-Herzegovina.*

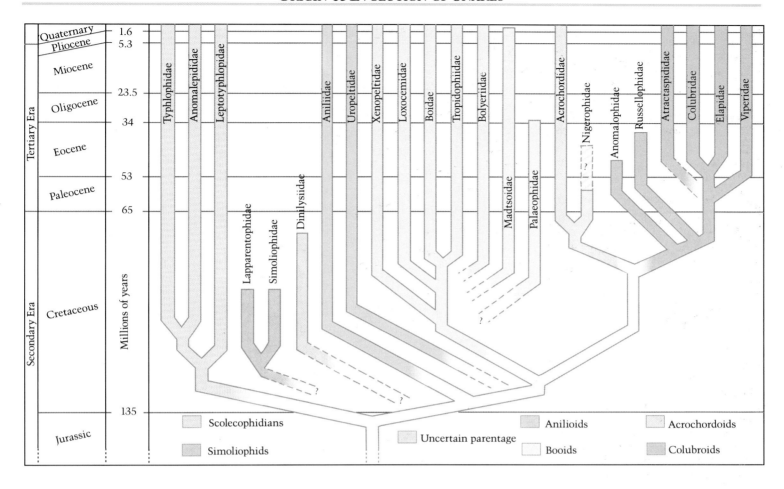

ILLUS. 2: Phyletic snake tree: A first divergence (dichotomy) may have occurred during the upper Jurassic; it gave rise to the Scolecophidians (left) and to the Alethinophidians (right). The oldest known snakes (Lapparentophidae and Simoliophidae) may be linked to Alethinophidians. The Dinilysiidae's relations are enigmatic; their position on this chart is only a compromise between various hypotheses. Notice how important the Booids' and colubrids' branches are.

▽ BELOW: Vertebra from Lapparentophis defrennei, the oldest fossil snake known.

On the other hand, the link between the bones of the upper jaw and palate with the skull (which link is quite weak in snakes) is incompatible with burrowing life. It must then be accepted that the skull's consolidation has been inherited from a burrowing past, while the upper jaw and palate's mobility are more recent acquisitions.

Furthermore, bodily elongation and limb loss are adaptations to the act of burrowing, and to the time spent in the burrows and fissures where small mammals live. These mammals were probably prey for the snakes' ancestors.

Taking the last two hypotheses into consideration, it is now believed that snakes' ancestors were semiaquatic and semi-burrowing, and lived in the mud, as do many present-day limbless amphibians.

EVOLUTION OF SNAKES

▶ The first stages: mute fossil remains

Paleontology tells us little about snakes' first evolutionary steps. The oldest fossils, found in Algeria, in middle Cretaceous deposits (100 to 96 million years old), consist of a few damaged vertebrae. Another Algerian fossil, *Lapparentophis defrennei*, of which we have only very partial remains, is either a contemporary of the former or slightly more recent. *Paryachis problematicus*, on the other hand, a complete fossil about 3½ ft. (1 m) long, from the middle Cretaceous, about 94 to 96 million years old, was found in the Middle East. Although it was serpentiform, it probably had very minimal hind limbs. Despite its remarkable state

of preservation, we do not know whether it was a Varanoid lizard with a very elongated body or a primitive snake. The problem remains unresolved, as indicated by its scientific name.

Others dating from the middle Cretaceous are snakes like *Pouitella* and *Simoliophis* and enigmatic fossils (lizards or snakes?) such as *Mesophis*, *Pachyophis*, and *Estesius*. This period, which lasted between 100 and 90 million years, appears to be a critical one in the history of snakes. They are believed to have appeared a little earlier, during the lower Cretaceous (135 to 100 million years ago), or perhaps even during the upper Jurassic (155 to 135 million years ago). While those impressive dinosaurs roamed the earth (middle Cretaceous), snakes were the same size as they are now.

▶ Snake diversification: from movement to capturing prey

During the course of their evolution, snakes have perfected various modes of limbless locomotion and a system for catching prey that have helped them become successful. We don't know in which order the various limbs were lost, as fossils are silent on the subject. No known snake, fossil or present-day, has any trace of a scapular belt or forelimbs. However, the more primitive present-day snakes, such as minute-snakes, boas, or pythons, retain a vestigial pelvic belt and hind limbs. These vestiges sometimes form small bulges on each side of the cloaca, but they're never involved in locomotion. The older fossils' state of conservation doesn't allow us to understand how important the pelvis and hind limbs were.

Thanks to new joints between the vertebrae and the specialization of intercostal and skin muscles, snake locomotion has adapted to various environments. These adaptations were probably responsible for the snakes' expansion. Their gripping devices (mouth and jaws in particular) evolved in two different directions from the primitive state best represented by the present-day snakes *Anilius* and *Cylindrophis* (Anilioids). Scolecophidians, or minute-snakes, have small mouths, adapted to the capture and ingestion of small prey.

Starting from the same primitive stage, Alethinophidians (which account for 90% of present-day species) have evolved to swallow prey of a diameter larger than their own. This adaptation has affected the jaws' bones, and the two bones (supratemporal and quadrate) which are arranged differently in these snakes. Alethinophidians have also developed an articulation between their jaw and snout, allowing them to swallow large prey. This mechanism is not found in lizards or Scolecophidians; *procinetism* probably didn't exist in snakes' ancestors; it is mildly apparent in present-day Anilioids and is developing in other Alethinophidians—colubrids in particular.

Due to their small size and generally fragile skeleton, Scolecophidians didn't fossilize very well, and we know little about their past. Alethinophidians, on the other hand, appear in fossil beds dating to the end of the Cretaceous (90 to 65 million years old), and perhaps even sooner, if earlier fossils can be classified as members of that family.

The archaic terrestrial snakes Lapparentophidae were probably related to the Simoliophidae, which were apparently contemporaneous with marine snakes that have sometimes been classified as lizards. All of these disappeared about 90 million years ago.

Booids appeared towards the end of the Cretaceous, with three fossilized families: Dinilysids (which may be Booids), Madtsoidae, and Palaeophids. The Dinilysiidae, which were probably the most primitive of all, have left a very well preserved fossil and two (Booids, Tropidophids) of the five families still in existence.

Booids, and Boidae in particular, dominated the snake world during the first two-thirds of the Tertiary Era (65 to 23.5 million years), especially in Europe and North America. Huge snakes measuring over 35 to 50 ft. (10–15 m) were part of the Madtsoids; these disappeared at the beginning of the Tertiary, except in Australia, where the genus *Wonambi* survived until the Quaternary.

The aquatic Palaeophids are known only by their vertebrae; these were related to the Boidae, and they also measured up to 35 ft. (10 m).

Anilioids also appeared towards the end of the Cretaceous. These primitive snakes still exist now, but we don't know whether the fossils belong to the Aniliids or Uropeltids.

Whereas Anilioids and Booids are primitive Alethinophidians, the younger Acrochordoids and Colubroids are more highly evolved members of the same family. Acrochordoids include two aquatic snake families: Nigerophidae, which are

known only from fossils, appeared in the early Tertiary (60 million years ago) and disappeared during the middle Eocene (45 million years ago), and the Acrochordidae, which are still in existence, and which date from 15 million years ago.

Colubroids appeared towards the beginning of the Tertiary (53 to 35 million years ago) within (more or less) aquatic families such as Anomalophidae and Russellophidae and then experienced an explosive evolution during the Miocene, 20 million years ago, when Colubroids supplanted the Boidae. The latter were clearly dominant in fossil deposits, but saw their area of distribution diminish with the climate's cooling, and they deserted their northernmost ranges. On a geological time scale, Boidae quickly became a minority compared to the Colubroids, which were quickly progressing.

Colubroids include the two fossil families from the early Tertiary (Anomalophidae and Russellophidae) as well as four present-day families. The first colubrid is quite old and not very well known; it comes from a badly dated fossil bed of the Thai Eocene (approximately 40 million years old). Viperidae appeared towards the beginning of the Miocene, 23 to 21 million years ago, and the Elapidae a little later in the Miocene, about 18 million years ago. The Atractaspidae have left no fossils. It is only in the Colubroids, after a lengthy evolution, that the venom apparatus appeared. Colubroids fossils with venom apparatus have been found; unfortunately they are too similar to present-day snakes to shed any light on this evolution. The Colubroids' domination is attributed to this specialization, which has proved to be more effective than the Booids' predation through constriction. This domination also long lent credence to the belief that venomous snakes are the most evolved, and that it was the fangless Colubridae that gave rise to them. However, although three present-day colubrid families are solely composed of venomous snakes, two-thirds of the species in that family are not venomous.

◁ *LEFT: Some primitive snakes have retained a vestigial pelvis, which has lost any link with the vertebrae and "floats" in the muscle mass between the spine and ribs. There is sometimes a bone, considered a femur, which, in males, can jut out on each side of the cloaca; it is then covered by a corneal spur. Here is shown the spur in the male* Epicrates cenchria.

▽ *BELOW: A vertebra from* Palaeophis colossaeus, *a giant aquatic snake which may have been close to 33 ft. (10 m) long. It was found in Mali, where it lived 40 million years ago.*

There are serious arguments leading to the belief that all colubrids were originally venomous, and that some lost their venomous function secondarily, which would make venom an earlier characteristic. Thus, the venomous Colubridae would be the forerunners in the Colubroid family, rather than the most evolved.

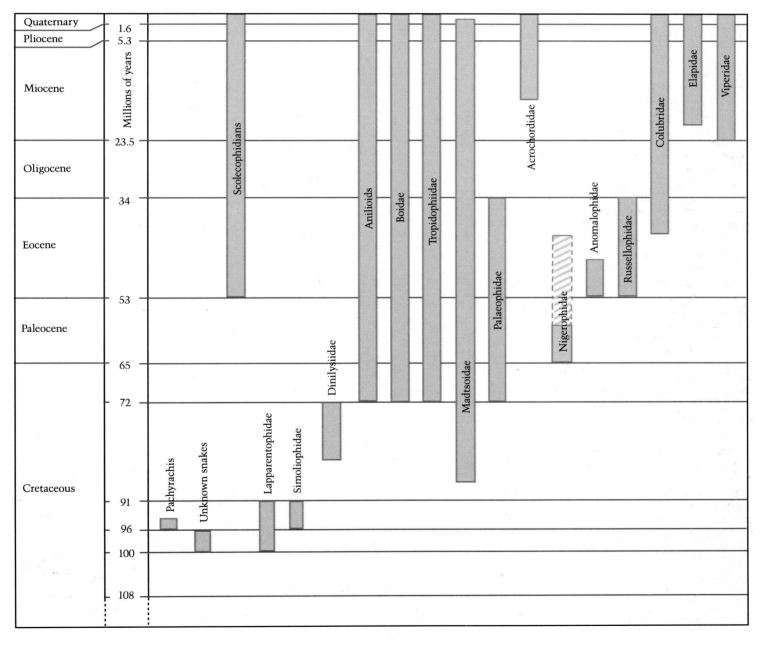

△ ILLUS. 3. Stratigraphic distribution of snakes. Not all snake families are included since some did not leave any fossils. The Cretaceous-Tertiary transition (65 million years ago) led to the extinction of dinosaurs and other animals, but not to the extinction of snakes. Note that Pachyrachis, which appears on this table, could very well not be a snake. Notice the Madtsoidae's distribution: It appeared 85 million years ago and was recently extinct, at an indeterminate date of the Quaternary. The oldest snakes are 100 million years old. For purposes of comparison, the oldest vertebrates are 470/450 million years old, the first reptiles appeared 340/330 million years ago, the first mammals 220/205 million years ago, and modern man (Homo sapiens sapiens) only 90,000 years ago.

THE SKULL TELLS THE EVOLUTIONARY STORY

THE BASIC LINES of reptiles' history can be read in their skulls.

Schematically, a primitive reptile's skull is composed of a bony cranial box which protects the brain and the internal ear. On the back and sides, a bony covering of dermic origin (the dermal tectum) surrounds the cranial box. On each side between the cranial box and dermal tectum, there is a space in the temporal region for the eyes, the middle ear, and the mandible's adductor muscles, which sit between the eyes and the ears. These adductor muscles help keep the mandible close to the upper jaw and are very important to the animal.

In the more primitive reptiles, only the nostrils and orbits open into the dermal tectum, and the skull is quite massive. These reptiles are called Anapsids, and turtles are their sole present-day representatives.

During evolution, windows (spaces) have opened in the temporal area, lightening the dermal tectum. Synapsids, which gave rise to mammals, have a window on each side, and Diapsids, which include all modern reptiles but turtles, and have given rise to birds, have two on each side. In Diapsids, the upper temporal window opens between the parietal (dorsal bone) (**pa**) and the upper temporal arc, composed of two bones: the squamosal (**sq**) and the postorbital (**po**). The lower window is found between the upper arc and the lower, composed of the quadratojugal (**qj**) and the jugal (**ju**). These two bones represent the vestigial remains of the dermal tectum's temporal region. The quadrate bone (**qb**), which plays a great role in snakes, is freed as temporal regression increases.

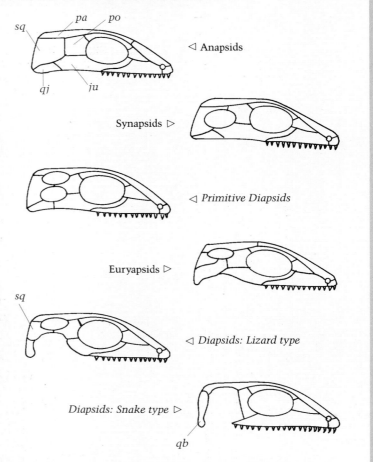

◁ Anapsids

Synapsids ▷

◁ Primitive Diapsids

Euryapsids ▷

◁ Diapsids: Lizard type

Diapsids: Snake type ▷

◁ *LEFT:* Naja romani *skeleton. This venomous snake lived in France 15 million years ago.*

REPTILE PHYLOGENY

THIS PHYLETIC chart shows the relations among the major reptile groups as well as among birds and mammals. Not all bird groups have been represented, in order to simplify the chart. The colored parts of the columns represent the known stratigraphy, while the cross-hatched extensions are hypothetical.

Notice that turtles, although they are classified as reptiles, are not as close to snakes, lizards, and crocodiles as are birds and mammals (there are varying opinions as to this). In the Diapsids, notice that there was a divergence after the first fossils (Araeoscelidians) appeared.

One, the Archosaurs, includes crocodiles, pterosaurs, and dinosaurs, as well as the birds descending from them.

Present-day forms dominate in the Lepidosauromorphs: Sphenodontians, lizards, worm lizards (whose parentage is controversial), and snakes. Plesiosaurs, which are marine fossils, seem to be real Lepidosauromorphs, as do Euryapsids (ichthyosaurs and placodonts), also marine fossils. Within Lepidosauromorphs, only Sphenodontians have kept the primitive diapsid configuration: the lower arc has been lost by the Euryapsids, the plesiosaurs, and lizards; worm lizards and snakes have lost both temporal arcs.

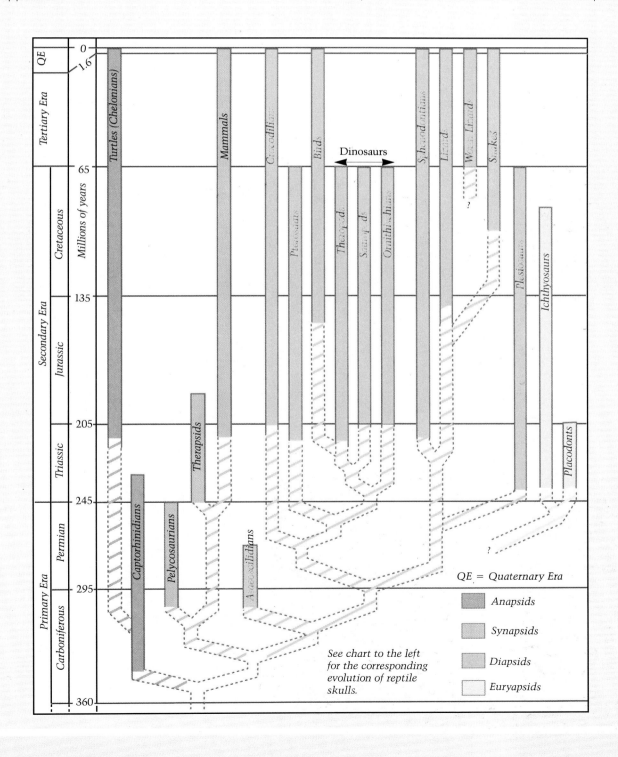

QE = Quaternary Era

Anapsids

Synapsids

Diapsids

Euryapsids

See chart to the left for the corresponding evolution of reptile skulls.

SNAKE DIVERSITY

Jean-Claude Rage

There are approximately 2600 species of snakes, varying from a few inches (centimetres) to about 35 feet (10 meters) in length. They occupy different habitats on every continent, except for Antarctica. They are also found in high latitudes: 67° in the Northern Hemisphere (Scandinavia, beyond the Arctic circle) and 50° in the Southern Hemisphere, in Patagonia and Chile. They are found at altitudes of 16,170 ft. (4900 m) in the Himalayas, but marine species do not live below 330 ft. (100 m) deep. There are two groups of snakes, with unequal numbers: Scolecophidians, with 260 species, and Alethinophidians, with over 2400 species. Each of these groups is further divided into families—in the case of Alethinophidians, these must be grouped by superfamilies. This chapter will concern itself only with present-day families, since fossil families have already been described.

SCOLECOPHIDIANS

Scolecophidians are small snakes 6 in. to 3½ ft. (15 cm to 1 m). They're often called minute-snakes, not because they are dangerous and able to kill very fast, but because of their small size (in Latin, *minutus* means small). These nonvenomous animals are, in fact, harmless to man.

Their geographic distribution is limited to tropical and warm-temperate climates. They are burrowers, living in tunnels they dig, or in burrows made by other animals, such as termites. This life-style is linked to a certain number of morphological and anatomical peculiarities. The lack of differentiation between the head and trunk, and the tail's obtuse shape, give these animals a strong resemblance to worms, which explains their name (from the Greek *scolex*, worm, and *ophis*, snake). They use their heads for burrowing: the rostral scale found at the front of the face is very developed, and the front part of the skull is quite rigid. Since they live away from light, their visual function is quite limited; some even appear to be blind. Their names in both English (blind snakes) and German (*Blindschlangen*) attest to this fact.

The eye is not covered by a special scale, as in the Alethinophidians, but it is either hidden by or barely apparent under the head's scales.

Scolecophidians eat small-sized prey and have a small mouth. The jaws are shorter than the skull. Both halves of the mandible are joined to each other at the front, which is not the case in Alethinophidians.

The ventral scales are small and similar to those on the back and flanks, as in lizards and worm snakes, whereas in most Alethinophidians the stomach is covered by large scales.

▶ ***Typhlopidae family: the typical blind snakes***
Typhlopidae (from the Greek *typhlos*, blind), are characterized by the mobility of their maxillary

---

SNAKE CLASSIFICATION

Snake classification follows this model (fossil families and superfamilies are followed by an asterisk*).

Snake Order (Ophidians)
Scolecophidian suborder:
Families: Typhlopidae, Anomalepididae, Leptotyphlopidae
Alethinophidian suborder:

Simoliophids superfamily*
Families: Lapparentophidae*, Simoliophidae*
Anilioids superfamily
Families: Aniliidae, Uropeltidae
Booids superfamily
Families: Dinylsiidae*, Madtsoiidae*, Loxocemidae, Boidae, Tropidophidae, Bolyeridae.
Acrochoroid superfamily
Families: Nigerophids*, Acrochordids
Colubroid superfamily
Families: Anomalophids*, Russellophids*, Colubrids, Elapids, Viperids, Atractaspidids

---

bone, which sports teeth, whereas the mandible has none. The intramandibular articulation is also lacking. These are vestigial remains of a pelvis, but these are not apparent from the exterior.

△ *ABOVE:* **Typhlops**, *a minute-snake from Turkey*

Typhlopidae comprise around 150 species that are widely spread between the two tropics. One of them (*Typhlops vernicularis*) lives beyond this zone and into Greece.

Rhamphotyphlops braminus, the flowerpot snake, and the aquatic Elapidae, *Pelamus plataurus*, are the snakes with the widest geographic distribution (from Iran to Mexico, and to the islands of the Pacific). This distribution comes from its interdependence with man. It lives among the roots of cultivated plants, and man probably ensured the snakes' propagation, although by accident. Furthermore, it appears that all of the species' individuals are females that reproduce through parthenogenesis, which is a type of reproduction that facilitates the colonization of new territories, since a single individual can ensure its descent and create a local population. Typhlopidae feed on small invertebrates, especially ants and termites.

▶ *Anomalepididae family*

As in the Typhlopidae, the mobile maxillary bone sports teeth, but in this case the mandible does too. The intramandibular articulation is lacking. There are no vestigial pelvic remains. This family is only composed of about twenty species, found in Central and South America. We know little about its way of life.

▶ *Leptotyphlopidae family: slender blind snakes*

These snakes, which are always small, owe their name to their long and slender body (from the Greek *leptos*, thin). Although these are burrowing animals, like all Scolecophidians, some Leptotyphlops have been observed climbing trees. In these snakes, unlike in those of the two previous families, the maxillary is firmly fixed to the skull, and is immobile. The maxillary has no teeth; these are found on the mandible instead. There is an intramandibular articulation.

Leptotyphlopidae retain vestigial remains of a pelvis and of hind limbs, which cannot be seen from the exterior.

There are approximately sixty species in this family, found in America, Africa, and Western Asia.

ALETHINOPHIDIANS

This large group includes snakes of all sizes, from 8 in. to 35 ft. (20 cm to 10 m), which are adapted to every way of life: they are terrestrial, arboreal, aquatic, burrowing, and some, like those of the *Chrysopelea* genus, even "fly" (see the chapter on locomotion).

Alethinophidians (from the Greek *alethinos*, real, and *ophis*, snake), are quite different from Scolecophidians, and represent typical snakes. Generally, the head is clearly differentiated from the trunk, although this is less true in burrowing species. The skull is procinetic (the mouth area is mobile). The eye is quite visible, and except for a few primitive species, the eye is covered by a specialized scale which is clear and perfectly fitted.

Alethinophidians are characterized by their

ability to swallow prey whose diameter is larger than their own. Their mouth is wide, the jaws being as long as, or longer than, the skull. Various adaptations help to open the mouth even wider. As opposed to the Scolecophidians, the mandibles are independent of each other and can open quite wide. Nonetheless, in certain burrowing species, the size of the mouth is reduced. The upper jaw and the mandible both sport teeth; in some Colubroids, some of the maxillary teeth (upper jawbone) are transformed into venom fangs. There is an intramandibular articulation. The ventral area is covered with large scales in most members of this family.

Four present-day superfamilies are recognized: the Anilioids, the Booids, the Acrochordoides, and the Colubroids.

ANILIOIDS

Anilioids are the most primitive of the Alethinophidians. The head and trunk are only mildly differentiated, the mouth opening is small, the mandibles' independence is limited, and the ventral scales are not, or only slightly, enlarged. This superfamily includes two families: the Aniliidae and the Uropeltidae.

▶ *Aniliidae family: ringed snakes*

This family is composed of the sole species *Anilius scytale*, the South American ringed snake. It is about 32 in. (80 cm) long and seems to be more or less a burrower in loose soil, feeding on apodal amphibians, lizards, and snakes. Alternating red and black rings give it a strong resemblance to the coral snakes, venomous Elapidae also found in South America.

The jaws' length is similar to that of the skull, and the upper jaw bones are only slightly mobile. *Anilius* retains a vestigial pelvis and femurs, which form anal spurs in the male. The head, which is in direct continuation of the trunk and tail, gives it a characteristic appearance; furthermore, its manner of defense consists in hiding its head while raising its rounded tail. Its eyes are not covered by a specialized scale, but appear in the middle of such a scale.

▶ *Uropeltidae family*

This family includes two relatively different subfamilies, the Cylindrophinae and the Uropeltinae.

Cylindrophinae subfamily: the tube snakes

Two south Asian genera, *Cylindrophis* and the very rare *Anomochilus*, known as tube snakes due to their cylindrical shape, barely blunted at both ends, are traditionally classified as Aniliidae, but seem to be more closely related to the Uropeltinae.

Cylindrophis differs from *Anilius* particularly by the presence of a specialized scale covering the eye. This genus is composed of eight species, generally called "two-headed monsters" by local populations. *Cylindrophis* defends itself in the same way as does *Anilius*. These animals are predominantly dark grey and brown. Some species are 3½ ft. (1 m) long. *Cylindrophis* is apparently more of a burrower than *Anilius* and can burrow tunnels. It spends time in rice fields and marshes and feeds on

▽ BELOW: *The false coral snake,* Anilius scytale, *from South America, is the Aniliidae family's only member.*

△ *ABOVE: South American giant anaconda* (Eunectes murinus)

▷ *RIGHT: The Asian reticulated python* (Python reticulatus) *is the largest snake species.*

snakes and eel. The second genus, *Anomochilus* (composed of two species) is not well known.

Uropeltinae subfamily: shield-tail snakes

This subfamily's geographic distribution is limited to peninsular India and Sri Lanka (Ceylon). It is composed of eight genera and a few over forty species. These are small snakes, ranging from 8 in. to 32 in. (20 to 80 cm), but rarely over 16 in. (40 cm), with a diameter of ¾ in. (2 cm) at the most. Unlike other Anilioids, they have lost all pelvis vestiges. They burrow actively with their heads, which are very pointed and have a massive skull with a firmly fixed upper jaw. The mouth is relatively small. The tail is truncated, which gives Uropeltinae the opposite morphology of other snakes: at first glance, the head is often taken for the tail and vice versa. Since these snakes also defend themselves with a hidden head and raised tail, the effect is rather startling, especially since two marks on each side of the tail simulate eyes. Large spiny scales form a shield over the tail. These scales are unique to these snakes. Uropeltinae live in loose soil (forests, gardens), where they burrow tunnels. Worms appear to be their staple.

BOOIDS

The large Booids group includes the largest present-day snakes as well as smaller ones. They exhibit more highly evolved characteristics than the Aniliidae, such as a clear differentiation between head and trunk (although this is less prominent in burrowing species), a large mouth, and large ventral scales. The upper jaw has some mobility in relation to the skull so as to facilitate the ingestion of large prey. This superfamily is composed of five families: Xenopeltidae, Loxocemidae, Boidae, Tropidophidae, and Bolyeridae.

▶ *Xenopeltidae family: rainbow snakes*

This family has a single species, *Xenopeltis uni-*

color, the South Asian rainbow snake. The oral opening is similar to that of the Aniliidae, and the mandibles are only slightly independent. On the other hand, there are no pelvic remains, which is a highly evolved characteristic. *Xenopeltis* is 3½ ft. (1 m) long. It is brown or black and rather lackluster, but it's iridescent under certain lights, from whence its name.

This is a more or less burrowing species that lives near water, in rivers and deltas, feeding on lizards, other snakes, and small rodents.

▶ Loxocemidae family: a dwarfish "python"

This also has but one species, the Mexican "dwarf python" (*Loxocemus bicolor*). Its evolutionary level is approximately equal to that of *Xenopeltis*, but it's distinguished by one primitive characteristic, its vestigial pelvis.

Loxocemus measures approximately 3½ ft. (1 m) and lives in southern Mexico and Central America. This brown snake, with its relatively well-defined head, is still somewhat unknown to us and is thought to be a burrower.

▶ Boidae family: the great constrictors & others

Boidae are well known thanks to the giant family members such as the reticulated python, the boa constrictor, and the anaconda, which can measure up to 35 ft. (10 m). Nonetheless, smaller snakes measuring around 3½ ft. (1 m) are also part of this family. Whether terrestrial, arboreal, aquatic, or burrowing, these powerful constrictors suffocate their prey in their coils. The head is clearly differentiated from the trunk, except in the burrowing species, and the mouth is large, with jaws that are longer than the skull—except, once again, for the burrowing species. The upper jaw moves easily in relation to the skull. The mandibles can part easily. Large scales cover the stomach. There are a vestigial pelvis and femurs; these form anal spurs in males, which is a rare example of sexual dimorphism. Three subfamilies are easily distinguished: pythons, boas, and sand boas.

Pythoninae subfamily: pythons

Pythons are distinguished from boas and from sand boas by some of the skull's anatomical details and by the fact that the pythons are oviparous, whereas the other Boidae are thought to be ovoviviparous (see the chapter on growth and reproduction). Most pythons have thermo-sensitive labial dimples on each side of the mouth which allow them to locate a warm-blooded animal found in close proximity (see the chapter on the nervous system and sensory organs).

There are four genera of pythons: *Python* (7 species), *Calabaria* (1 species), *Aspiditae* (2 species), and *Morelia* (17 species). *Python* is found in Africa, South Asia, and Indonesia. The Calabar python (*Calabaria*) is a small burrowing python measuring around 3½ ft. (1 m) that lives in eastern Africa. *Aspidites* and *Morelia* are found in the Australia–New Guinea region and in Indonesia.

Five genera have usually been attributed to the *Pythoniae* subfamily, but recent research has shown that there is less diversity in these pythons than had been believed, and that these two genera alone are valid; they comprise nineteen species. The Asian reticulated python (*Python reticulatus*) is the largest of all snakes: a length of 35 ft. (10 m), perhaps even more, appears possible. The African rock python (*Python sebae*) can reach 30 ft. (9 m), while in Australia the amethyst python (*Morelia amethysina*) is over 20 ft. (6 m) long. Giant individuals, nonetheless, are quite rare, and the average length in all of these species is much shorter. These giant types coexist with much smaller ones: for example, the African royal python (*Python regius*), rarely reaches 5 ft. (1.5 m), and the splendid green arboreal python from Australia and New Guinea, *Morelia* (previously *Chondropython*) *viridis* doesn't exceed 6½ ft. (2 m) in length.

△ *ABOVE: South American boa constrictor* (Boa constrictor)

Boinae subfamily: the true boas

Boas are usually less stocky than pythons and are more often arboreal. Members of three genera have thermo-sensitive labial dimples. All boas are ovoviviparous. The subfamily includes eight genera (around twenty species), and its curiously disjointed distribution is different from that of pythons; it is found in North and South America,

▷ RIGHT: *the Round Island boa (Casarea dussumieri), a very rare species*

Madagascar, and some islands of the Pacific. Only a few of these islands accommodate both pythons (*Python, Morelia*) and boas (*Candoia*). The most popular species is the *Boa constrictor*, a large snake from South America that tends to be terrestrial and can reach 17½ ft. (5 m). The Amazon basin is home to the anaconda (*Eunectes murinus*), a giant snake that is both aquatic and arboreal and whose size has given rise to numerous legends; it may indeed attain 35 ft. (10 m) or more, but it is particularly fat. There are also some relatively small boas: the arboreal boa, *Corallus enydris*, is 7 ft. (2 m) long, the *Xenoboa cropanii* is 3½ ft. (1 m) long, and although some species of the genus *Epicrates* are over 17½ ft. (5 m) long, many do not exceed 6 ft. (1.5 m).

Erycinae subfamily: sand boas

Sand boas are small burrowing Boidae, 3½ ft. (1 m) at most, that live in loose soil, sand in general. Their geographic distribution is to the north of that of pythons and boas, although they share some areas. Erycinae comprise four genera (and twelve species): *Eryx, Gongylophis* (sand boas) in the Old World, *Charina* (rubber boas), and *Lichanura* (rosy boas) in western North America. The head and trunk are not differentiated and their tails are truncated. *Eryx* and *Gongylophis*, both of which live in arid zones, can easily disappear in the sand without burrowing tunnels, since the soil just collapses after they have passed. The terrestrial *Lichanura* is found in arid and semiarid zones. *Charina* usually lives on the ground, hidden under debris, but it's apparently able to climb trees.

▶ Tropidophidae family: forest boas

Tropidophidae were long classified as members of the Boidae, with whom they share characteristics like a vestigial pelvis and anal spurs in males. Nonetheless, Tropidophidae exhibit certain more highly evolved characteristics; for example, they have lost all traces of a larger left lung. The length of their jaws approaches that of their skull. They are found in disparate areas in Central America, the Caribbean islands, and South America. Twenty species are grouped in four genera: *Trachyboa* and *Ungaliophis* (Central American boas), *Exiliboa* (Mexican dwarf boas), and *Tropidophis* (which is found in the Caribbean islands, where insularity favors speciation, and thus includes fifteen or so species by itself). These are small terrestrial Booids, which are rarely more than 3½ ft. (1 m) long and exhibit a clear differentiation between head and trunk.

▶ Bolyeridae family

Both species of this family, *Bolyeria multocarinata* and *Casarea dussumieri*, have lost all vestigial remains of a pelvis and hind limbs. Their skull recalls that of the Tropidophidae, but it displays one enigmatic characteristic: the maxillaries, which form the larger part of the upper jaw, are composed of two anterior and posterior halves, which is a characteristic unique to tetrapods. Although these snakes are the only ones with this

characteristic, which shows that they are related, they are rather dissimilar in other aspects. *Bolyeria*, which can attain 6 ft. (1.8 m), has a cylindrical body, a head that is undifferentiated from the trunk, and a relatively short tail. This morphology suggests that this relatively unknown snake is a burrower. *Casarea*, which probably doesn't exceed 3½ ft. (1 m), has a slightly transversally flattened body, a distinct head, and a long tail, which suggests an arboreal way of life. Both genera have only been found on Round Island, with an area of 61 acres (151 hectares), 12½ miles (20 km) to the north of Mauritius, where they are the only snakes. Both are endangered, and *Bolyeria* may already be extinct. It is, obviously, quite strange to find these two endemic species on a small island off Mauritius, which is itself a volcanic island only a few million years old. It would certainly be interesting to discover how these animals, or their ancestors, found their way there.

ACROCHORDOIDS

This superfamily is composed of a single present-day family, the Acrochordidae, which is composed of snakes that are stunningly well adapted to aquatic life. Their head is flattened and widens to the back, and is quite distinct from their thick trunk. They have a large head with mobile jaws. The ventral scales are small, and there are no vestigial remnants of hind limbs or of a pelvis. The scales are disconnected, and they are the only snakes to have small tubercles equipped with small hairs, the function of which is still mysterious. These snakes are ovoviviparous.

▶ Acrochordidae family: wart snakes

This family contains three species belonging to the *Acrochordus* genus: *A. javanicus, A. arafurae*, and *A. granulatus*. *A. javanicus* can reach 7 ft. (2 m), while the others are smaller. These thick and apathetic snakes live along the coasts of South Asia and on the Australasian islands. *A. granulatus* mostly frequents salt water while the other two are found in the fresh or briny waters of rivers and estuaries; they mostly feed on fish. Acrochordidae can occasionally move on land, but with difficulty; all are ovoviviparous and eject their young directly into the water. Their grainy, loose skin gives them a bulgy look and has led to their being called "wart snakes." Their skin is used for leather goods, known as *karung*.

sometimes very much so. Both mandibles can spread quite wide. Colubroids have lost all vestigial remains of a pelvis and hind limbs. Some are venomous. Three families are generally recognized (Colubridae, Elapidae, and Viperidae), and four if the Atractaspididae are included for the genus *Atractaspis*, which was once classified as part of the Viperidae but whose origins remain enigmatic.

COLUBROIDS

Colubroids comprise around 2950 species and account for up to 85% of all snakes. The head is generally well differentiated from the trunk, the mouth is big, and the jaws are longer than the skull. Large scales cover the ventral area, except in marine Elapidae. The upper jaw bones are mobile,

▶ Colubridae family: grass snakes

With over 1650 species distributed in some 300 genera, Colubridae is the largest snake family. In every continent on which colubrids are found (except for Australia, where the Elapidae dominate), Colubridae account for the largest part of the snake fauna. Their size varies from around 8 in. (20 cm) for the North American *Carpophis* to 12 ft. (3.5 m) for rat snakes like the Asian *Zaocys*. Their anatomical organization is that of Colubroids, with Colubridae being characterized by an aglyphic or opistoglyphic dentition (see the chapter on portraits of snakes). Subdividing the Colubridae is difficult, if not impossible; to this day no satisfactory proposition has been made, which is why the subfamily names appear in quotation marks.

Opistoglyphic colubrids, accounting for about a third of Colubridae, are mostly found among the "Homalopsinae" (aquatic, and found in the rice fields and deltas of China and South Asia) and the "Boiginae" (terrestrial and arboreal), but they are also found in other groups of colubrids. These animals are theoretically harmless to man because of the position of their venom fangs, which are found in the back of their mouth. However, the fangs of *Dispholidus typus*, an arboreal snake from tropical and southern Africa, are closer to the front of the mouth due to a shortening of the maxillary, and its venom is extremely toxic. Opisthoglyphs like *Dispholidus* have been the cause of mortal accidents when handled. Whether aglyphic or opistoglyphic, colubrids exhibit a wide variety of adaptations. In Asia, crabs constitute *Fordonia's* main prey. American "Dipsadinae" and Asian "Pareatinae" eat snails (see the chapter on predation and nutrition). Another specialization that deserves to be mentioned is the ability to swallow eggs, particularly evident in *Dasypeltis*.

Beyond these special cases, vertebrates constitute colubrids' main source of nourishment: fish, amphibians, birds, mammals, and other reptiles. The main ophiophagous (snake-eating) colubrids are the North American king snake (*Lampropeltis getulus*) and the South American mussurana (*Clelia clelia*).

△ ABOVE: *Western hognose snake,* Heterodon nasicus, *a burrowing colubrid*

◁ LEFT: *A small subfossorial colubrid* (Phyllorhynchus browni), *adult size*

▶ Elapidae family

Elapidae live in the warm regions of every continent but Europe, and in most oceans. They include all of the proteroglypic Colubridae, that is, those whose venom fangs are implanted towards the front of the maxillary. Otherwise, they are anatomically quite similar to Colubridae. A further specialization lets some species, known as "spitting cobras," shoot their venom a few feet (meters) out of their mouth. Due to both the poisonous quality of their venom, which contains substances that are harmful to the nervous system, and to the position of their fangs, Elapidae are quite dangerous, in most cases.

Classifying Elapidae, although it is easier than with Colubridae, is still quite difficult. We recognize two groups, terrestrial and aquatic Elapidae, without attaching a systematic importance to this subdivision. Elapidae represent over 60 genera and 170 species.

Elapinae subfamily: coral snakes, cobras, and taipans

These snakes resemble colubrids. They are generally terrestrial, and sometimes they burrow; arboreal forms are rare and there is only one freshwater genus. Cobras are the Elapinae's best-known representatives. They include a number of genera, *Naja* being the most representative. They live in Africa and Asia, and feed on vertebrates, essentially frogs, lizards, birds, small mammals, and other snakes. They are fast and slender, and intimidate their adversaries by raising the front part of their bodies and showing their hoods by spreading out their ribs; this strategy is not available to all of them. The Southeast Asian royal cobra (*Ophio-*

phagus hannah), a great snake eater, exceeds 17½ ft. (5 m), and sometimes even 20 ft. (6 m). It can raise its head 4 ft. (1.3 m) above the ground and is the largest venomous snake. Although it has the potential to be extremely dangerous, it causes few accidents, unlike the Indian cobras *Naja naja*, which don't exceed 5 ft. (1.5 m).

The cobra group also includes the African *Boulangerina*, which lives in freshwater, the arboreal *Pseudohaje*, and the spitting cobras, like the black-necked cobra (*Naja nigrocollis*) and Ringhal's cobra (*Hemachatus haemachatus*). These can project their venom up to 10 ft. (3 m). They target the eyes of their prey and can cause temporary blindness. Other Elapidae (which do not belong to the cobra group) can be found in Africa, such as large mambas (genus *Dendroaspis*). The black mamba (*D. polyepis*), which is mostly terrestrial and generally brown and grey, despite its name, measures up to 15 ft. (4.5 m). Other mambas are green and arboreal. Asian Elapidae that are not cobras belong to the genus *Bungarus*. These are unaggressive ophiophagous snakes with black and yellow or white rings, measuring up to 7 ft. (2 m).

The three genera of American Elapidae are *Micrurus*, *Micruroides*, and *Leptomicrurus*, which have red, black, white, and yellow rings and are known as coral snakes. The largest of these rarely exceeds 3½ ft. (1 m). They are terrestrial animals with burrowing tendencies that often feed on other snakes. There is a rich fauna of Elapidae in Australia, with more than 20 genera and 70 species.

Australia is the only continent with more venomous than nonvenomous snakes. Some are quite dangerous, like the taipans (*Oxyuranus*), which can measure up to 13 ft. (4 m), the tiger snake (*Notechis*), the Australian copperhead (*Austrelaps*), or the death viper (*Acanthopis*). There are also many Australian Elapidae which are considered harmless to man despite their venomous quality. This is true of the bandy-bandy (*Vermicella*) and of the Australian coral snake (*Simoselaps*).

Hydrophinae subfamily: marine snakes

These snakes live in saltwater except for two species, *Hydrophis serpenti* and *Laticauda crockeri*, which have adapted to lakes. They feed almost exclusively on fish. Their adaptation to water is shown in part by the lateral flattening of at least part of the lower body, which facilitates swimming. These snakes' venom is more toxic than that of terrestrial species, but they only rarely bite man. The most primitive have enlarged ventral scales. This is the case of *Laticauda colubrina*, which measures up to 5 ft. (1.5 m) and occasionally comes ashore, especially to lay eggs. It is the only oviparous Hydrophinae. Most of the others have small ventral scales, are ovoviviparous, and never come ashore. They tend to live in coastal areas, but one of them, *Pelamis platurus*, is pelagic and lives from the eastern coast of Africa to the American western coast. These snakes sometimes form huge groups; one such group was seen between Malaysia and Sumatra that was 10 ft. (3 m) wide and 63 miles (100 km) long.

▽ *BELOW:* Naja melanoleuca, *raised. Notice the hood.*

▶ *Viperidae family: vipers, rattlesnakes, fers-de-lance*

The Viperidae family includes all solenoglyphous snakes, except *Atractaspis*. They are able to point their fangs ahead, and thus have the most efficient venom injection apparatus. In the larger species, such as those of the genus *Bitis*, often found in tropical Africa, or the bushmaster, *Lachesis muta* from Central America, the fangs can reach 1½ in. (3 cm). The venom provokes internal hemorrhages. These snakes are generally shorter than the Elapidae, with a short tail, a massive body, and a head that widens towards the back. Some scales occasionally form "horns" around the eyes or nose.

The Viperidae's pupil is vertical, except in *Causus*, where it is round. They adapt very well to sandy areas, for they have perfected sidewinding (see the chapter on locomotion). Some live in colder areas than snakes of other families: the northernmost of snakes, the peliad viper (*Vipera berus*), lives well beyond the Arctic Circle in Scandinavia, and the southernmost snake, the Argentine fer-de-lance (*Bothrops ammodytoides*), are both Viperidae. The snake living at the highest altitude, up to 16,000 ft. (4900 m), *Agkistrodon himalayus*, is also a Viperidae. These snakes most often feed on small vertebrates. The family, which includes 180 species, can be divided into three subfamilies: Azemiopinae, Viperinae, and Crotalinae.

Azemiopinae subfamily: the most primitive vipers
This subfamily has been created for a single species, *Azemiops feae*, which is considered the most primitive of vipers. It is rare and not very well known, and measures 32 in. (80 cm) at most; it lives in the mountainous regions of Asia, southeastern Tibet, and north Vietnam.

Viperinae subfamily: vipers
Eight to ten genera (approximately 40 species) are found in this subfamily. Viperinae live in Europe and Africa, excluding Madagascar. Many genera are found in Africa. *Causus* has very large venom glands, but its bite is not particularly dangerous; its venom is not too harmful to man. *Bitis* includes species of all sizes. The largest and very powerful ones have a considerable diameter, up to 6 in. (15 cm). Both the colorful Gaboon viper (*B. gabonica*) and the duller puff adder (*B. arietans*) measure over 5 ft. (1.5 m) long and are very dangerous. The *Cerastes* genus, which does not exceed 32 in. (80 cm), includes horned vipers, which are well adapted to desert life. *Atheris* and *Adenorhinos* are two green arboreal vipers with prehensile tails. The *Echis* genus is composed of a few species measuring 30 in. (75 cm) at most, spread from eastern Africa to India. Its aggressive behavior, the strength of its venom, and the fact that it frequents areas populated by man means that one of its species (*E. carinatus*) has been involved in a number of fatal accidents. Only the genus *Vipera* is found in Europe, with small or medium-sized species. *V. ursinii*, for example, does not exceed 20 in. (50 cm). Many *Vipera* species live in Asia, and they are sometimes classified as belonging to the separate genus *Daboia*. One of them, Russell's viper (*D. russelli*), a species measuring 5 ft. (1.5 m), has been the cause of numerous deaths in India and southeast Asia. Two other small vipers,

Eristicopis and *Pseudocerastes*, occupy small areas of Asia.

△ *ABOVE:* Pelamis platurus, *an extremely venomous member of the* Hydrophinae. *This one appears stranded on the beach, but the picture provides a good portrait of the species. Note the typical flattening of the tail.*

▷ RIGHT: *Gaboon viper (Bitis gabonica).*

▽ BELOW: *Close-up of the horns of* Cerastes cerastes, *the horned viper.*

▽ BELOW: *Sidewinder (Crotalus cerastes). Note the opening between the eye and nostril, where the thermosensitive organ is found.*

Crotalinae subfamily: pit vipers, rattlesnakes, fers-de-lance, and moccasins

Crotalinae differ from other Viperidae because of a thermo-sensitive organ located in the maxillary, on each side of the head, that opens towards the exterior by a characteristic dimple placed between the eye and the nostril. This organ can detect infinitesimal variations in temperature and allows the snakes to locate warm-blooded animals within a certain proximity (see the chapter on the nervous system and sensory organs). Crotalinae are the only American Viperidae, but they are also found in large parts of Asia, and they have penetrated into Europe to a certain extent. Depending upon the author, six to twelve different genera are recognized, for approximately 150 species.

The rattlesnakes *Crotalus* and *Sistrurus* are two essentially North American terrestrial genera whose rattles, formed by a series of fitted horned rings, are found on the end of their tail. When rattled, they make a characteristic noise that signals the animal's presence. *Sistrurus* only includes small species, whose bites are usually not very dangerous: the pygmy rattlesnakes, which feed on frogs and lizards. *Crotalus* includes both small harmless species and larger ones that are dangerous to man. Among these, the diamond-back rattlesnakes, *C. atrox* and *C. adamanteus*, measuré over 6 ft. (2 m). The large and feared cascavel, *C. durissus*, is South America's only rattlesnake. Other Crotalinae have no rattles. *Agkistrodon*, both North American and Asian, is represented by moccasins

PRINCIPLES OF SYSTEMATIC CLASSIFICATION

Yannick Vasse

ALL LIVING BEINGS, animal or vegetable, have been classified according to a formal nomenclature since Linnaeus' initiative in 1758. The hierarchy used today to express the various degrees of relationship between organisms is that which he suggested in his book *Systema naturae*, although the criteria used at the time were different.

Systematics are a branch of biology, concerned with the classification of living beings. It refers itself to a certain number of levels which determine degrees of relation, and are called taxons. The basic unit is the species, which is the only biological reality and which is mostly defined by the interfertility of natural populations.

All of the higher-ranked categories attempt to facilitate the understanding of various families' relationships, and to incorporate the precision of scientific language.

Close species are grouped by genera,

and a species is usually characterized by two names: the generic name (with a capital) and the specific name (without a capital). The asp, for example, a European viper, is called *Vipera aspis*. Other species belong to the genus *Vipera*: *V. berus* (the adder), *V. ammodytes* (the long-nosed viper), etc. The specific name alone is meaningless, for it can be attributed to any number of species belonging to various genera, or superior taxons.

For example, *viridis*, which means green, is found in *Dendroaspis viridis* (the green mamba), *Lacerta viridis* (green lizard), *Picus viridis* (woodpecker), and *Lavandula viridis* (a lavender), which is a plant.

This classification is comparable to that of first and last names in humans.

There is an established hierarchy above the genus, which can be subdivided as required by the group's complexity. Let's

return to *Vipera aspis*:
Kingdom: Animal
Phylum: Chordates
Subphylum: Vertebrates
Class: Reptiles
Superorder: Squamates
Order: Snakes
Suborder: Alethinophidians
Superfamily: Colubroids
Family: Viperidae
Subfamily: Viperinae
Genus: Vipera
Species: Vipera aspis

Some taxons are easily identified by suffix.
Superfamilies: -oidae
Families: -idae
Subfamilies: -inae

There are variations within scientific literature, due to different interpretations by various authors.

◁ *LEFT:* Vipera seoanei, *a European viper*

▷ *RIGHT:* Crotalus viridis, *which lives in western North America, from Canada to Mexico.*

and copperheads, the only Viperidae with aquatic tendencies.

In Latin America and the Lesser Antilles, the *Bothrops* genus includes a number of terrestrial and arboreal species (palm vipers). "Fer-de-lance" refers to a number of feared species, including *B. lanceolatus* in the Antilles as well as *B. atrox*, which can reach 6 ft. (1.8 m). The smaller jararaca (*B. jararaca*) is also quite dangerous. *Lachesis muta*, the 12 ft. giant (3.5 m) of Viperidae, known as the bushmaster or surucucu, lives in South and Central America; it is probably very dangerous, but it's also quite rare.

A number of genera coexist in Asia: *Trimeresurus, Agkistrodon, Deinagkistrodon, Calloselasma, Hypnale, Tropidolaemus, Ovophiss.*

Trimeresurus, which is similar to the American *Bothrops*, includes arboreal species which are usually green and have prehensile tails; bites inflicted by these snakes are rarely fatal.

Agkistrodon halys, living in the northwest Caspian area, is the only European rattlesnake.

▷ *BELOW: Burrowing or mole viper* (Atractaspis)

▶ Atractaspididae family: burrowing vipers, or mole vipers

This family is solely comprised of the genus *Atractaspis* (15 or so species), one of the enigmas in snake classification. Long classified as Viperidae due to the solenoglyphous structure of their fangs, they are nonetheless quite distinct by other anatomical details. *Atractaspis* is now classified close to proteroglyphs (Elapidae) or opistoglyphs (Colubridae), and sometimes in a separate family.

Atractaspis are burrowing snakes measuring around 3½ ft. (1 m), whose head is not differentiated from the body, with a small eye with a round pupil, and a short tail finishing in a point. These snakes from eastern and southern Africa (one species, *A. engaddendis*, lives in the Sinai and southern Israel) feed on other burrowing reptiles: *Typhlops, Leptotyphlops*, worm lizards, and other members of the genus *Feylinia*.

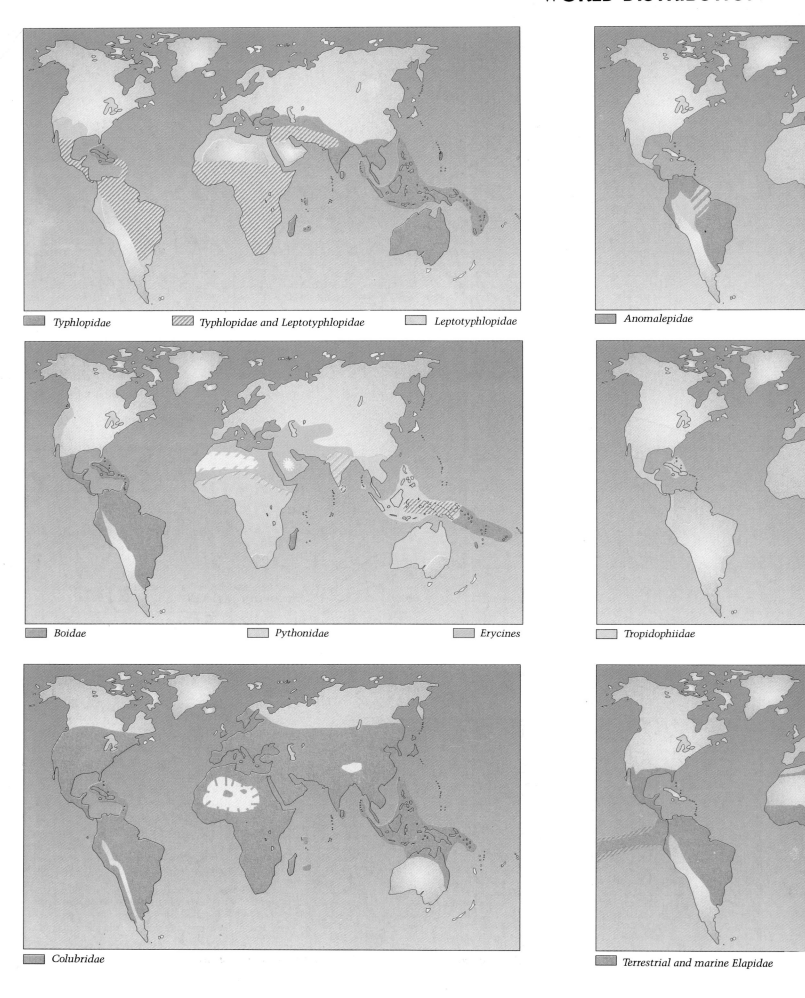

Typhlopidae

Typhlopidae and Leptotyphlopidae

Leptotyphlopidae

Anomalepidae

Boidae

Pythonidae

Erycines

Tropidophiidae

Colubridae

Terrestrial and marine Elapidae

OF SNAKE FAMILIES

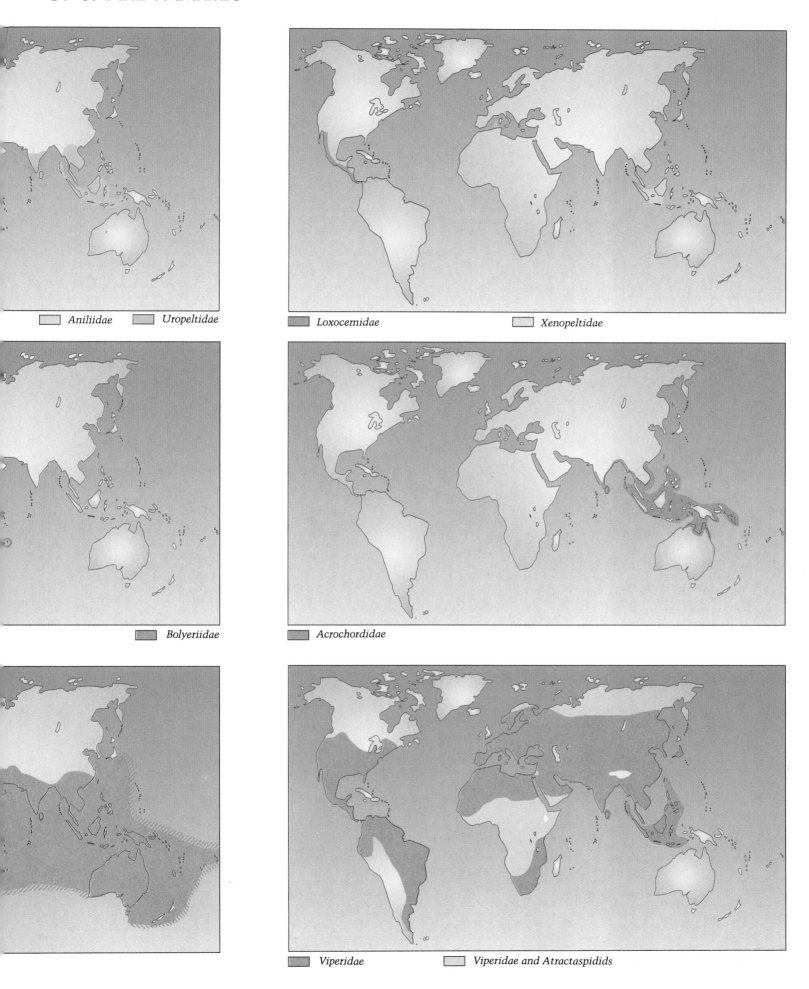

▢ Aniliidae ▢ Uropeltidae	▢ Loxocemidae ▢ Xenopeltidae
▢ Bolyeriidae	▢ Acrochordidae
	▢ Viperidae ▢ Viperidae and Atractaspidids

BIOLOGY OF SNAKES

NERVOUS SYSTEM & SENSORY ORGANS

Roland Platel

Snakes' central nervous system is organized along the same basic lines as that of other reptiles, and is an improvement over those of amphibians. It also exhibits certain particularities that show it to be quite evolved in relation to those of other reptiles, such as turtles and crocodiles. Indeed, snakes have remarkable sensory equipment: beyond the organs they share with other terrestrial vertebrates, they have developed highly sophisticated ones, such as the vomeronasal sense and thermic detection.

PRESENTATION OF THE NERVOUS SYSTEM

Comparing the brains of frogs and vipers shows that the latter is proportionally larger. An "encephalization index" is calculated in order to understand the relative importance of the brain to the rest of the body, and to compare this development across several groups: it reflects the species' evolutionary level. The higher the index, the more evolved the species is considered (see the table on page 51).

Snakes range from 32 for the *Boa constrictor*, from the Boidae family, to 104 for the water moccasin (*Agkistrodon piscivorus*), a Viperidae.

These numbers differ only slightly from those found in amphibians (35 to 174), and are low compared to those found in other reptiles such as turtles (43 to 234) or lizards (72 to 337). See Illus. 2.

One shouldn't conclude that snakes are no more evolved than amphibians, since it is well known that this brain index puts long-bodied animals at a disadvantage, because apodia generally leads to a regression of the brain volume. Snakes must thus be compared to morphologically similar species. One then sees that the amphiume, a long-bodied amphibian, has an index of 35, while various serpentiform reptiles have numbers close to those of snakes: 44 for the worm lizard, 72 for the glass snake, 74 for the blindworm, and 104 for the serpent lizard. Snakes are thus quite comparable to other reptiles with respect to their brain development. Life-style also affects this index: a relatively inactive terrestrial species that carries out most of its activity at dusk, like the smooth snake (*Coronella austriaca*), has an index of 48, while a diurnal, active, and occasionally arboreal species like the ladder snake (*Elaphe scalaris*) has an index of 79.

Although the encephalization index gives us some information on species' evolutionary level, the detailed analysis of the relative importance of certain parts of the brain gives us a much richer picture. Indeed, zones dedicated to processing sensory information are more or less developed in an animal according to those zones' role in the animal's behavior.

The accessory olfactory bulbs, which are linked to the vomeronasal sense, are quite developed in terrestrial species, which stalk their prey on the ground. The nervous centers dealing with visual information are particularly developed in the aquatic Colubridae, demonstrating sight's importance in such an environment. The cerebellum, which plays a fundamental role in maintaining balance, is much more developed in aquatic or arboreal species, which move in all three dimensions. Each adaptation to a particular way of live thus gives rise to the development of one or more centers of the nervous system. Studying them can thus give us important information on the animals' way of life.

THE CENTRAL NERVOUS SYSTEM: BRAIN AND SPINAL CORD

Observing the brain reveals the large size of the cerebral hemispheres, which, although smaller

▽ *BELOW: Illus. 1. Dorsal view of a viper's brain*

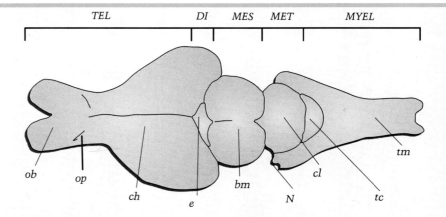

ob: olfactory bulbs (main and accessory); **e:** epiphysis location; **ch:** cerebral hemisphere; **cl:** cerebellum lamina; **bm:** bone marrow; **op:** olfactory peduncle; **tc:** tela choroidea of the 4th ventricle; **tm:** tectum mesencephalicum; **N:** nerve

TEL: telencephalon; **DI:** diencephalon; **MES:** mesencephalon; **MET:** metencephalon; **MYEL:** myelencephalon

than those of birds and mammals, are much more developed than those of amphibians. There is, in fact, a clear progression, as the development of new structures allow for information to be integrated in a more complex manner. The appearance of a cerebral cortex partially heralds the structures which become preponderant in mammals.

The cerebral hemispheres contain an encephalic formation that is typical of snakes and of some lizards: a spherical core where the information obtained by the accessory olfactory bulbs is projected.

Farther back, between tubercles are stratified by cellular layer, which is quite complex in reptiles, where the peripheral zone (the dermal tectum) receives the nervous fibers of retinal origin. Comparing these layers in lizards and both typical and burrowing snakes has led to interesting observations on the phylogenic relations between these two groups of squamates. The semicircular toruses, which are homologous to the posterior quadrigeminal tubercles found in mammals, contribute largely to the auditory function.

The cerebellum is found towards the back and looks like a thick blade. It is involved in posture, and although developmental variations appear, based on different species' way of life, it remains small compared to that of legged reptiles.

The spinal cord, found in the vertebral canal, is obviously quite long. It can be up to 100 times longer than a colubrid's brain. The lack of limbs give the cord a constant diameter. It is the seat of much reflexive activity and is somewhat autonomous, despite being under the brain's control through many connections. A decapitated snake can still move, sometimes even with relatively complex movements, such as those used for catching prey.

SENSORY ORGANS

▶ *Hearing, a relatively undeveloped sense in Ophidians*
Snakes' ears exhibit certain characteristics which differentiate snakes from other reptiles as well as from other vertebrates.

Like most other reptiles, except crocodiles, snakes have no external ear. Furthermore, their middle ear is virtually nonexistent. The tympanic plate, eustachian tube, and eardrum are absent; only the columella, shaped like a small stick, subsists, articulated onto the oval window (which opens on one side of the inner ear) and to the quadrate bone.

On the other hand, the inner ear is generally organized like that of other vertebrates, and if various families of lizards are characterized by morphological variations, these variations are not so important among snakes.

The sensory formations of the semicircular canals, the utricle and saccule, ensure balance (vestibular sense). The cochlear canal, and the basilar papilla, a membrane that picks up and reacts to vibrations (in particular) are given over

▽ *BELOW: Illus. 2. Brain-size index for amphibians and reptiles. Each column represents the different groups studied.*

BRAIN-SIZE INDEX

A formula allows for the comparison of brain development and the calculation of a brain-size index. This formula takes the volume (or weight) of the brain, B, and the volume or weight of the body, W, at a power close to ⅔. It is written $B = kW^a$

Calculating k gives us the brain-size index, independent of the animal's size. Ten is taken as a reference number, which corresponds to the lamprey, which has the lowest brain-size index of any vertebrate. Since the brain is the nervous center which deals with all information and organizes all behavior, it is agreed that a higher index signifies a more evolved species.

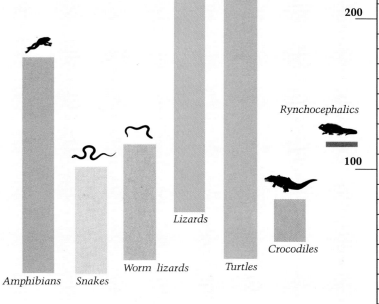

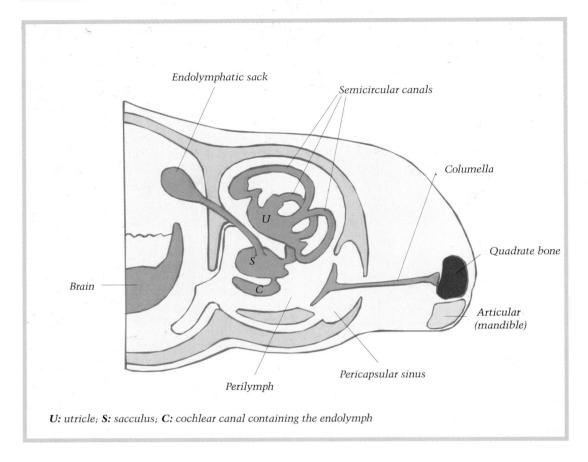

U: *utricle;* **S:** *sacculus;* **C:** *cochlear canal containing the endolymph*

◁ LEFT: *Illus. 3. Theoretical diagram showing the different parts of a snake ear. The middle ear is reduced to the columella, found between the oval window and the quadrate bone.*

to hearing. The lack of external and middle ears could lead one to expect to find a greatly reduced basilar papilla, especially in the burrowing species, as this is the case in lizards with the same life-style. In fact, the opposite is true: this papilla is larger in burrowing than it is in arboreal or terrestrial snakes, and it has only regressed in marine snakes.

This is the problem we find in snakes' auditory universe: although their middle ear is not particularly favorable to receiving sound vibrations, the part of the internal ear devolved to hearing is well developed in most species. Is snakes' hearing efficient? How are sound vibrations transmitted to the internal ear?

Experiments recording the cochlear nerves' electric activity have shown that colubrids, notably the *Thamnophis* and *Natrix* genera, perceive vibrations of 100 to 700 Hz (for man, the range is from 50 to 1500 or 2000 Hz). Since removing the quadrate bone eliminates hearing much more obviously than does removing the columella, it is obvious that this bone plays an essential role in the transmission of sound vibrations.

In natural conditions, the snake's hearing system seems to perceive vibrations emitted by the substratum in contact with the head. Again, it is the quadrate, along with the upper jaw, that ensures transmission. The case of arboreal snakes is different, since their head rarely comes into contact with the substrate. Since vibrations applied to the body's soft tissue quickly lose their intensity, these species may detect aerial vibrations, but this has not yet been proven.

So hearing is not absent from the snakes' universe, but it does not play a pivotal role.

▶ Smell

Olfactory messages start in the sensory epithelium, which covers the back part of the cavum, one of the three areas of the nasal fossa along with the vestibulum and preorbital area. The epithelium, which is large in snakes, allows for the detection of prey—or predators—when the stimulus is composed of volatile substances.

Snakes' olfactory performances are difficult to evaluate for they are often associated with other senses, whether vomeronasal or visual. But the sheer volume of the olfactory nervous centers leaves no doubt as to the fact that snakes are macrosmatic animals: the perception of volatile chemical substances plays an important role in their behavior.

▶ The vomeronasal sense: an important asset

The vomeronasal function exists in lizards and mammals (except for cetaceans and superior primates), but nowhere is it as highly perfected as in snakes. Although it has long been considered a component of the sense of smell, it differentiates itself by the nature of the stimulus and the nerve centers called into play. It gives rise to many of the snake's behaviors, of which we are only beginning to measure the importance.

△ *ABOVE LEFT:* **Chironius carinatus,** *tongue out*

▷ △ *ABOVE RIGHT: Seen from the top, the head of a grass snake (*Natrix natrix*) with its tongue out*

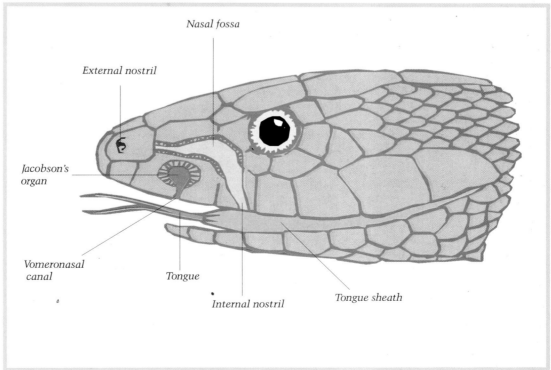

Nasal fossa

External nostril

Jacobson's organ

Vomeronasal canal

Tongue

Internal nostril

Tongue sheath

▷ *RIGHT: Illus. 4. Colubrid head, showing the nasal fossa and Jacobson's organ*

LOCATING & TRACKING PREY

Yannick Vasse

Locating & tracking	Senses used
When an asp viper has located a rodent (vole or mouse) that could make a meal, it follows it with its eyes and flicks its tongue, remaining immobile until the animal is in its reach.	The viper lies in wait for game, and finds prey by sight, since the snake is alerted by movement.
At that moment it surges forward and bites its victim with its venom fangs.	The snake prefers to bite if the prey or decoy has skin and fur, but a dismembered body or another decoy may also be bitten. Vision is also important at this stage: a viper that is used to feeding on white mice will have difficulty accepting a grey mouse, and vice versa.
The victim immediately flees, but the venom immobilizes by the time it gets a little farther away. The viper waits for two or three minutes, during which it yawns, and slowly goes in search of the rodent, following its direction. The snake searches for the animal's traces, keeping its head close to the ground, flicks its tongue repeatedly, and follows the animal's tracks.	A viper with covered eyes reacts normally, but with a haphazard or random start. Obstructed nostrils do not keep it from tracking. But if the tips of the tongue are cut, it cannot find the prey's tracks, which proves how important the vomeronasal sense is. A dismembered body or decoy is never followed, while a skin gets the same reaction as an entire mouse.

Ringed snake (Natrix natrix) *faces down its prey, a green frog.*

Once near the dead or agonizing animal, the viper goes all around it; all the while, the snake touches the prey with its tongue.	The prey is identified thanks to Jacobson's organ, which analyzes the nonvolatile chemical particles picked up by the snake's tongue. Only entire mice, skins, or freshly skinned bodies are accepted at this stage. So it is, in fact, a chemical stimulus emitted by the skin which leads to the prey's capture.
It searches for the prey's head, which is usually swallowed first.	Recognizing the head and swallowing it put many senses into play: smell, the vomeronasal sense, and, perhaps, touch. The head is recognized even if it is affixed to another part of the body. If the head is taken away, the viper is disturbed, but ends up eating the prey anyway.

Catching prey is a complex behavior that puts a number of senses into play: sight, which predominates in the first stage, but is not indispensable, and the chemical senses afterwards, which are indispensable.

The grass snake can follow the tracks of a live frog without any preliminary contact. Some hobbyists feed their frog-eating snakes with "frog-flavored" mice, i.e., mice that have been soaked in the thawed water of frozen frogs.

△ *ABOVE: Group of garter snakes,* Thamnophis sirtalis parietalis, *Manitoba, Canada*

The snake darts its thin and forked tongue in and out of its mouth at various rhythms, and it picks up nonvolatile molecules from the substratum, which it then carries to the receptive organ: the vomeronasal organ, or Jacobson's organ. This organ is found in the nasal cavity, and it opens towards the roof of the oral cavity through two orifices. Its sensory cells react on contact with certain molecules by nervous influx, which reach the accessory olfactory bulbs, and from there the other encephalic centers as well as the nucleus globosus. This is a highly developed sense in some snakes, such as the colubrids. In certain Colubridae, the vomeronasal bulb is much more developed than the main olfactory bulb. Observing an asp viper (*Vipera aspis*) under experimental conditions has shown that its first behavior is exploratory darts of the tongue. It can thus recognize prey, stalk it if it moves, attack it so as to be able to catch it if it escapes after having been bitten (see table).

The vomeronasal function is not the only reason for these behaviors, but it is much more important than other functions (smell, sight, heat detection) in most species.

This function also favors interspecies relations, helping to find fellow creatures so as to form the famous snake balls which are often found towards the beginning of dormancy. These balls help maintain social coherence and help to join the sexes for spring.

Sexual behavior in the male garter snake is triggered by the detection of an estrogen-dependent pheromone emitted by the female's skin. Such behavior starts with rapid tongue darting, followed by a raising of the partners' bodies, and a joining of the cloacas, followed by copulation. For species living in temperate regions, only males who hibernate partake in the nuptial ritual, and the vomeronasal organ's role is essential. Sexual hormones have been found in those males that act upon the brain structures connected to the vomeronasal function: the nucleus globosus. We don't know if this behavior exists in every snake, for the number of species that have been studied is still too small.

▶ Vision

Although the vomeronasal function plays an extremely important role in snakes' perception, sight dominates, except in burrowing species, like Typhlophidae and Leptotyphlopidae, whose eyes are atrophied.

Snakes have a wide field of vision: 125° for the grass snake (*Natrix natrix*), 135° for the rock python (*Python molurus*).

Snakes also have binocular vision, which allows them to appreciate distance and perceive depth. In snakes, the area seen by both eyes is approximately 30°. It is 45° in arboreal species like *Ahaetulla*, with its horizontal, keyhole-shaped pu-

RETINAL STRUCTURE

THE DIVERSITY AND COMPLEXITY of the snake's retina's visual cells are explained by two complementary interpretations.

The first interpretation refers to the origin of snakes (as is generally agreed upon); snakes evolved from burrowing lizards whose retinas were modified for this type of life-style.

The second interpretation involves a cellular redifferentiation arising from leaving a burrowing life-style and passing through snakes' various present-day adaptations, including a return to underground life.

The most archaic type of retina, which characterizes Typhlopidae and Leptotyphlopidae, only contains rods (simple scolecophidian type). Boas' and pythons' retinas recall those of most vertebrates: there are cones (for color vision in bright light) and rods (for crepuscular vision). This is called duplex vision. Snakes are the only group to present variations on this model.

Colubrids' retinas have four types of visual cells: rods, cones similar to those of Booids, and two new types of cones: thick simple and thick double. This type of retina is called viperine duplex, as it is found in the genera *Vipera*, *Bitis*, and *Causus*, as well as in some terrestrial Elapidae, and in the smooth snake (*Coronella austriaca*). By simplifying this duplex type, one finds the two other types of retina found in snakes:

Cones like those of Booids have disappeared in rattlesnakes (*Crotalus*), fers-de-lance (*Bothrops*), and water moccasins (*Agkistrodon*), which only have three types of visual cells: one rod and two cones.

In many Colubridae (*Natrix*, *Thamnophis*, *Coluber*), the rods disappear and there are three types of cones.

Malpolon monspessulanus, a diurnal species with good vision, has not only lost rods, but the cones resembling those of Booids.

Let us also note that in species from the *Phyllorhynchus* genus, the cones resemble rods, but without their characteristic pigmentation, the visual purple.

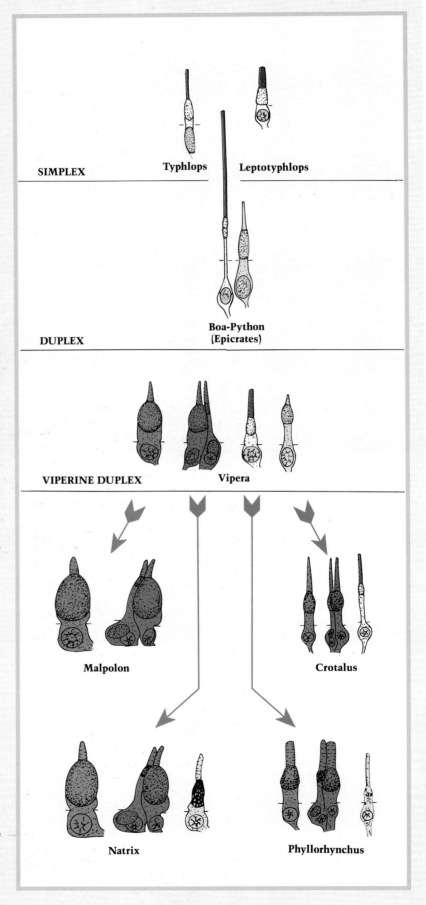

Illus. 5. Shape variations and types of association of visual cells in the major snake groups. Rods are recognizable by their distal segment, which carries rhodopsin (in red); the different colors show the three types of cones. The arrows suggest the relation between the different types.

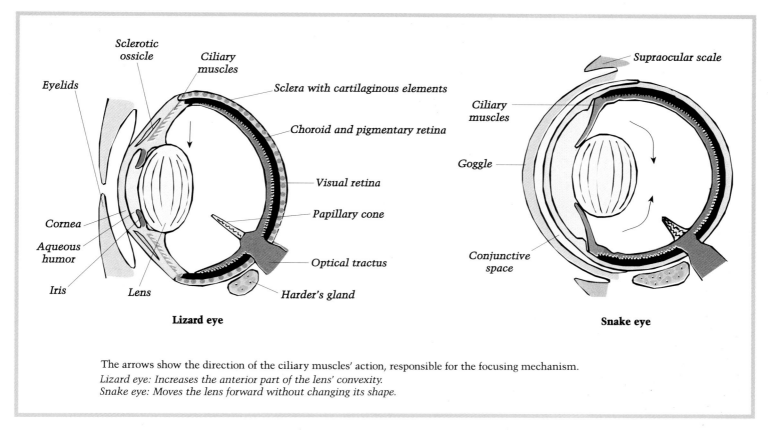

The arrows show the direction of the ciliary muscles' action, responsible for the focusing mechanism.
Lizard eye: Increases the anterior part of the lens' convexity.
Snake eye: Moves the lens forward without changing its shape.

△ *ABOVE: Illus. 6. Comparative sketches of a lizard's and a snake's eye*

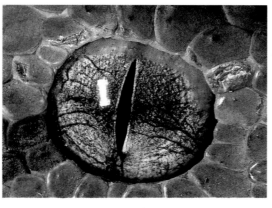

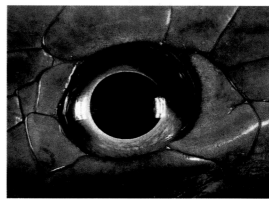

▷ *NEAR RIGHT: Gaboon viper's* (Bitis gabonica) *eye, with slit pupil*

▷ *FAR RIGHT: Grass snake* (Natrix natrix) *eye, round pupil*

pil, and with the two depressions on each side of its face that help to minimize the nasal area. This binocular vision of a 45° represents a real adaptive advantage for snakes that move in a three-dimensional area.

Snakes' eyes can generally accommodate, that is, they can focus on images forming on the retina. This is original among reptiles and close to what happens in squid (Cephalopods), sharks, and amphibians, and puts the ciliary muscles, which are peripheral to the iris, into play; their contraction increases pressure in the vitreous body and pushes the lens towards the front. In some species of the genus *Natrix*, the front of the lens can change shape, as it does in certain mammals. In marine species, air vision is accompanied by a considerable diminution of the pupil's diameter, sometimes to the size of a pinhead.

Snakes, diurnal species at least, seem to have good color vision. Many diurnal colubrids have a round pupil and a yellow lens, as well as a retina made entirely of cones, which ensures color vision that functions in intense light. It has been proven that *Natrix (Tropidonotus)* has cones that are sensitive to red, green, and blue.

Crepuscular species have a paler lens and their retina contains both cones and rods, which allow for vision in dim light. In nocturnal snakes, finally, the pupil is a vertical slit, the lens is colorless, and the retina contains mostly rods.

This outline shouldn't be generalized as there are numerous exceptions. For example, European vipers, which are diurnal rather than crepuscular, have vertical pupils and the retina contains both rods and cones of many types. In crepuscular or nocturnal pythons, the pupil is round, but the retina contains both a large quantity of cones as well as rods.

The visual cells on snakes' retinas are both more diverse and more complex than those found

in other vertebrates. This complexity, which is obvious when looking at the cells' structure (cones and rods), probably also extends to their physiology, which is still not well known (see the table on the next page).

Despite its importance, vision rarely works alone in a snake's perception: It precedes or accompanies another sensory function. It is closely linked with heat detection in both rattlesnakes and pythons.

▶ Heat detection: sensing infrared rays

Crotalinae and Pythoninae detect the infrared rays emitted by a heat source. This sense is extraordinarily useful in locating and catching warm-blooded prey, such as birds and mammals. The perception apparatus differs among groups. Crotalinae have loreal dimples; these are deep cavities found on each side of the head, between the eye and the nostril, closed by a thin membrane with over 7000 sensory endings. In pythons, the labial scales have up to 13 pairs of depressions called labial dimples; the sensory endings are found in the epithelium, which covers the bottom of these dimples.

In certain boas (*Boa constrictor*), the infrared receptive apparatus is only composed of a few infrared-sensitive cephalic scales.

Even the mildest of stimuli (a difference of $\frac{3}{1000}$ of a degree to the nerve ending) gives rise to a message which reaches the brain. This entire mechanism is still relatively unknown.

Snakes prove to be remarkably precise in locating the sources of infrared rays, their receptor

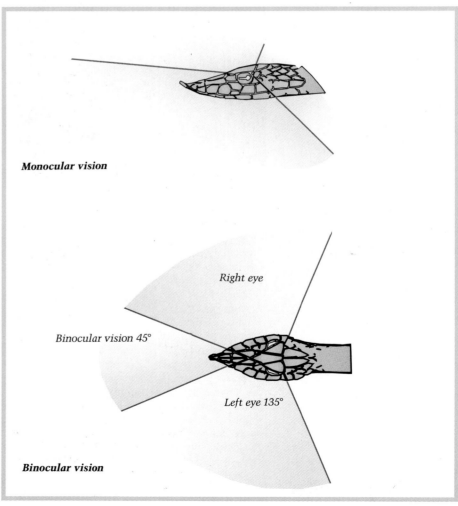

Monocular vision

Right eye

Binocular vision 45°

Left eye 135°

Binocular vision

 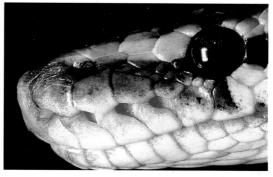

◁ LEFT: *Tree snake* (Ahaetulla), *with its keyhole-shaped pupils*

▷ NEAR RIGHT: **Crotalux atrox's** *loreal dimple*

▷ FAR RIGHT: **Python regius's** *thermoreceptive dimples*

functioning like a lensless camera. The nerve paths coming from these infrared-sensing organs is radically different from those found in classic sensory models. These paths serve as relays in structures of the brain stem, which exists only in the Crotalinae and Pythoninae, and then reach the brain, where visual information is decoded: the dermic tectum. So there are possibilities for superimposing the visual function upon heat detection. Certain multimodal neurons of the optic region simultaneously deal with both types of information.

▷ RIGHT: *Illus. 8. Thermic and visual perception of a rattlesnake*

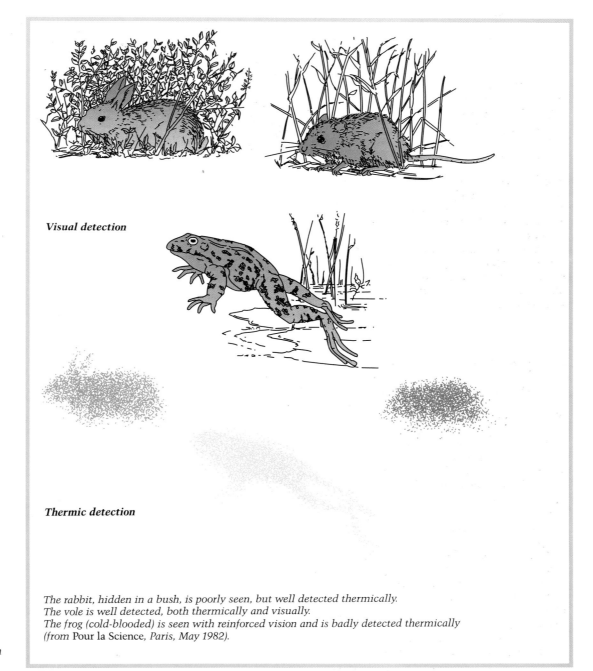

Visual detection

Thermic detection

The rabbit, hidden in a bush, is poorly seen, but well detected thermically.
The vole is well detected, both thermically and visually.
The frog (cold-blooded) is seen with reinforced vision and is badly detected thermically (from Pour la Science, *Paris, May 1982).*

◁ LEFT: *Illus. 7. Monocular field of vision, and binocular field of vision in a tree snake* (Ahaetulla)

LOCOMOTION

Jean-Pierre Gasc

While a snake's shape often seems strange to man, its movements give the impression that its body never changes shape. Anatomical studies and analysis of snake movement have made it possible to solve some of the mysteries of their reptation, as well as certain specializations of this apodal means of locomotion.

SNAKES ARE SUBJECT TO THE LAWS OF PHYSICS

An animal's movement comes from the environment's response to the force produced by its muscular system. In quadrupeds or bipeds, the limbs push off the substratum, and the force comes from muscular extension. Snakes, of course, have no concentrated point to push off from: any part of their body can push against the ground. A horizontal flexure runs through the spine from front to back, which tends to press the body against the ground. Propulsion results from the sum of the reaction against the ground. As in all other apodal vertebrates, the entire spine and its surrounding muscles are the snake's locomotive organ.

Although some snakes (Typhlopidae, Leptotyphlopidae, and Boidae, in particular) have retained a vestigial pelvis and back limbs, these play no role whatsoever in movement. The mechanisms responsible for movement are found in the skeleton and the vertebrocostal system's muscular structure, as well as in the sheath formed by the skin and muscles.

THE SKELETON

Snakes have at least 130 vertebrae between head and cloaca, and thus number can exceed 300. Fewer vertebrae are found in the Viperidae, the most in the Boidae and burrowing vipers (*Atractaspis*). All vertebrates whose limbs (and their locomotive role) are restricted have a cylindrical, elongated body, with a circumference equal to a tenth of total body length, and sometimes even less.

The snakes' system of vertebral articulation, which is close to that of lizards, is among the most complex found in vertebrates. Manipulating a few vertebrae gives an idea of the possibilities: Only a

▷ RIGHT: *This young boa constrictor (Boa constrictor) ensures its grip by a grasping action with the back of its body. The rest of its body hangs and is ready to surge towards a prey. The front of the snake's body is kept rigid by the double action of articular blocks and a strong musculature. Seen both from above in the front and below by the suspended part, the animal shows the two types of scales most snakes have: small scales in oblique rows on the back, and large scales covering the stomach.*

ANATOMY OF A VERTEBRA

EXCEPT for the first three or four, each vertebra carries a pair of ossified ribs, articulated by a single head on a lateral face, finished by a small cartilaginous piece. On the lower side of the vertebra, the hypophases extend obliquely towards the back, found either on the front part of the spine (up to the heart) or all the way down to the cloaca.

The vertebra is composed of a massive body on which the neural arc rests, which delimits the space occupied by the bone marrow. The vertebrae form a cavity in front, the cotyle, and a jutting in the back, the condyle. This type of procoeleus vertebrae allows for the rotation of each condyle into the following cotyle; the surfaces are covered with cartilage.

Neural arcs are laterally extended by lamella, which form gliding surfaces: zygapophyses (the front ones oriented towards the top, the back ones oriented towards the bottom). Each vertebra's neural arc rests on the following one.

The neural arc also forms a jutting area above the neural canal: the zygosphene, which has a gliding facet oriented outside and towards the bottom on each side (Illus. 1). The whole forms a mortise-and-tenon joint; the zygantrum is hollowed out into the posterior face of the preceding vertebra's neural arc.

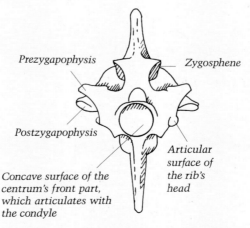

Prezygapophysis

Zygosphene

Postzygapophysis

Articular surface of the rib's head

Concave surface of the centrum's front part, which articulates with the condyle

◁ LEFT: *Illus. 1. Snake vertebra seen from the front*

few movements are possible, and these have a limited amplitude. Movements are defined according to the three spatial dimensions, the entocondyle acting as frame of reference; rotation and translation are possible along each axis.

The articular facets' position only seems to offer three of the six theoretical degrees of liberty: lateral flexion (rotation around the vertical axis), dorsoventral flexion (rotation about the transverse axis), and dislocation (translation along the longitudinal axis). However, taking the facets' dimensions into account, the first two movements' course is limited, and dislocation is blocked by ligaments and muscles.

In fact, each movement's amplitude is quite limited. Lateral flexion, which is by far the largest, often ranges between 10° and 20°, while ventrodorsal flexion is of only a few degrees. Finally, only a tiny torsion of the spine is possible (rotation around the longitudinal axis). There is only a slight loosening between facets of the zygosphene-zygantrum on the one hand, and the zygapophyses on the other.

These limitations may appear contradictory with snakes' obvious ability to curve their bodies into balls, as the small African python *Calabaria* does when it feels threatened, but the body's mobility is, in fact, the sum of the small movements of many vertebrae. The python's spine can curve 60° through the addition of the articular play in a portion of the body with 40 vertebrae (see Illus. 2, on page 61). The dominant movement is a lateral flexion, which translates the generally horizontal orientation of the zygapophyses' facets, on which the different modes of reptation rest. Dorsal flexion is also used, particularly towards the front of the body, as shown by the *Najas*' ability to raise their heads by raising the front third of their bodies. Sidewinding (a type of reptation) is accompanied by a torsion of the spine between the static and mobile parts of the body.

MUSCULATURE

The musculature, which activates ribs and vertebrae, is disposed in cords composed of a succession of muscle fibre fascicles prolonged by tendons,

▷ *RIGHT: Illus. 2. Morphological characteristics of snake vertebrae.* **A:** *lateral and ventral view of two python vertebrae. The vertebral bodies are interarticulated thanks to a posterior condyle (**pc**) inserted into the next vertebra's anterior cotyle (**ac**). Each side has an articulation facet for the ribs (**r**). The neural arcs, topped by a crest, the neural spine (**n**), glide in relation to their neighbors thanks to a double system of zygapophyses (**Zap**) and the group formed by the zygosphene (**Zys**), found towards the front, and the zygantrum, at the back.* **B:** *the maximal amplitude of lateral flexion between two successive vertebrae*

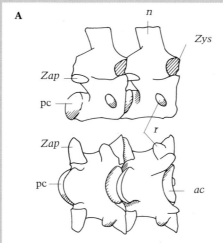

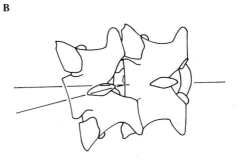

Despite a very small play in the zygophysis-zygosphene system, a 60° twist is possible over 40 vertebrae. Snakes' twisting capacities thus do not endanger the bone marrow, since there is no large movement between any two vertebrae.

each of which covers a number of vertebrae, affix-
ing to specific points of the vertebrae and ribs. The
whole system is composed of various units. Pythons have 9 fascicles, sand vipers (*Cerastes*) have
12, *Hierophis viridiflavus* has 16, and *Oxybelis* has
33. These fascicles are covered so as to ensure the
autocohesion of the whole by keeping any one
from pulling away when movement starts, much
like a twisted cord.

△ *ABOVE:* Crotalus viridis nuntius
pushes onto its environment's
surface through the propagation of a
wave that begins at the head.

Skin: interfacing with the environment

While animals with limbs have concentrated
mechanisms on the bottoms of their extremities
(rugged pads, claws, lamella, etc.) that ensure a
good static contact, avoiding skidding or too great
a loss of strength by deforming the substratum, the
situation is quite different for snakes. Most of their
points of body surface come into contact with the
environment; furthermore, each one of these
points is confronted, either alternatively (accordion reptation) or simultaneously (sidewinding)
with the antagonistic conditions of good static
contact and of gliding without excessive friction.

The skin surface's configuration plays an important role in locomotion. It is usually covered with
scales whose backs are loose and which slightly
cover the scale behind them. The scales' geometric
disposition and their bodily distribution (network

LATERAL UNDULATION

IN REPTATION by undulation, two parts of the snake's body are on the same circumference, led by the undulation in its horizontal plane, moving from one side to the other and with the forward progression. The speed at which the flexion is propagated from back to front determines the interval between the movement of these two points.

Transverse movement can be studied independently of longitudinal movement, as if the animal stayed in place and undulated like a vibrating cord. There are two longitudinal periods for each transverse period, so that a continuous oscillation can be perceived by the naked eye.

When a snake travels an experimental area made up of a flat surface with pitons spread at regular intervals, it uses lateral undulation. Its motor flexion can thus be observed. This flexion isn't rigorously sinusoid; its length and amplitude increase towards the back, where the body is thinner. There is nonetheless a relative consistency at any given moment of the number of periods along the body.

There is an exchange of forces at each contact point with the ground. The flexion wave determines a more or less oblique push on the ground, which leads to an equal and opposite push from the body. The motor effect depends upon the intensity and orientation of the result of these two forces, push and reaction, and is represented by horizontal movement.

Despite a distribution of weight along the length of the body, snakes are subject to gravity and to the added effect of the push on the ventral side. In natural conditions, they often travel on uneven or even discontinuous substrates, such as branches. The resulting force must have a vertical component, gravity's opposite; the flexion wave pushes down and back.

It's easy to understand how important some characteristics, like lighter bodies (a reduction in the weight of contractile muscles in relation to the tendons, which diminishes the friction between skin and ground), and body elongation, allowing for a multiplication of points producing motor reactions, are to arboreal species. These conditions are sometimes opposite. Body elongation increases friction, and the multiplication of contact points is limited by the flexion capacities between two successive contacts. Various compromises expand the diversity of specializations.

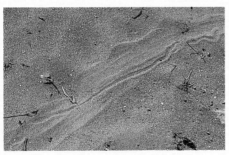

◁ OPPOSITE, ABOVE: *Tracks of the Egyptian cobra (*Naja haje*)*
◁ OPPOSITE, BELOW: *Tracks of the puff adder (*Bitis arietans*)*

△ ABOVE: *Illus. 3. Tracks left by lateral undulation*

with diamond-shaped links on the sides and back, and transverse rows on the stomach) facilitate the meeting of resistance points and unattached sides of the scales, where they are subjected to a push towards the back by flexion impulse. Furthermore, no bodily relief is opposed to forward gliding.

The exact same principle is revealed upon examining the skin's surface at a microscopic level. Those scales that appear to be the smoothest are in fact covered with tiny indentations that leave some tiny contours in back. Their back-to-front alignment creates gliding tracks. Arboreal species like the tree snake (*Oxybelis*), which must also establish a static vertical contact (against gravity), have quadrangular networks.

CHARACTERISTICS OF THE VARIOUS MODES OF REPTATION

Instead of being handicaps, the lack of limbs, the considerable elongation of the body, and the particular mode of locomotion have allowed snakes to expand into diverse environments. Snakes rival limbed species, sometimes even beating them. One of snakes' assets is their ability to immediately respond to a new environment by changing reptation modes. Snakes are also so diversified that they include many examples of specialization, in which one reptation mode is favored.

▶ *Lateral undulation*
Lateral undulation is practised by most apodal

vertebrates, and consists of a continuous movement by the entire body, where the animal glides
on the substrate. Each part of the body successively
passes on the same part of the ground, without
there ever being any static contact. The snake
alternates contracting and relaxing the muscles,
and sides, from head to tail.

Lateral undulation is the most common reptation mode, particularly when the snake escapes or
attacks. The longer the snake and the more con-
toured the ground, the more efficient this mode is.
Those snakes that are particularly long and slender, like racers (*Coluber*), can curve their bodies
more than vipers can with their short and stocky
bodies, and thus the former use more points as
"launching pads." But the more contact points
there are, the greater the force pushing against
forward movement; the theoretical efficiency of a
great number of curves is limited. The fastest
snakes are those whose length is no more than 10
to 13 times their circumference.

These fast snakes are represented by the North
American racers and whipsnakes (*Coluber* and
Masticophis), which reach 4 mph (6 to 7 km/hr)
on flat surfaces, and the record-holding East African black mamba (*Dendroaspis polyepis*), which
was observed doing 7 mph (11 km/hr) over 142 ft.
(43 m) in 14 seconds.

In natural conditions, snakes use available supports (grass, stones) and the undulation's regularity can be modified. The animal adapts its
curves to the contours encountered by its head or
cervical area. The theoretical undulation model is
thus changed during the trip towards the back of
the body. Peripheral data (of cutaneous, muscular,
and articular origin) probably inform the motor
centers of the distance between supports, the
amount of pressure exerted, and the degree of
curve.

▶ Skidding

Snakes in search of prey, or in seasonal movement
between a wintering site and an activity zone, must
travel through different environments. They are
sometimes confronted with physically difficult situations, such as when they encounter a smooth
surface (a stone slab, e.g.). They must then make
wide lateral undulations, which allow them only to
advance slowly.

In order to get a maximum push from a surface
that is not particularly favorable to their means of
locomotion, snakes rest their head (or cervical
region) on the ground and, starting from this
static point, send a flexion wave through their
body. Lateral skidding exerts an oblique push on
the substrate (Illus. 4). When the wave reaches
the tail, a new one creates an identical but sym-
metrical push. The center of gravity thus receives
reaction from one side and then from the other, so
that instead of a straight trajectory, it travels in
zigzags. This travel mode, which is quite costly in
energy and inefficient (since two-thirds of the
movement is lost), is only used in an emergency, as
when the snake must cross an open space.

▶ Accordion

The snake engaged in this movement seems alter-

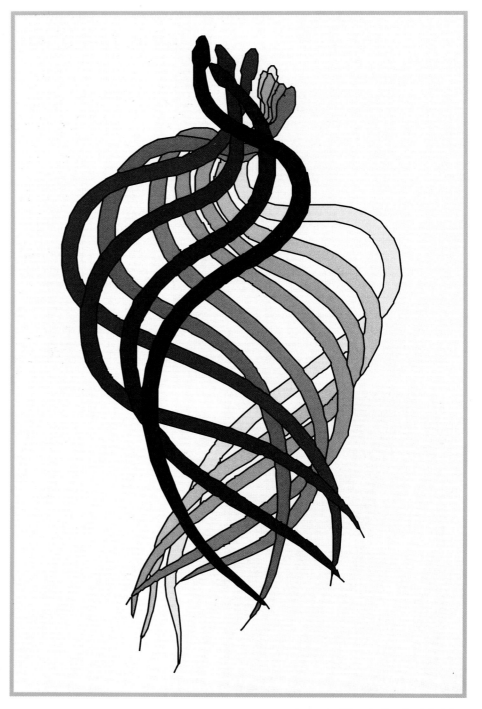

△ ABOVE: *Illus. 4. Sketch of skidding movement*

nately to stretch and fold. The work is divided along the body: one portion, grouped by a number of curves, enters into static contact with the substrate, while another is pushed or pulled thanks to this contact (see Illus. 5). The roles are then reversed between both parts. Two situations make snakes move this way. Short and stocky snakes like the Viperidae use this method on smooth surfaces, and all snakes use it when they are in a large enough tunnel.

When the tunnel is sufficiently larger than the snake's diameter, static contact occurs between the lateral walls and the body's meanders. These meanders are greater the narrower the tunnel, although when the two diameters are too similar, and the snake can no longer curve its body, this mode of locomotion cannot be carried out.

Although in theory long and thin snakes are favored by this kind of movement, in reality their capacity is determined by their curving ability, that is, the number of vertebral articulations per foldable body segment, taking the diameter/length ratio into account. It turns out that relatively short snakes which, like Viperidae, have a minimum number of vertebrae (150), are the best "accordionists," for their vertebrae allow pronounced flexions. However, certain elongated colubrids,

like *Elaphe* and *Coluber*, use the accordion to climb rough trees or even walls. Since these colubrids are long and lightweight, they can use any bumps as a cramping point for their scales.

▶ *Sidewinding*

Sidewinding is practised by snakes in level and moderately rough areas, usually a sandy environment, where they leave characteristic traces consisting of a series of parallel bars.

Cinematographic observation has made it possible to see the various phases of movement. The snake raises its head as well as a loop of its body, which is thrown ahead and to the side and comes back into contact with the ground. At the same time, another loop is formed, and so on. The snake proceeds by taking "steps" to the side. The general orientation of the head and body are oblique in relation to the direction of movement. The movement nonetheless gives an impression of continuity, for the loops are only a few millimetres above the ground.

Among the species that practise sidewinding, the best known are the horned viper (*Cerastes cerastes*), which goes up to 2 mph (3 km/hr), the Namibian viper of southwestern Africa (*Bitis peri-*

▷ RIGHT: *Illus. 5. Sketch of accordion movement. The zones in static contact with the walls of a tunnel, or with the ground, are constituted by a tightening of the body's undulations; the animal pushes or pulls its body from these zones.*

ngueyi), the Pakistani McMahon's viper (*Eristi-cophis macmahoni*), and the sidewinder, a desert rattlesnake which also moves at up to 2 mph (3 km/hr), the maximum speed for this type of reptation. Some semiaquatic colubers, like the grass snake (*Natrix natrix*), as well as terrestrial Boidae with great flexion abilities, can also use sidewinding to move on smooth surfaces. All of these snakes use sidewinding on rough ground.

▶ Straight or linear progression

Straight progression is practised by thick-bodied snakes (boas, terrestrial pythons, and large vipers from the *Bitis* family) when on a smooth surface. The young can even climb a very smooth vertical wall, especially if their bodies are damp, which facilitates adhesion by a superficial tension phenomenon. These snakes can even climb the glass walls of a terrarium.

The snake's body does not flex at all and stays straight while gliding.

This mode of reptation depends upon the active role played by the scales and muscles, and especially by the anchoring of the ventral scales, from neck to cloaca.

Small groups of scales are successively lifted, moved ahead, re-anchored to the ground by their loose edge, and the body is pulled along by this support, bringing the abdominal wall's costo-cutaneous muscles into play.

In fact, these small groups of scales act as tiny legs, and the repetition of these small "steps" by the contraction waves gives rise to a reaction important enough to move the animal's center of gravity at uniform speed. This travelling method only allows for slow speed, a few inches (cm) per second, or a few hundred feet (metres) per hour, but heavy snakes can travel across smooth surfaces by expending less energy than by other methods requiring the mobilization of the entire body in a violent movement.

Straight progression is also useful for a snake slithering in a narrow tunnel, but such movement cannot be done by every species.

ORIGINAL METHODS OF MOVING ABOUT

▶ Burrowing

Some snakes are accomplished burrowers, like the

◁ *LEFT: The horned viper's (*Cerastes cerastes*) sidewinding leaves discontinuous marks in the sand. One can easily make out the two areas in static contact, which are separated by those areas that are slightly above the sand, and which leave no marks, except for the tail, when it moves from one support to the next.*

SIDEWINDING

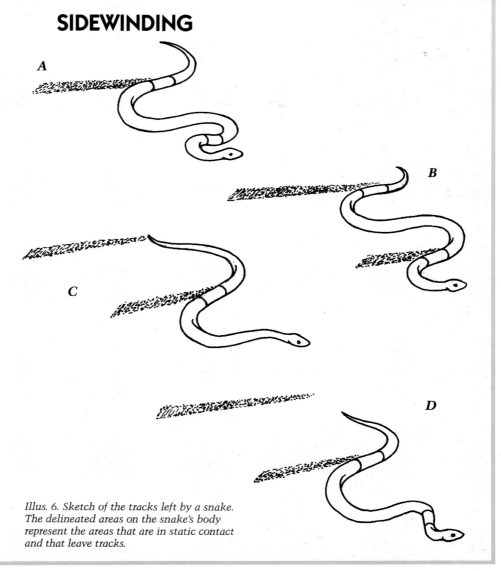

SIDEWINDING is fundamentally different from other reptation modes. If parts of the body are in static contact with the ground, as in any accordion reptation, for one thing these parts are straight and not flexed, and for the other their anatomical situation is forever changing. Each part of the body establishes a brief static contact, and such body parts are then included in a curved and mobile area held a few fractions of an inch (mm) above the ground.

This strange movement is based on the propagation of a lateral and asymmetrical flexion wave, which is accompanied by a vertical flexion, which raises the mobile parts.

The snake appears to roll on its side like a spiralling object. In reality, the rolling is compensated for by the vertebral articulations. There are usually two static portions along the body, each one leaving an oblique imprint in the sand in relation to the snake's direction. The two marks are parallel. Their orientation is determined by the head's lateral flexion when it sits on its new support. The body's center of gravity follows a linear trajectory at a regular speed.

Illus. 6. Sketch of the tracks left by a snake. The delineated areas on the snake's body represent the areas that are in static contact and that leave tracks.

NERVE COMMANDS & COORDINATION

WHEN MOVING, snakes appear as if they are absolutely one with the ground's surface, and considering the number of contact points, this suggests an extraordinary power of central coordination. We do not know exactly which nerve circuits are involved, but it doesn't seem as if an exceptional organization of the motor centers is necessary in these animals.

Analyzing the electric activity that accompanies the muscular contraction during movement does show the motor response to be essentially segmentary. The nerve impulse propagates from the bone marrow's front to back and successively activates the rachidian motor nerves it encounters. These, in turn, activate the muscles found in their territory. Many of these muscles then transmit the message to faraway skeletal parts by a system of tendons.

It has been shown that the contracted zone, around the force's field of application, and shifted on both sides of the curved body, is found slightly ahead of contact on the convex side, and slightly behind on the concave side.

Musculature is thus successively, and not synchronically, active, and only for a few elements at a time.

The shape to which the body adapts in a given situation is not only the result of muscular contraction. It also depends on articular guiding, on the musculotendonous system's geometry, and on the sensory information transmitted by the skin and by the tendonous and articular receptors.

The initial and relatively simple motor command is modulated by local reflexes, which explains how every point in the body theoretically follows the same trajectory.

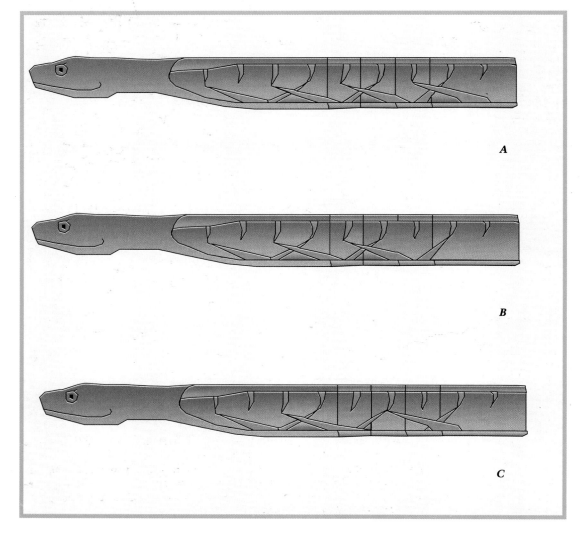

◁ *Illus. 7. Linear progression mechanism. The ribs are immobilized and act as anchors for a muscle system uniting them to the scales' internal wall. Each scale is alternately pulled back and forth by different muscle groups, and its posterior edge hugs the ground, creating a motor reaction.*
A. Snake at rest;
B. Successive groups of ventral scales are moved towards the front;
C. The subjacent body is brought back to its original level.

A

B

C

△ ABOVE: *Snakes that burrow in the sand (*Eryx, *in this case) use their heads as penetrating tools, pushed by the rest of the body's supports.*

▷ RIGHT: *The rostral scale's particular shape is probably due to the use of the head for prospecting the terrestrial environment, as* Salvadora hexalepis *does here.*

Typhlopidae and Leptotyphlopidae (blind and minute-snakes), which are from primitive families. These small animals, usually measuring under 3 ft. (1 m), hide under stumps, rocks, and roots. They have vestigial eyes, a small, compact head, a cylindrical body covered by small, overlapping scales all of the same size, and a short tail that ends in a sort of spine.

The skull is heavily consolidated and is the tip of a soil-boring apparatus in which the joint movements of the vertebrocostal axis and the skin play a part.

Some Aniliidae are specialized burrowers. They present some of the same specializations as Uropeltidae: a solid and compact head, no narrowing to mark the neck, and a short tail that fixes itself to the ground and serves as a point of support.

Uropeltidae, whose tail ends in a shield, offering increased resistance, exemplify a remarkable adaptation to burrowing and movement in tunnels. The motor part of the body is concentrated towards the front, with a strong musculature, while the back, which is passively pulled along, contains the viscera.

Some burrowing snakes are iridescent, the most typical case being that of the rainbow snake, *Xenopeltis unicolor*. This phenomenon (see pigments on page 16) is due to the particularly smooth texture of the epidermis, which acts as a dry lubricant, facilitating burrowing.

Boidae include moderately specialized burrowing species, like the sand boa (*Eryx*), found in North Africa and India, and the Mexican dwarf python (*Loxocemus*). Finally, some more highly evolved snakes are occasionally burrowers, such as the colubers *Heterodon* and *Prosymna*, and the burrowing viper *Atractapsis* (Atractaspididae).

▶ Swimming

Snakes are all apt to swim occasionally, undulating laterally in water like the eel, so as to move a mass of water behind them. Those that feed on aquatic prey in ponds and small streams swim close to the surface and are often able to flatten their bodies by spreading their ribs out (*Natrix*, *Xenodon*).

Marine snakes, on the other hand (Hydrophinae and the more specialized freshwater snakes, Colubridae and Homalopsinae), are laterally flattened in the caudal area, which helps form a scull; the caudal vertebrae's neural spines and ventral processes are lengthened.

▶ Climbing

Some arboreal species, like the southeast Asian *Ahaetulla*, with their long, thin bodies, use lateral undulation to advance horizontally in trees and bushes, taking support on relatively distant points, leaving parts of their body in the air. They can move rather rapidly.

The slower and heavier arboreal species, like arboreal boas (*Corallus*), the emerald tree boa

△ *ABOVE LEFT: Undulation is also effective in an aquatic environment.* Natrix maura, *the colubrid viperine snake, which is often confused with the viper, hunts in small waterways.*

◁ *LEFT:* **Eryx jaculus,** *a sand boa*

△ *ABOVE:* **Natrix natrix,** *the smooth snake, moves among the immersed vegetation of ponds, slowly approaching frogs, which are its favorite prey.*

▷ *RIGHT:* **Hydrophis,** *one of the many venomous sea snakes, exemplifies one of the most extensive adaptations to an aquatic environment. The posterior region and tail are flattened, constituting a propulsory organ. These animals can no longer move on land.*

(*Corallus caninus*), the boa constrictor (*Boa constrictor*), and the parrot snake (*Bothriopsis bilineata*), have an ovoid section, the largest part of which is found towards the back, which, along with the narrowed ventral scales, helps to provide an oblique push against gravity. These species also use their constricting abilities to grab branches when they must cross large spaces. The *Boa* and *Trimeresurus* genera also use their prehensile tails as an aid to climbing.

▶ *Jumping*

A few snakes, like the rattlesnake *Bothrops (Portidium) nummifer*, from Central America, an extremely stocky animal, tend to jump, either when they hit a prey or to clear a height of up to 3 ft. (1 m), starting from a low point. They push their tails onto the substrate for support, curve their body into an S to serve as a spring or coil, and jump while stretching their body over 3 ft. (1 m). The golden tree snake (*Chrysopelea ornata*), a southeastern Asian Colubridae, glides by throwing itself from tree to tree, its body rigid, oblique in relation to the ground, like an arrow. Its ventral area caves in, which offers greater resistance to air, and it can cross impressive distances of over 33 ft. (10 m).

▽ *BELOW: Adaptation to an arboreal life-style is sometimes accompanied by a lateral flattening of the entire body, with the back exhibiting a thin spine and ventral scales that don't cover the entire width of the body. These characteristics are obvious in the green Indonesian python (*Morelia viridis*), seen here as a juvenile, and by the South American tree boa.*

△ *ABOVE:* Philodryas olfersi, *a species living in South American forests, has a long body that lets it move in trees with few supports.*

◁ *LEFT:* Chrysopelea ornata, *the golden tree snake, can slow its fall by spreading its ribs and staying rigid.*

A CARDIOVASCULAR SYSTEM WORKING AGAINST THE FORCES OF GRAVITY

Yannick Vasse

IN A TERRESTRIAL ENVIRONMENT, gravity's effects are particularly felt by the fluid-filled cardiovascular system. Of all vertebrates, snakes are those which present the most varied adaptations to gravity, and their remarkable diversity is partly due to the efficiency of their circulatory system.

Blood vessels, small tubes with thin and pliable walls, could undergo deformations when in a vertical position. The walls, distended by the aerial pressure added to that of gravity, would let the plasma escape, which would flow outside the capillaries. Blood pressure would drop and the principal organs would not be sufficiently irrigated.

And yet, there are arboreal snakes which evolve along vertical surfaces. The North American colubrid *Elaphe guttata* climbs trees in search of bird eggs. Arboreal boas can hang upside down when chasing prey. How do they maintain their blood pressure when their head is either up or down? These behaviors would be impossible without a cardiovascular system that is able to maintain normal blood pressure when the body leaves a horizontal position.

An experimental device lets us know the blood pressure in different parts of the body. The animal is placed in a plastic tube, which is mobile around a central pivot, and catheters containing a physiological liquid are introduced into the blood vessels and measure blood pressure. Gravity's effect on the cardiovascular system is read through the angle of the tube's inclination.

The tiger snake (*Notechis scutatus*) is an Australian terrestrial snake with varied habitats, from the floodplains to tropical forests. When it is vertical, with its head up, its blood pressure increases in the middle of its body, that of the skull decreases slightly, blood accumulates in the tail, but there is no circulatory faltering. This snake thus has the physiological equipment to regulate blood pressure.

Hydrophinae, members of the Elapidae, are strictly aquatic, but they evolved from terrestrial forms. Can they still stand gravity's pressure? The body is lifted in water, as gravity is balanced by Archimedes' principle.

As the angle of the tube is more inclined, and the snake's head is higher, the heart

◁ *LEFT: The creviced surface of some tree bark offers enough support for colubrids to climb vertically. Fluid distribution in the body of this* Elaphe obsoleta quadrivitata *creates some adaptation problems for the blood pressure's regulating system. The very anterior position of the heart, the thin body, and tight skin are arboreal adaptations.*

beats faster without managing to compensate for the decrease in blood pressure in the brain. A 39 mm mercury decrease in a marine snake leads to the closing of its blood vessels. Blood accumulates in the back of the animal's body, the heart receives less of it, the cardiac flow and blood pressure decrease. If a marine snake is maintained in a vertical position, head up, and out of the water, the brain is not irrigated by blood and the snake will die.

The same experiment carried out on an arboreal snake reveals that gravity's constraints are small, even when the snake is held head up. Arterial pressure remains high, thanks to the capillaries' better muscle tone. When the vascular muscles are contracted, blood is compressed and blood pressure rises. It remains steady between 20 and 60 mm mercury. Blood accumulates in the posterior part of the body, but only one-third as much as would accumulate in an aquatic or strictly terrestrial species.

If a semiarboreal snake is held at a 45° angle, head up, the irrigation of the lower half's muscles and organs decreases, but irrigation to the main organs (heart, lungs, brain) barely changes.

The selective decrease of the blood-flow rate is due to vasoconstriction, which is the contraction of the smooth muscles within the blood vessels' walls. When the vessels of the lower half of the body have a decreased diameter, blood pressure rises in the middle of the body, and blood irrigates those areas where the vessels are least contracted.

When an arboreal snake is held vertically, head down, the cardiovascular reactions are inverted: Cardiac rhythm is lowered, and the vessels' smooth muscles loosen to partially compensate for the increased gravitational pressure in the head. Blood does not accumulate in the head, for the vein volume is less than it is in the tail, and the brain is held in a rigid skull.

Blood pressure depends on behavior and habitat. Arterial pressure for the five aquatic species studied varies between 15 and 39 mm mercury, and 50 and 90 mm mercury for arboreal species. Semiaquatic and nonarboreal species exhibit intermediate values.

Another adaptation to various habitats is the heart's placement in the body (see Illus. 8). In nonarboreal terrestrial snakes, the heart is often closer to the head (in the body's first quarter). When held vertically with its head up, the snake's blood accumulates in its tail, as the vessels dilate easily. The heart is towards the middle of the body in marine

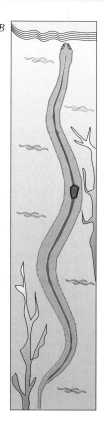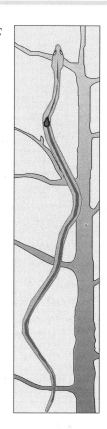

Illus. 8. *Blood circulation in three types of snake (**A:** terrestrial; **B:** aquatic; **C:** arboreal) in vertical, head-up position*

A: *The heart is close to the head; since the animal is in an unusual vertical position, the tail receives extra blood thanks to the blood vessels' dilation.*

B: *Found in the middle of the body in a marine snake, the heart limits the pumping effort. Blood pressure is compensated for by the external water pressure, and blood doesn't accumulate in the tail.*

C: *The heart is close to the head, which allows for good blood infusion to the brain, no matter what position the snake is in.*

snakes, thus limiting the pumping work to the two extremities. Blood does not accumulate in the tail, for blood pressure is compensated for by the exterior water pressure.

In arboreals, the average distance between the head and heart is about 15% of total body length. The closer the heart is to the head, the easier brain irrigation is.

The heart's anterior position in the body has two inconveniences. When a snake's head is down, the tail may not be well irrigated; but the tail isn't of vital importance. What is problematic is that when the head is up, blood coming from the tail must travel all the way to the heart, and against gravity. Snakes' veins do not have valves, those membranous folds that keep the blood from flowing away from the heart. Blood flow is helped in three ways: the contraction of the smooth vessel muscles, the contraction of the skeletal muscles, and

skin compression.

One often sees an arboreal snake stop while it is climbing a tree and undulate its body, creating waves of muscular contractions from tail to head. These movements compress the veins and push blood towards the head. The central venous pressure thus increases in the heart area.

Arboreal snakes have very thin bodies, they're muscular, and their skin is stretched tight, unlike aquatic and terrestrial snakes, which have looser skin and a softer, less slender body.

This taut skin plays the role of an "anti-gravity suit." The same characteristic is true of some large mammals, like the horse, giraffes, and man.

From Harvey Lillywhite, *Pour la Science*, Paris, Feb. 1989.

PHYSIOLOGY

Hubert Saint-Girons

Like all living beings, snakes must maintain the characteristics of their inner environment within limits that are compatible with their survival. They are wrongly considered "cold-blooded." In fact, they are ectotherms, which means that their internal temperature depends on that of their environment. They expend little energy when at rest, for the energy used for thermic regulation is minor. Reptiles are nonetheless thermophilic animals, unlike many fish and amphibians: They can carry out most of their functions only at high temperatures. They must also avoid extreme temperatures, which would quickly be fatal to them. This necessitates a thermoregulating activity, at least in certain parts of the world or during certain seasons, which allows them to maintain their internal temperature at a level compatible with their survival. As they are incapable of producing heat, unlike birds and mammals, snakes adapt behaviorally, mostly by searching for the right thermic conditions. Their vital functions more or less depend on temperature, but they also possess various mechanisms to help cope with changes in ionic level and retain internal fluids.

THERMOREGULATION

▶ Temperature

Temperature plays a crucial role in a snake's life and affects various biological functions. It quickens any and all of the chemical reactions that occur within the organism when it rises within a range that doesn't threaten the individual. When the animal's temperature is too high, it kills all the enzymes responsible for these vital chemical reactions.

The chemical reactions' speed or efficiency generally doubles for an 18°F (10°C) increase in temperature. They are then said to have a thermic quotient (TQ) of 2. This number is not necessarily the same for a physiological function taken as a whole. The TQ varies with temperature. This is the case for enzymic reactions, which become more efficient up to a certain temperature and then lose efficiencyh. This TQ is often used to measure the influence of temperature on this or that function, as well as to measure the differences that exist between species.

▶ Metabolism

The production of metabolic energy (measured through the consumption of oxygen per weight) in reptiles, which is quite feeble at 41°F (5°C), increases almost exponentially as the temperature rises. In homeothermic birds and mammals, internal temperature is maintained constant through energy consumption, both to cool down and to warm up. But at 98.6°F (37°C), a snake's basal metabolism will be quite inferior to that of a mammal of the same weight. In general, snakes living in cool regions have a higher basal metabolism

than those living in warmer areas, although these differences are minimized at high temperatures (see Illus. 1).

The basal metabolism's TQ varies in large part according to the species and experimental conditions. It is most often found in the 2 to 4 range between 59°F (15°C) and 95°F (35°C). But it can be as high as 10 at the lowest tolerated temperature.

All cellular activity, whether muscular or glandular, leads to increased oxygen consumption. However, for a given muscular effort, the energy expenditure is independent of temperature, so that

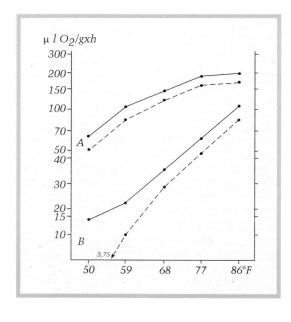

◁ LEFT: *Illus. 1. Oxygen consumption in* Vipera berus *(—) and* Vipera aspis *(---) according to temperature.*
A. *During moderate exploratory activity.*
B. *Individuals at rest*

△ *ABOVE: Water moccasin* (Agkistrodon piscivorus) *getting into the water after having basked in the sun*

during a slow movement, the total oxygen consumption (basal metabolism + activity) is multiplied by 10 at 50°F (10°C), but only by 2 at 86°F (30°C). See Illus. 1. According to the rare available data, it appears that in a snake engaging only in habitual, moderate, and intermittent activities the daily consumption is about half that of the basal metabolism. Violent efforts like catching prey, a quick escape, or a fight with a predator demand a considerable burst of energy, which the oxygenated metabolism (aerobic) cannot supply, although it can be multiplied by 10 at 86°F (30°C). Another mechanism, the breakdown of glycogen or glucose into lactic acid (anaerobic metabolism) then enters into play, but only for a limited amount

of time. Snakes, especially the young, tire very quickly during intense activity and recuperate slowly. In general, Colubridae and Elapidae, which hunt on the prowl, have higher aerobic capacities than Boidae and Viperidae, which hunt by remaining hidden, and the former can sustain more extensive efforts longer.

The influence of other functions on the metabolism are milder and not very well known. It has been observed that in the first days of prey digestion, the basal metabolism could be multiplied by 3 to 7 in Boidae.

▶ *Temperature's influence on other functions*
The possible intensity of muscular activity is

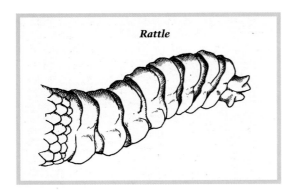

Rattle

△ ABOVE: Rattle. Its vibration is
closely related to temperature (see
Illus. 3).

linked to temperature, as are all other functions.

Depending on the species, snakes are almost
paralyzed when the temperature ranges from 34°F
(1°C) to 48°F (9°C). The maximal locomotion
then increases to attain an optimal level, usually at
around 86°F (30°C). The locomotion environment is also an influence. The garter snake, *Thamnophis elegans*, a semiaquatic colubrid, sees its
swimming speed increase faster than that of its
terrestrial reptation between 41°F (5°C) and 59°F
(15°C), but the opposite is true above 68°F (20°C).
The heartbeat also rises along with temperature,
which lets the blood carry an increased supply of
oxygen and nutrients to the organs using it.

Other activities, like vibrating the rattle in
rattlesnakes (see Illus. 2 and Illus. 3) or the
tongue's exploration for chemical messages are very
much dependent on temperature.

Some functions require high temperatures.
This is the case of digestion, which must be
quicker than the prey's rotting, which would lead
to intoxication. When placed in too low temperatures after eating, snakes regurgitate their prey. It
is difficult to determine what the limits of digestive
temperature are, and it certainly depends on the
species. It is lower in species living in colder regions. The European viper (*Vipera berus*), for example, a northern species living up to the Arctic
circle, can completely digest a mouse at 50°F
(10°C), while other, more southern European vipers need a temperature of 59°F (15°C).

Starting at minimal temperature, the length of
digestion lessens with the rise in temperature, first
rapidly, and then more slowly, becoming almost
constant as of 77°F (25°C) to 86°F (30°C), depending on the species.

Spermatozoid production (spermatogenesis)
ceases below 54°F (12°C) to 59°C (15°C), and its
last part, spermiogenesis (sperm production),
needs even higher temperatures, over 68°F (20°C)
to 69.8°F (21°C), in the semiaquatic colubrid
Nerodia sipedon. Its speed then increases considerably. All functions stop when nearing the lethal
maximum. In many cases, their efficiency stops
increasing before reaching this level. This is quite
clear in the case of digestion, but is also true for
most muscular activity.

It is obvious how important it is for snakes to
maintain their body temperature at a level that
is compatible with those necessary for vital
functions.

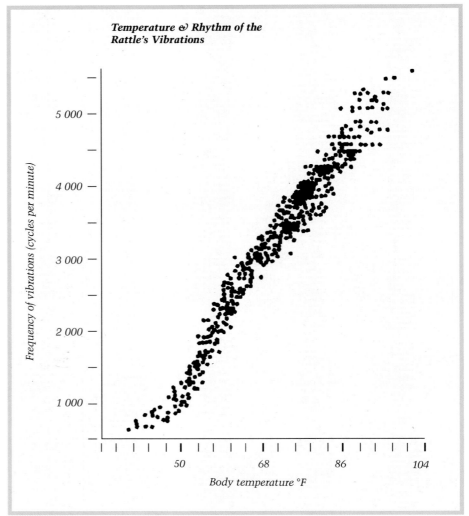

**Temperature & Rhythm of the
Rattle's Vibrations**

Frequency of vibrations (cycles per minute)

5 000 —

4 000 —

3 000 —

2 000 —

1 000 —

50   68   86   104

Body temperature °F

△ ABOVE: Illus. 3. Relations between
temperature and rhythm of the
rattle's vibrations (Crotalus atrox).
(From Martin & Bagby, 1972.) One
can see that the TQ (Q10) is higher
between 50°F (10°C) and 64°F (18°C)
than above and below these
temperatures.

▶ *Critical temperatures & thermic comfort*

Lethal maximal and minimal temperatures can be determined for each species, as well as critical temperatures beyond which the animal is incapable of coordinated movements. There are also *maxima* and *minima*, which are voluntarily tolerated and frame the thermic activity zone within which the "favorite" temperature is found (temperature preference range).

Lethal temperatures are still difficult to determine precisely because they depend on the length of exposure. The lethal minimum is generally found to be between 19°F (−7°C) and 28°F (−2°C), and the short-term lethal maximum between 107.6°F (42°C) and 113°F (45°C). Marine snakes (Hydrophinae) may be much more sensitive to extreme temperatures, since for *Pelamis platurus*, the only species studied in regards to this matter, the lethal minimum is around 52°F (11°C) and the lethal maximum 96.8°F (36°C).

Critical temperatures are particularly interesting from an ecological point of view. When placed outside and subjected to these temperatures, a snake is virtually condemned to death, since it cannot move. But when sheltered, it can often survive temperatures below the critical minimum, as often happens during dormancy.

The critical minimum for terrestrial snakes is usually found between 37°F (3°C) and 46°F (8°C), and the maximum is between 100°F (38°C) and 108°F (42°C)—perhaps a bit higher for certain desert-dwelling colubrids. There again, the margin is reduced for marine snakes and probably also for burrowing snakes.

The voluntarily tolerated *maxima* and *minima* are the highest and lowest temperatures recorded for active animals outside their shelters, in natural or seminatural conditions. The voluntarily tolerated minimum ranges from 46°F (8°C) to 73°F (23°C) depending on species, seasons, and lifestyle. For example, in early spring in cold temperature regions, species like the garter snake (*Thamnophis sirtalis parietalis*) and the European adder (*Vipera berus*) leave their cold (around 46°F [8°C]) underground shelters and take some sun. Later in the season, their minimal temperature ranges from 50 to 54°F (10 to 12°C) and rises to 57–61°F (14–16°C) by summer. The latter numbers are the voluntarily tolerated minimum for many temperate-region snakes, but they are also those of nocturnal Viperidae living in arid Mediterranean-type zones, like the sidewinder (*Crotalus cerastes*) of the southwestern United States. However, many species have never been found at temperatures below 68–73°F (20–23°C), which may be because they were not observed at the right moment. The voluntarily tolerated maximum lies within a smaller range, usually 93–96.8°F (34–36°C). Some higher numbers have been found, particularly in desert-dwelling snakes: 105.4°F (40.8°C) in the sidewinder, which is dangerously close to that animal's lethal maximum of 107.6°F (42°C). The security margin between voluntarily tolerated maximum and critical maximum is generally quite narrow, around 9°F (5°C).

The favored temperature is that which an animal chooses when it has a large choice (when caged with a variable heat source, for example). It varies slightly with the physiological state, but proves to be remarkably constant within a single species. This temperature is often between 86 and 91°F (30 and 33°C) in Boidae and Colubridae, as well as in Elapidae and Viperidae, which live very differently from the Arctic Circle to the equator.

Some desert-dwelling colubrids' and vipers' favored temperature is slightly higher, between 90 and 93°F (32 and 34°C), while that of burrowing species is lower, around 77°F (25°C). Favored temperature is in no way equal to optimal temperature. Under natural conditions, terrestrial reptiles are generally subject to nocturnal cooling, and captive animals, when they have a choice, pick lower temperatures at night than they do during the day, the difference being sometimes as much as 27°F (15°C) in diurnal heliophilous species from temperate regions, like the smooth snake (*Coronella austriaca*). When constantly kept at its favored temperature, a snake of this type usually dies within a few months. This is probably why fossorial burrowing species, which are subject to mild variations between day and night, have low favored temperatures. The same is also probably true of strictly aquatic snakes, which, unfortunately, have not been closely studied in this respect.

Although a favored temperature is not affected by sex or season, it may be influenced by the animal's physiological condition. The only precise data we have concerns digestion, during which snakes search for a slightly higher temperature. The value difference for preferred temperature for an animal that has not eaten and one that is ingesting a large prey is of almost 4°F (2°C), especially in European vipers (87°F and 90°F; 30.5°C and 32.4°C).

▶ *Thermic exchanges*

A snake's body temperature depends partly on the heat gained from directed or reflected solar rays, conducted by the ground or convected by ambient air, and partly from the heat lost by radiation, conduction, convection, and evaporation.

The amount of energy absorbed by radiation depends on the skin's absorption and reflection spectrum, on the surface exposed, and on the radiation angle of incidence. The intensity of thermic exchanges by conduction depends on the con-

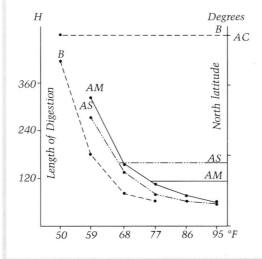

▷ RIGHT: *Illus. 4. Length of digestion, in hours, according to temperature and in relation to the species' northernmost distribution, indicated in degrees of northern latitude (Arctic Circle: AC). (From Naulleau, 1983.)*
AM: *long-nosed viper* (Vipera ammodytes)
AS: *asp viper* (Vipera aspis)
B: *European adder* (Vipera berus)

△ ABOVE: *Ringed krait* (Bungarus fasciatus); *this Elapidae, which is active and dangerous at night, remains strangely passive if it is exposed to daylight.*

▷ RIGHT: *Viperine snake* (Natrix maura). *This snake regularly heats itself on riverbanks after having hunted (in water that can be quite cold) for the fish and amphibian larvae on which it feeds.*

tact surface between animal and ground, and the latter's conductivity: It is high for sand and rocks, low for bark and plant litter. Thermic exchanges by convection with air are minimal without wind. At high altitudes, the internal temperature of a snake

in the sun can be up to 86°F (30°C) above that of the air.

Heat is lost not only through radiation, conduction, and convection, but also by evaporation, which is particularly active the drier and hotter the

◁ LEFT: *Asp viper* (Vipera aspis), *basking in the morning sun on a stump that insulates it from the cold ground. Except during early spring, this thermoregulation stage, during which the animal is quite visible and exposed to predators, lasts just a short while.*

△ *ABOVE: Horned desert viper* (Cerastes cerastes), *burrowed in the sand. Sand-dwelling vipers simultaneously hide and thermoregulate by burying parts of their body in the sand.*

air. Nonetheless, reptiles' evaporation rate is generally lower than that of other terrestrial vertebrates, and only plays a minor role in their thermoregulation, except when fighting exceptional cases of overheating. The animal then opens its mouth and pants rapidly, which helps it lose heat through evaporation. Size also affects thermoregulation; an ectotherm's thermic exchanges are grossly proportional to its surface, which increases at a much slower rate than its volume. Thus, a large snake heats up and cools down much more slowly than a smaller one. By curling onto itself, a snake can reduce its exchange surface by half.

▶ Mechanisms ensuring thermoregulation

Due to the snake's low metabolic level, heat production has little influence on its internal temperature, except for giant species and in very particular cases.

Snakes have a number of different ways of keeping their internal levels at the required level at their disposal. Some are physiological adaptations, others are behavioral.

There are a few physiological thermoregulation mechanisms, the most important of which deals with blood modification and distribution. A speedier cardiac rhythm and the dilation of surface blood vessels quickens the pace of thermic exchanges, and the inverse phenomena slow them down. Thanks to these mechanisms, a snake can change temperatures at various speeds.

Nonetheless, behavior plays the largest part in thermoregulation. Snakes can, for example, change from diurnal to nocturnal, and vice versa, unlike lizards. Burrowing species, which are thigmotherms (their heat exchanges occur through contact), use the ground's temperature, which is usually warmer close to the surface during the day. In humid tropical forests, this heat gradient is low and the snakes' internal temperature varies little, not just between day and night, but year-round. The species from warm, temperate regions have a wider gradient at their disposal during summer, but the thermic variations remain mild and the favored temperatures low. Viperidae with a tendency to burrow, like the Saharan *Cerastes*—their head always right at sand level—manage to maintain their temperature at a surprisingly constant level by burying their bodies at varying depths, despite the considerable temperature variations between the air and the ground surface. Nonetheless, in summer they must sometimes choose shady areas or return to their shelters. No truly burrowing species exist in the cooler temperate regions, where only direct exposure to the sun lets reptiles reach sufficiently high temperatures.

Terrestrial snakes all use underground shelters (rodent burrows, cracks in rocks, etc.), which shelter them from both cool nights and hot days. In cool temperate regions, thermoregulation problems are mostly those of finding heat. In the morning, snakes bask in the sun, lying on stumps or bark that can isolate them from the still-cold ground. Some species, like the European adder (*Vipera berus*), flatten their body, ribbonlike, to expose a greater area to the sun's rays. When the sun is intermittent, this behavior can last all day.

▽ BELOW: *Avicenna viper* (Cerastes vipera), *burrowed in the sand. This animal is more strictly a sand-dwelling snake than the horned desert viper. The Avicenna viper has a flat head with small eyes oriented towards the top.*

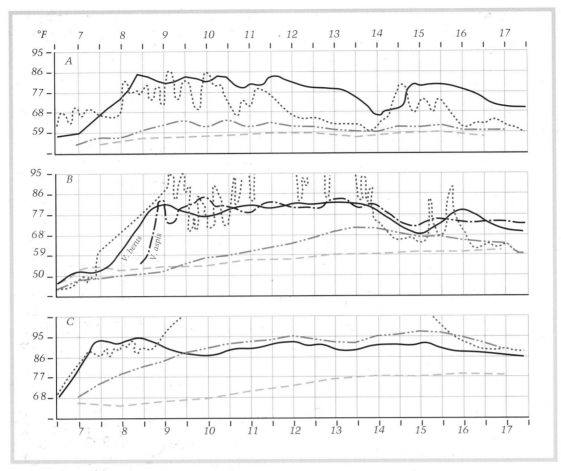

◁ LEFT: Illus. 5. Thermoregulation
for European vipers, in summer, in
different atmospheric conditions
A. On a relatively cloudy day
(Vipera berus)
B. On a sunny day (Vipera berus
and V. aspis)
C. On a very hot day (V. seoanei)
——— or —·—·— viper's stomach
temperature, recorded by telemetry
········· temperature of a metallic
atmospheric probe in the sun 20 in.
(50 cm) above ground
—·— temperature in the shade
20 in. (50 cm) above ground
— — — temperature of a burrow
8 in. (20 cm) below ground

Usually, once the internal temperature is at the desired level, the snake maintains this equilibrium by placing part of its body in the shade, or it limits its exposure by folding part of its body on itself. When moving (looking for prey or a sexual partner), the animal worries less about thermoregulation, and its internal temperature varies as it moves from sunny to cool areas. During the late afternoon, snakes often lie on rocks that have stored the sun's heat and then return to their subterranean shelters, now warmer than both the air and the ground's surface.

During warm summer months, the morning sun exposure is quite brief. Snakes then ensure their thermoregulation by coiling up in the shade or under bark, sometimes even returning to their underground shelter. Continuous recordings carried out by biotelemetry prove how adept snakes are at maintaining a constant internal temperature, except on cloudy or rainy days (see Illus. 5).

Thermoregulation methods are the same in warmer temperate areas, but the search for heat becomes less essential, especially during summer, and the various species have more diverse lifestyles. For example, the smooth snake (*Coronella girondica*), from the Mediterranean region, moves only at dusk and spends the day under bark and vegetal matter, searching for small lizards. Such behavior would obviously spell its death in colder regions.

In hot and arid zones, snakes must fight against overheating. Due to their modes of locomotion, the hot ground is particularly dangerous for them, and some diurnal species become more or less nocturnal during the summer months. All these snakes spend their days in deep underground tunnels. In these regions, the wintertime fight against the cold is quite simple, since the sun always shines brightly; it is dealt with in the same manner as in temperate regions.

In humid tropical forests, with relatively constant and hot weather, thermoregulation poses no problems to the various snake species. Again, the

▽ BELOW: The smooth snake
(Coronella girondica), which only
moves at dusk

△ *ABOVE: Marine oviparous snakes from the* Laticauda *genus hunt at sea but often come ashore to mate, lay eggs, and digest prey.*

▷ *RIGHT: Viperine snake (*Natrix maura*) hunting in the fresh waters of France's Languedoc region*

same methods are used: The preferred temperature is obtained either by placing part of the body in the sun and part of it in the shade, or by choosing an area of the right temperate underground, above ground, or, for the many arboreal species, at different heights in the vegetation.

Aquatic and semiaquatic snakes use different methods; those species that never leave water, like Hydrophinae (marine) and Acrochordidae (lake waters), as well as the tentacled snake (*Erpeton tentaculatum*), only have a mild thermic gradient at their disposal, especially when they are far from the shore. By taking the sun at the water's surface, they can raise their internal temperature by 2°F/1°C above that of the water, but are nevertheless forced to live in warm areas.

Semiaquatic species may be more or less tied to water. Marine snakes of the *Laticauda* genus, which are oviparous, search for their food at sea in hunts that can last many days, but return to digest their big prey on solid ground, at least in winter.

At that time, they maintain their internal temperature at around 86°F (30°C) during the entire day by the usual methods. Freshwater snakes regularly warm themselves in the sun while on solid ground, where they generally spend most of the day.

Many maintain their temperature at the required levels by keeping part of their body submerged under water. In areas where water is cold, snakes go on short hunting missions and then return to warm up on the ground. Physiological adaptations that quicken the increase in temperature and slow down heat loss are particularly useful under such conditions.

DAILY RHYTHM

All snakes have a highly developed chemical sense and can find prey in the dark. Unlike lizards, no snake species lacks a sense of smell which would render them obligatorily diurnal. However, if most snakes are active day or night depending on temperature and type of prey, others live according to a much stricter, and probably innate, circadian rhythm. When looking at two rattlesnakes from a semidesert area of the United States (the Colorado desert), one, Mitchell's rattlesnake (*Crotalus mitchelli*), is diurnal during spring and fall and nocturnal during summer, while the other, the sidewinder (*Crotalus cerastes*), is fundamentally nocturnal (see Illus. 6). The average temperature of an active individual is obviously much lower in *C. cerastes* (78°F [25.8°C]) than in *C. mitchelli* (88°F [31.2°C]), yet both species have the same preferred temperatures and maximal voluntarily tolerated temperatures.

Activity is difficult to define because many snakes hunt from a hiding place. An animal rolled in a tunnel that protects it from either heat or cold is obviously at rest. But the smooth snake (*Coronella girondica*), for example, which only moves at dusk and spends all day under vegetal matter or a stone looking for small lizards, cannot be considered strictly crepuscular. The same could be said of the Avicenna viper (*Cerastes vipera*), which moves a lot during most of the night, but is still lying in wait during the day, which it spends mostly burrowed in the sand, with only its head emerging.

DORMANCY

No matter how perfect, ectotherms' thermoregulation depends on an external heat source, and in most areas at latitudes above or below 20° (tropics), winter is too cold for snakes to exercise their main functions (digestion, in particular). They must absolutely avoid the lethal minimum temperature and must also hide from predators and possible floods.

In temperate regions, snakes usually winter alone or in small groups in a rodent's burrow or a hollow stump.

In areas with very cold winters (northernmost regions, or those with a continental climate), snakes must find and move into deep cracks in rocks to avoid frost, going deeper and deeper by the end of autumn and coming closer to the sur-

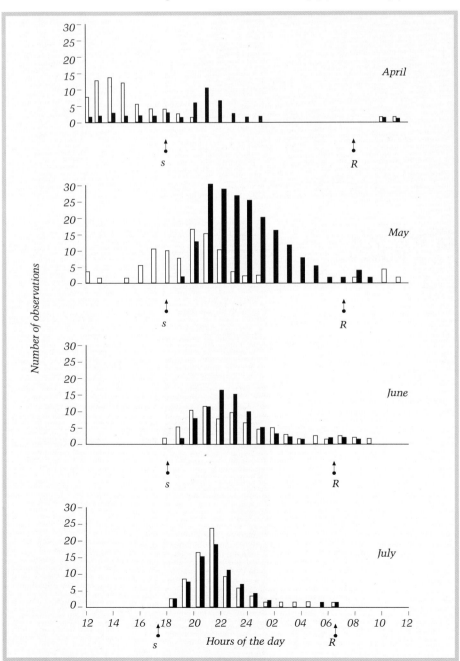

▽ ▷ *BELOW AND RIGHT: Illus. 6. Circadian rhythm of two rattlesnakes' activity in different months (from Moore, 1978) Light columns:* Crotalus mitchelli *Dark columns:* Crotalus cerastes *The arrows indicate the average sunup* (**R**) *and sunset* (**S**) *time.*

face in spring to be ready to emerge as soon as exterior conditions are welcoming. Such shelters are generally rare, or at least grouped in a small area, so snakes often winter there in large numbers. These groupings also favor the joining of the sexes for species with summer or fall delivery.

In the Viperidae family, gestating females do not eat and spend the entire year in close proximity to the wintering grounds, while the rest of the population disperses during the summer feeding season. Other conditions lead to migrations towards wintering grounds. Smooth snakes (*Natrix natrix*), for example, which spend the summers in humid valleys rich in prey, return to the drier and sunnier hills in the fall, where they spend the winter without gatherings. The wintering season's duration varies according to climate and species. It can last up to eight months around the Arctic Circle and as little as two to three months in subtropical zones. Within a single region, mem-

bers of the species living in the southern areas winter a shorter time than those in the northern areas. There are also differences linked to the environment. In the northern Sahara, Avicenna vipers (like *Cerastes vipera*) winter for about five months, as opposed to those living in a rockier environment like the horned desert viper (*Cerastes cerastes*).

The weight lost during this season is insignificant, adding up to only a low percentage of total body weight. Snakes do become much thinner, however, although this happens mostly right before and after wintering, when the individuals are active but not feeding anymore, or not yet. Winter mortality is quite low, save in newborns; the adults that die are usually unhealthy to begin with. However, a long period of abnormally cold weather or the flooding of a wintering area can lead to a much higher mortality rate.

WATER & MINERAL SALTS

Like most living terrestrial beings, snakes are constantly confronted with problems of storing and losing water, especially because of evaporation through the skin, while breathing, and while rejecting urine and feces. These are even greater problems for the desert-dwelling species. Aquatic species must deal with different problems.

The movement of water within an organism or the exchanges between an organism and a given aquatic environment depends on the quantity of salts or organic substances dissolved in the water, which exert a force called osmotic pressure. Water always goes from low osmotic pressure areas (where the salts are not very concentrated) to high ones. Depending on the circumstances, it tends to go towards or away from an organism, which can, in both cases, imperil it. The salts tend to go from an area of high to low concentration. Maintaining hydric equilibrium depends on regulating the balance of minerals. This is called osmoregulation.

▶ Limiting losses

The first solution to the problem of maintaining a good hydric balance is to limit losses.

Evaporation is very much limited by snakes' skin structure, which varies from one species to the next and with the weather. The mechanisms are still unknown. The absence of sweat glands helps to limit cutaneous evaporation. Another cause of water loss is respiration. The expired air is charged with warm mist and the loss of water increases with heat. This is nonetheless a somewhat limited loss.

Water loss due to total evaporation increases with temperature and can reach large proportions in dry environments. Snakes from dry and arid regions adapt behaviorally, spending their days in deep, cool, and humid shelters, most often rodents' burrows. In tropical zones with a long dry season, numerous terrestrial snakes practise estivation, disappearing in spring, the hottest period, and reappearing during the rainy season of June and July; one such example is the ball python (*Python regius*).

Curiously, desert-dwelling species do not estivate. They may be better adapted to heat, unless

Light columns: Crotalus mitchelli
Dark columns: Crotalus cerastes

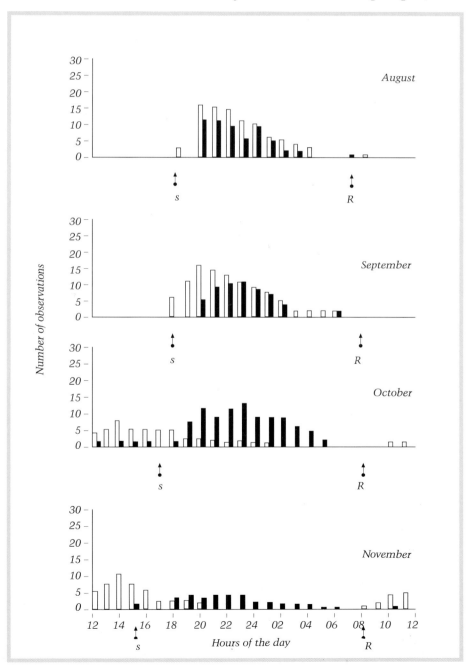

Number of observations

Hours of the day

DORMANCY & HIBERNATION

THE TERM HIBERNATION was initially applied to mammals whose endothormia is temporarily suspended during the cold season. This lets them survive without eating, but implies no energy output and, sometimes, profound physiological changes. The ectothermic reptiles are part of this group, and their wintering or dormancy is not really the same as mammals' hibernation, which is why most herpetologists use a different term. The problem is slightly more complex in that although any snake can, at any season and without damage, live for a few months at temperatures barely above the critical minimum, a dormancy period appears necessary to the good health and reproduction of some species. Even a snake like the asp viper (*Vipera aspis*), which lives and reproduces perfectly in practically constant laboratory conditions, whenever given a choice chooses to winter for a few months during the cold season.

∧ *Garter snakes (*Thamnophis sirtalis parietalis*) emerging from hibernation*

▷ RIGHT: **Corallus caninus,** *a South American arboreal Boa, in its characteristic resting position.*

▷ RIGHT: *European adder (*Vipera berus*) in a snow-covered area. In high altitudes or latitudes, the vipers' first outings can occur in recently cleared areas, basking on stumps or rocks that have been exposed to the sun.*

estivation in tropical species is directly linked to the disappearance of potential preys.

Water loss through feces is quite low. Water loss due to urination varies greatly. Losses depend essentially on the quantity of salts and wastes that the metabolism must eliminate, nitrogenous products in particular. Reptiles' kidneys are incapable of producing concentrated urines, so the greater the amount of salts needing to be eliminated, the more abundant the urine and thus the amount of water needed to dilute it. Nevertheless, these nitrogenous byproducts can be stocked as nontoxic and insoluble urate, and their excretion does not lead to any further water losses.

▶ *Rehydration*

Snakes must rehydrate in order to counterbalance these fluid losses.

Water is stored through drinking and the ingestion of prey, some of which are quite rich in water,

Hydric balance of the desert-dwelling colubrid Spalerosis diadema cliffordi *at 86°F (30°C)*
Water losses and gains in ml/kg/day, for colubrids weighing 274 g on average, and fed mice (from Dmi'el & Zilber, 1971).

		Gains		Losses
Food:	water	15.27	Urine	0.15
	Metabolic water	1.46	Feces	1.18
Drink		0.00	Various	0.80
			Evaporation	12.35

◁ LEFT: *Laboratory studies give us some indication of the hydric balance in a desert-dwelling snake. At 86°F (30°C), most water loss is due to evaporation and most water gains come from prey. Other factors have little effect as long as there's sufficient prey.*

and which also furnish the energy necessary for making "metabolic water." In most regions, drinking water is available as dew or rainwater. Early in the morning or after a rainfall, one can often observe snakes coming out of their shelters and patiently swallowing drops of water, one by one, from vegetation.

Aquatic snakes, or those that glide in wet grass, stock a small amount of water by cutaneous absorption.

In arid zones, some species, like the desert *Cerastes*, never drink. These snakes must make do with the water contained in their prey and metabolic water.

▶ Mineral salts

Snakes feed mostly on vertebrates, which tend to have an internal environment similar to their own. Terrestrial species thus have few problems concerning osmoregulation.

▶ Avoiding imbalances

Aquatic species must confront more difficult problems.

Semiaquatic freshwater snakes swallow water when catching their aquatic prey, usually fish or amphibians. They also absorb some through their skin when submerged, since their internal liquid environment is more concentrated than freshwater. They can suffer from a loss of salts. On the

one hand their cutaneous evaporation can be quite important when they are on solid ground, and on the other hand they produce, in large quantities if need be, a highly diluted urine that lets them get rid of water without losing salt. It may also be the case, although this has not been proved, that sodium is reabsorbed through the cloaca, as it is in freshwater turtles.

Some semiaquatic colubrids, like the American species *Nerodia fasciata*, also spend time in brackish waters, in estuaries and coastal marshes; their osmoregulation problems are concerned with avoiding excessive concentrations of salt.

There do not appear to be any physiological differences between individuals of a same species who live in fresh and briny waters. And, as we have seen, their regulatory capacities are quite developed. Furthermore, individuals from brackish waters do not drink, and, like the desert-dwellers, make do with metabolic water and the water held in their prey.

On the other hand, freshwater individuals drink when placed in briny water and, even when well fed, cannot survive long in such an environment. Of course, when they have the opportunity—after a rainfall, for example—all semiaquatic snakes from briny waters drink freshwater, but they can do without it. Strictly marine snakes, which have no access to freshwater and live in a highly mineralized environment, must employ other methods to assure their osmoregulation. They have a particular gland which can secrete a

△ *ABOVE: Rattlesnake* (Crotalus viridis) *drinking dew. Most terrestrial and arboreal snakes have no ponds or streams to drink from. Instead they drink dew or rainwater, drop by drop. The drops are not lapped up, but inhaled by the rostrum's groove. The individual in this picture has its tongue out for olfactory exploration, not for drinking.*

very concentrated solution, containing five to six times more dissolved salts than plasma. This organ's maximal secretion rate (50 to 200 μg of sodium per hour per 100 g of body weight, the same amount of chlorine and 3 to 9 μg of potassium) is not very high, but it allows them to eliminate excess salts with a minor loss of water.

All marine reptiles, as well as vegetarian desert-dwelling lizards, have salt glands, but curiously these organs differ according to the different groups: posterior orbital gland in turtles, external nasal gland in lizards, lingual glands in crocodiles, and, in snakes, a modified and hypertrophied salivary gland, the posterior sublingual gland.

▶ Surviving dehydration

Like other reptiles, snakes have an ultimate resource to face their osmoregulation problems: They can survive for quite a while rates of dehydration or salt excess that would quickly kill a mammal.

The normal sodium rate in plasma, often not quite as high in freshwater snakes, can double in dehydrated or saltwater species. In fact, the proportion of water in the tissues (approximately 70%) and the rate of plasmatic electrolytes in an osmotically balanced snake appear to be constant regardless of systematic position and life-style.

△ ▷ *ABOVE AND RIGHT: The semiaquatic colubrid* Nerodia fasciata *has a wide distribution in North America, where its life-style recalls that of European colubrids* Natrix maura *and* N. tessellata. *It lives in brackish waters on the East Coast, but these populations differ little, either physiologically or morphologically, from freshwater populations. A behavioral difference is that they do not drink the water, thus avoiding a high concentration of salts.*

GROWTH & REPRODUCTION

Hubert Saint-Girons

Due to their great variety of life-styles snakes of each family or even of each species face particular problems that must be resolved in order to ensure reproduction. Their sexual physiology is quite close to that of lizards, but snakes are, nonetheless, surprisingly uniform in terms of sexual behavior. Parthenogenesis, relatively common in lizards, is only known to occur in one snake: the flowerpot snake (Rhamphotyphlops braminus), a small burrowing species that is common in tropical regions. Indeed, as opposed to having populations where the two sexes live in equal proportions, many islands of the Pacific have solely female populations.

THE SEXUAL PARTNERS' MEETING

Other than in their winter groupings, terrestrial snakes lead solitary lives, and while they are not hostile to their fellow creatures during occasional meetings, they tend to isolate themselves as much as possible to avoid competition for food. This situation changes during reproductive periods.

A male who is ready for sexual activity immediately approaches any other snake he sees, and the second one's reaction determines the rest of the former's behavior. If the other snake is a male and acts aggressively, a battle immediately ensues. It is, in fact, a ritual combat during which the adversaries don't bite, but test each other's strength. They move towards each other with a jerky motion and intertwine their bodies along half to two-thirds of their length, their heads high. The heads occasionally bump each other, as each protagonist attempts to push the other and bring its body back into a straight line. The weakest one soon gives in, unharmed.

These fights vary somewhat between species. Although ritualized battles are the rule for Viperidae and most Elapidae, they are much more violent in Colubridae, who really do bite each other. The various types of battles, or at least their early stages, also happen between females or the young, in cases of competition for food. Many species, on the other hand, especially those of the Natricinae subfamily, are not at all sexually intolerant. Male garter snakes (*Thamnophis sirtalis*) gather outside wintering areas in large groups and court females as they emerge, without manifesting any aggressiveness (see the chapter on ecology).

When faced with an animal that is not reacting in any particular manner, the male begins with the preliminaries of the sexual act. At this point, the sex and species are recognized chemically, mostly by the vomeronasal organ, which gets its data from the tongue. If the partner in question is not a

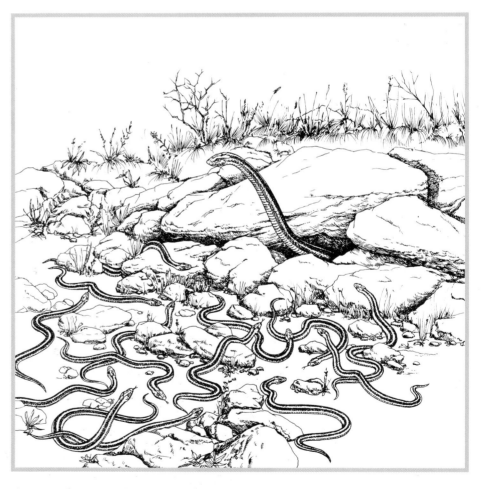

△ *ABOVE: The garter snake's sexual behavior during spring consists of a short but intense phase. For a period of time lasting from three days to three weeks, males take to the sun close to their shelters. Females then emerge, covered with pheromones.*

▷ *RIGHT: Males (up to a hundred of them), attracted by these pheromones, encircle a female, forming a ball. One of the males pulls itself out of the ball and mates with the female.*

▷ RIGHT: *Prairie rattlesnakes* (Crotalus viridis) *mating. The male, with its slightly darker markings, is to the right.*

Drawings from Scientific American, *November 1982*

receptive female, recognizable by the pheromones, chemical substances produced by sexual hormones and emitted by her skin, the male quickly loses interest.

With the bottom of its head placed on its partner's back, the male progresses slowly, following her body's curves, and covers her completely. Then he winds his tail around hers, attempting to join her cloaca. The female does not consent immediately, and either shies away with a precise movement or moves slightly. In many colubrids, like the smooth snake (*Coronella austriaca*), the male takes the female's head into its mouth after the usual preliminaries. It is often only after many hours—and sometimes even days—that the male manages

△ ABOVE: *Smooth snakes* (Coronella austriaca) *mating*

VITELLOGENESIS & SPERMATOGENESIS

Ovule production

Like birds, reptiles produce large eggs containing all of the necessities for embryonic development. Ovulation is preceded by a vitellogenesis period lasting a number of weeks, during which period reserves are made. This is costly in energy, since the calories contained in the ovocytes can account for up to a third of the female's body. This energy can either come directly from prey ingested during this period or from previously accumulated reserves, usually in the form of abdominal fatty tissues.

On the other hand, vitellogenesis does not seem particularly demanding from a thermic point of view. It usually occurs during the two months preceding ovulation (spring in temperate regions); however, it starts as early as the preceding summer in some rattlesnakes.

Ovulation is the rupture of the ovarian follicles and the passage of the ovocytes contained therein into the oviducts. These ovocytes are fertilized in the oviduct's upper area, and covered in its middle part by a sheath made by the uterine glands. In oviparous species, these glands are quite large and they form a thick, slightly calcified shell. They are much less developed in viviparous species and only surround the ovocyte with a thin, supple, and transparent membrane. The thick-shelled eggs spend at least two weeks in the oviduct, sometimes more, and are then expelled by muscular contractions and dropped in the incubation area.

Spermatozoid production

This requires relatively high temperatures, and the last phase in particular, spermiogenesis, is extremely sensitive to thermic factors.

Under favorable conditions, the evolution of the seminal lineage, from the multiplication of spermatogonia to the production of a sufficient number of spermatozoid, takes a minimum of three months. As their formation progresses, spermatozoid pass through the epididymis, then through the vas deferens, where they accumulate for up to a few months.

Unlike many lizards, snakes have no seasonally developed, external secondary sexual characteristics. But they do have glands that are adjunct to the genital tract, the epididymis, and the kidney's sexual segment, whose secretions are essential to the activation and survival of spermatozoids during mating. Sexual behavior only takes place when these glands are hypertrophied, but the opposite is not always true.

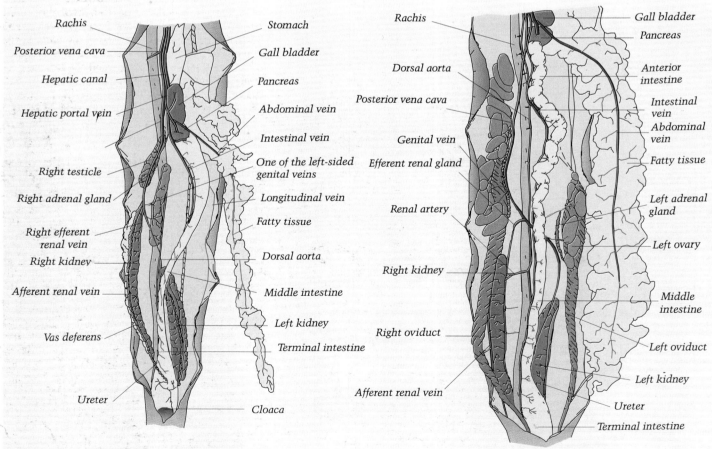

ILLUS. 1. Male sexual apparatus

(from Lecuru and Platel, 1970)

ILLUS. 2. Female genital apparatus

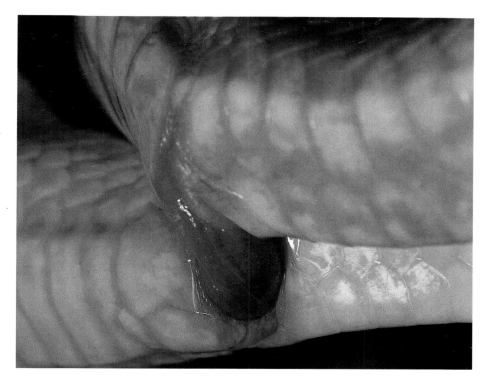

△ *ABOVE: Corn snakes (*Elaphe guttata*) mating; the hemipene's penetration is quite visible.*

to insert one of its hemipenes into the female's cloaca. The male organ immediately inflates and stays fixed thanks to the keratinized spines that cover it. The coupling generally lasts one to two hours, but can vary from ten minutes for colubrids to over two days for a viper of the *Cerastes* genus. The couple generally stays still, although the female can pull her partner to a nearby shelter. The two animals can separate right after coupling, but the male often stays close to the female for a few days, and usually couples again. Unfortunately, there have been few long-term observations of snakes' sexual behavior in nature.

OVIPAROUS SNAKES

Most snakes, probably 70%, are oviparous, which means that some time after coupling, the female lays eggs that are protected by a hard shell. The choice of where to lay the eggs has not been studied in any great detail. Most species are able to clear away loose soil and furnish cavities under a rock or in decomposing vegetal litter. Eggs may also be placed in natural cavities, hollow stumps, or small mammals' burrows. Arboreal snakes generally lay eggs in tree holes.

Good places for laying eggs that provide the right temperature and humidity favorable to incubation are not always simple to find. One place often holds many different females' eggs. Females do not hesitate to travel great distances in order to find the right place, and they probably return yearly. Eggs must be placed in a relatively humid and sufficiently warm environment, which, in cool temperate regions, means a sufficiently sunny place. Eggs placed in the ground are generally left alone. Nevertheless, some Asian cobras (*Naja naja*

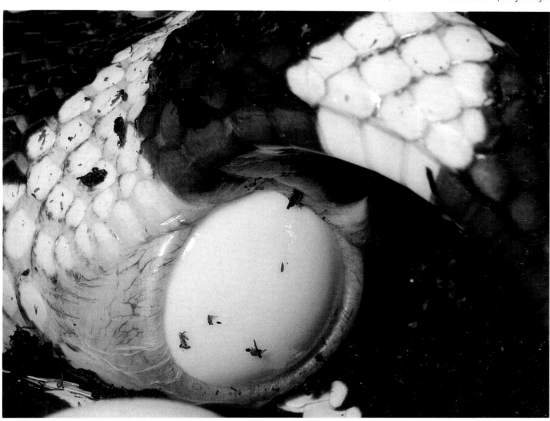

▷ *RIGHT: Egg being expelled from the common king snake (*Lampropeltis getulus*)*

△ ABOVE: *Captive Montpellier snake* (Malpolon monspessulanus) *and its eggs. The eggs are never exposed in such a way under natural conditions.*

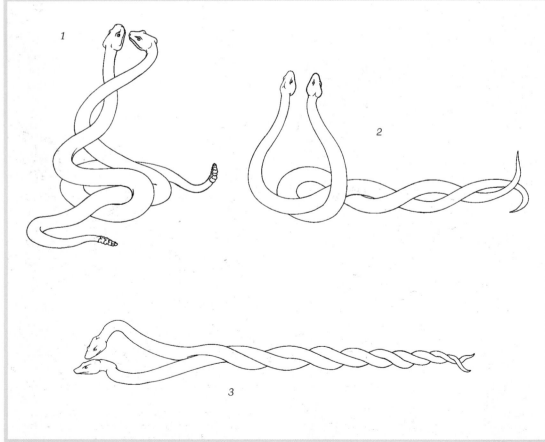

◁ LEFT: *Male battles*
1—Intertwined rattlesnakes (Crotalus atrox)
2—During ritual combat, two Aesculapian snakes (Elaphe longissima) *adopted a lyre position. This is rare in colubrids, which rarely raise their heads during fights.*
3—Characteristic position of many male colubrids during more-or-less ritualized fights.
From C. M. Bogert & V. D. Roth, 1966

▷ RIGHT: *Hatching of a smooth snake* (Natrix natrix). *After having ripped the parchment-like shell, sometimes in more than one place, the newborn puts its head out.*

▽ BELOW: *Kingsnake* (Lampropeltis triangulum nelsoni) *hatching. The newborn will explore its environment and, in case of danger, return into its shell.*

and *Ophiophagus hannah*) have been observed staying close to the nest for some time, repulsing any intruders. They have even been seen coiled around the eggs. Since many snakes are sedentary, it may be that the female continues living in the burrow after laying its eggs. Various observations suggest

△ ABOVE: *Last step in the smooth snake* (Natrix natrix) *hatching. The snake emerged completely out of its egg since it didn't sense any danger.*

that if there is not a real guard over the eggs, there is a strong tendency not to stray too far. The same is true in one of the rare oviparous southeast Asian rattlesnakes, *Ovophis monticola*.

Many pythons, on the other hand, take real care of their eggs, for the female coils around them and raises their temperature a few degrees above that of the environment by rapidly contracting her muscles. In this case, the female is both protecting and "hatching" her eggs.

OVOVIVIPAROUS SNAKES

In ovoviviparous snakes, the eggs are held in the mother's stomach until they hatch. These conditions ensure a constant humidity and regular temperature within the limits of the female's thermoregulative capabilities.

△ *ABOVE: Rock python* (Python molurus) *hatching. Many python eggs are almost "sat upon."*

1 to 4. Birth of the long-nosed viper, an ovoviviparous species (Vipera ammodytes)

1—The young, still wrapped around itself and surrounded by a thin and transparent membrane, appears at the cloacal opening.
2—The ejection progresses.
3—The young is "laid," but it must still "hatch" and rip the membrane.
4—The newborn is now ready to start its independent existence. In the middle, on top, notice the umbilical cord, which will soon fall off, and the limp and empty yolk sac.

At far northern latitudes or in high altitudes, only ovoviviparous snakes are found, as the ground is too cold for eggs to develop. Furthermore, eggs hidden in the mother's body are less exposed to predators than those left on the ground or in cavities. These advantages are counterbalanced by a number of disadvantages, as the gestating female is very much disabled. It moves more slowly, must concern itself more about thermoregulation, and is more vulnerable to predators. Furthermore, the eggs' mass only lets her swallow small prey, which are not always available, at a time when vitellogenesis has deprived her of her energy and mineral stocks. Ovoviviparity, which is necessary for snakes living in cold regions, is also relatively common in terrestrial species from warm areas.

It seems that ovoviviparity has appeared in snakes numerous times, and it is found in almost every family. It is particularly frequent in Viperidae and constant in some subfamilies like the Boinae, Homalopsinae, and Hydrophinae. Very often, both oviparous and ovoviviparous species are found within the same genera, for example in the French smooth snakes. The two reproductive modes can be found in very closely related species, which are sometimes only considered subspecies, but which never live within the same population.

INTERMEDIARY MODES & VIVIPARITY

Obviously, the change from oviparity to ovoviviparity has come about rather easily. There are, among reptiles, many intermediaries between "regular" oviparity and a viviparity resembling that of mammals.

In a number of species, eggs with a normal shell are held in the mother's oviduct much longer than usual, up to halfway or more through the embryonic development (*Opheodrys vernalis*). In the extreme, the young are ready to hatch when the eggs are laid (*Typhlops diardi*). With a well-formed shell, the incubation could take place on the ground. But when the shell is nothing but a thin membrane, as in European vipers, ovoviviparity becomes necessary. Such eggs cannot normally survive outside the mother's body, although they contain all the elements necessary for the embryos' development, and it is possible to obtain normal newborns from sterile, heated, and humidified chambers.

In the last case, that of real viviparity, the ovocyte is small and the mother must make a great contribution of nutritive elements. This is a rare phenomenon, found in some lizards of the Scincidae family, but not in any snakes.

EMBRYONIC DEVELOPMENT

Fertilization, the meeting of spermatozoid and ovule, takes place in the upper part of the oviduct. The egg cell, constituted by the fusion of the two sex cells, migrates to the middle part of the genitals, where uterine glands secrete the substance that will surround it. As we have seen, this envelope differs as to whether the eggs will stay in the mother's body until they hatch or if they will be laid before.

The length of embryonic development depends on the species, and, within the species, on temperature. It generally ranges from 2½ to three months, the extreme known limits being two and five months. The shortest durations are seen in small terrestrial species from subtropical or tropical regions, like the southeast Asian *Oligodon*, and the longest are seen in ovoviviparous marine snakes.

There are also important variations in length within a single species depending on latitude, altitude, and even from one year to the next in accord with summer sunshine. An example from western France: Depending on the year, the asp viper's (*V. aspis*), average parturition date ranges from August 11 to September 27, while the ovulation date—within the first two weeks of June—remains relatively constant.

There are also specific differences, which can be illustrated with two vipers, the asp (*V. aspis*) and the European adder (*V. berus*). At a constant temperature of 88°F (31°C), embryonic development lasts 46 days in *V. berus* and 59 days in *V. aspis*. This development requires high average temperatures, close to those required for digestion or spermatogenesis. Under laboratory conditions, eggs are usually incubated at between 77 and 86°F (25 and 30°C).

Laboratory observation of asp vipers shows significant variations in gestation length depending

THE LARGEST SNAKES

Yannick Vasse

THE LARGEST SNAKES are found among the Boidae: pythons (Pythoninae) and boas (Boinae). The *Boa constrictor*, a mostly terrestrial South American snake, measures up to 16½ ft. (5 m). In Australia, the amethyst python (*Python amethystina*) measures over 20 ft. (6 m), and the African rock python (*Python sebae*) may reach 30 ft. (9 m). Giant individuals are very rare, and in certain species, the average size is much smaller.

The giant anaconda (*Eunectes murinus*) and the reticulated python (*Python reticulatus*) are more or less in competition for the record. The maximum confirmed size is 32⅓ ft. (9.83 m) for the Asian reticulated python, versus 28 ft. (8.5 m) for the South American giant anaconda.

The anaconda, both arboreal and aquatic, found in the Amazon basin, has given rise to many legends; it is said that it can measure up to 49½ or 66 ft. (15 or 20 m), but this seems unlikely. The good faith of those reporting these numbers cannot be doubted if the live or freshly killed animal was measured, and not just the trophy skin. The treated skin can stretch up to 50% of its original length.

In fact, the anaconda is no longer than 30 ft. (9 m), although there is a believable report of one measuring about 36 ft. (11 m) that was killed and measured by geologists with their surveyors' chain. If the reticulated python is considered the longest snake, the anaconda is much heavier and much more massive, with an impressive diameter and measuring up to 220 lbs. (100 kg).

One may be the longest, and the other is probably the heaviest.

EMBRYONIC ADNEXA

EMBRYONIC DEVELOPMENT in both oviparous and ovoviviparous species, like that of all reptiles, passes through characteristic stages that distance them from snakes and birds. The most striking of these stages is the appearance of adnexa, or secondary embryonic structures, which are characteristic of vertebrates that have no need of the aquatic milieu for reproductive purposes. On top of the yolk sac, which holds reserves, other adnexa (chorion, amnion, allantois; see drawing) develop early during embryogenesis and play fundamental roles in embryonic development.

• The amnion is a membrane surrounding a sac, the amniotic cavity, in which the embryo is bathed. This membrane plays a role of mechanical protection, and the liquid protects the embryo from shocks and maintains humidity.
• The chorion lines the shell.
• The allantoic cavity begins as a diverticulum from the posterior intestine. It never stops growing during embryonic development, and the allantoidian membrane finishes by lining the chorion. Its roles are many. The allantoic cavity stocks the embryonic metabolism's debris.

The vessels lining the allantois-chorion whole come in contact with the shell, through which gas, water, and probably some mineral substances are exchanged.

The yolk sac's wall, containing the eggs'

△ *ABOVE: Embryo of a ringed snake (**Natrix natrix**), emerging from its egg one-third of the way through the incubation period. On the right can be seen the umbilical cord and the yolk sac.*

reserves, can also come into contact with the chorion-shell ensemble and with the uterine wall in ovoviviparous species. This forms a rudimentary placenta, through which amino acids and steroids pass.

Whatever the structure, the exchanges between mother and embryo are never as

important as those in mammals.

Like lizards, snakes have a single tooth with which they break the shell in order to hatch. This tooth is inserted in the premaxillary at the tip of the snout, and is also found, although regressed and nonfunctional, in ovoviviparous species.

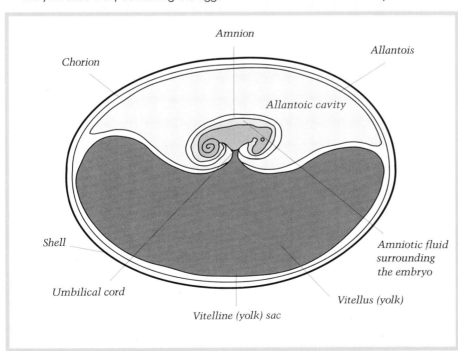

Chorion

Amnion

Allantois

Allantoic cavity

Shell

Umbilical cord

Vitelline (yolk) sac

Amniotic fluid surrounding the embryo

Vitellus (yolk)

◁ *LEFT: Illus. 3. Embryo in its amniotic cavity.*

HEMIPENES

Yannick Vasse

HEMIPENES HAVE a seminal groove facilitating sperm flow. That of *Typhlops* and *Leptotyphlops* has a simple groove, as does that of *Cylindrophis* (Uropeltidae) or of *Dasypeltis* (Colubridae). The groove bifurcates in other species, either with a simple hemipene (the Boidae *Epicrates*), or the hemipene itself is bilobal (Elapidae, Viperidae). Most colubrids have an asymmetric hemipene with a simple groove ending on a large lobe. The hemipene's surface is covered with scales, or papilla, as is the case with the bamboo rattlesnake (*Trimeresurus stejnegeri*). African burrowing colubrids of the *Prosymna* genus have extraordinarily lengthy hemipenes, almost reaching the tail.

Hemipenes have various shapes—they can be spherical, club-shaped, or like "snail horns." Others, like those of some *Trimeresurus*, are smooth. The hemipenes can also be long and thin, as in *Psammophis*, *Malpolon*, or *Psammophylax*.

△ *ABOVE:* Daboia mauritanica *with erect hemipene. In this species, the organ's tips are covered with spines.*

on average temperature: 92 days at 78.8°F (26°C), 74 days at 82.4°F (28°C), and 59 at 87.8°F (31°C).

FECUNDITY

The average number of eggs per lay or young per litter ranges from 2 to 50, depending on the species, but it is usually between four and sixteen. Within a single species this number depends in large part on the mother's size. For example, a young and newly mature python female lays about fifteen eggs, while an older, bigger one lays one hundred. This is an extreme example, but the difference in fertility between a newly mature and an older female is always significant. There is no systematic difference in fertility rates between oviparous and ovoviviparous species. The number of eggs or young doesn't depend solely on the mother's size, for the same reproductive effort can result in a small number of large young or a large number of small young. This is a specific characteristic, probably linked (at least in part) to the newborns' feeding opportunities.

A female's fertility also depends on the annual number of layings. While the unique laying seems to be the rule in oviparous snakes from temperate regions, like the smooth snake (*Natrix natrix*), many tropical species lay three to six times a year (*Ptyas*). The African viper (*Causus rhombeatus*), when in captivity and well fed, lays monthly. Although the reproductive effort of each of these multiple layings—that is, the proportion of the mother's body weight they represent—is almost always inferior to that of a single annual laying,

▷ *RIGHT: Newborn arboreal boa* (Corallus enydris). *This individual is ready to strike and has adopted a typical position. Juveniles exhibit most adult behaviors.*

annual fertility is clearly superior. Most ovo-viviparous snakes have a single yearly litter, and only a few tropical species have two. In colder temperate regions, many species and almost all Viperidae reproduce only every other year and sometimes even less frequently. For these females, which cannot move during the last two-thirds of gestation, the active period is too short to reconstitute the energy stocks necessary for the following year's vitellogenesis. They devote one year to reproduction and the next or more to feeding. In extreme cases, a population's natality coefficient can be 0.5 (one young per year per two adults). Obviously, under such conditions, only a very low mortality allows for the population's survival.

GROWTH & SEXUAL MATURITY

Except for its head, which is proportionally larger, a newborn snake is a miniature replica of an adult, and capable of the same activities. The newborns are nonetheless fragile in many respects, and seem less well adapted to the environment than are adults. This is probably due in part to a lack of experience, although we still know little about the snake's learning processes.

Furthermore, an organism's maximal efficiency, with respect to physiology and functional morphology, probably corresponds to a young adult's size. Whatever the reasons, the mortality rate is high during the first months of life, both from predation and wintering. Young snakes must also find appropriate food, as they are too small to swallow the adults' usual prey. Yet it is rare for their diet to be fundamentally different (see the chapter on predation and nutrition). In order to grow, young snakes must eat proportionally more than adults.

Snakes' growth is both continuous and indeter-

minate. Their size at any given age depends in part on their feeding opportunities, and they keep growing, although at an increasingly slower rate, to an advanced age. There is also a genetic component, for in captivity, snakes of a same litter, equally well fed, often have different growth rates and can be of very different lengths at the same age. Of course, growth rates also depend on temperature, and tropical species grow faster than those who winter for lengthy periods. Growth is usually quite slow during the first few weeks of life, becomes much quicker afterwards, and then keeps slowing down, with the shift in the growth curve usually happening after sexual maturity, rather than during.

▶ Females

Sexual maturity, which is species specific, varies quite widely between individuals, mostly due to climatic factors. For example, the prairie rattlesnake (*Crotalus viridis*) attains sexual maturity at three in Utah but only in its seventh year in Canada.

Viperidae from temperate regions are sexually mature between three and five years, while at the same latitude the Colubridae are mature between two and three years. Data for subtropical and tropical regions are insufficient, but reproducing age seems to be around nine months for certain small colubrids and 2½ for large species and marine snakes.

▶ Males

Males' sexual maturity is generally earlier than females'. It is not marked by the appearance of seasonal secondary sexual characteristics, like nuptial finery, as it is in lizards. Only the development of testicles and the hypertrophy of the annex glands (epididymis and sexual segment of the kidney) testify to the male's reproductive ability.

△ *ABOVE: Group of young and adult European adders (*Vipera berus*)*

SEXUAL CYCLES

THERE ARE A NUMBER of necessary conditions for the completion of a sexual cycle: a temperature high enough for spermatogenesis and embryonic development, sufficient alimentary resources before and during vitellogenesis, and an environment favoring the newborn's survival.

Cool temperate regions
In cool temperate regions, the active period is much too short for the entire reproductive cycle, from the beginning of spermatogenesis to birth, to take place within a single year. Embryonic development must take place during the summer for thermic reasons. Female sexual cycles are thus quite uniform, ovulation taking place at the end of May or beginning of June, and birthing in late August or early September, before dormancy. Vitellogenesis always takes place in the spring, during April or May, although in some rattlesnakes it starts the preceding summer, and the ovocytes reach one-third of their definitive weight before the dormancy season. Males' spermatogenetic cycle is more varied. In colubrids and rattlesnakes, spermatogenesis takes place during the summer, and the spermatozoids are stocked in the vas deferens during winter; spermatogenesis starts again, or continues, in the spring.

Mating usually occurs in April, but many species also mate during the fall, right before wintering. In such cases, spermatozoids are stocked in both the males' and females' genitals during dormancy. Finally, some rattlesnakes only mate at summer's end, and the spermatozoid are stored in the females' oviducts.

This type of fertilization is actually the rule in snakes, since even after a springtime mating, a few weeks go by before evolution begins.

Warm temperate regions
These different reproductive cycles are also found in warmer regions. However, when the active period is long enough, the cycle can complete itself uninterrupted.

Spermatogenesis begins at the end of dormancy, late February or early March, but males are not ready to mate until late May or early June, and the female's cycle is pushed back by one or two extra months. This cycle, with vernal and prenuptial spermatogenesis, is the rule in subtropical regions, arid or not, where the active period is quite long but winter is still cool. Some oviparous snakes, however, lay twice a year, in early June and late July-August, with the second births taking place in mid-fall.

Tropical regions
In tropical regions, the long and dry winter and spring season is not particularly favorable to newborn survival. Birth usually occurs during the rainy season, at least in terrestrial species, which means that spermatogenesis, as well as vitellogenesis, take place during the dry season. Most oviparous species lay more than once during the rainy season. Most ovoviviparous and some oviparous species reproduce only once a year, but the birth dates vary according to the species, throughout the rainy season. Many semiaquatic species, such as Homalopsinae, reproduce much earlier than terrestrial species from the same regions, so that births take place before the dry season is over, and while water levels are low. In such a case, spermatogenesis happens during the summer and fall, and ovulation in winter.

Equatorial regions
Many snakes living in equatorial zones have no fixed reproduction period, either because they lay throughout the year or because birth dates vary from individual to individual within the same species.

In temperate and subtropical regions, the temperature increase in spring plays the essential chronological role in reproductive cycles, even in individuals kept in artificial darkness, whereas light usually plays the determining role in birds and mammals. In tropical zones, the newborn's requirements appear to be the determining factor.

△ ABOVE: *Nuptial finery in the smooth snake* (Natrix natrix)

TERATOLOGY

Gilbert Matz

TERATOLOGY IS THE *lato sensu* study of monsters. Like other vertebrates, snakes present a number of teratologic cases. Any deviation from the expected results from a mistake in embryonic development. Such an error either provokes a minimal anomaly which poses no threat to the individual, or a viable malformation that leaves the snake handicapped, or a monstrous deformity that is usually lethal because it affects vital organs.

The most common anomalies are those of the tegument. Albinism is known in pythons, vipers, and cobras, and especially in thirty North American colubrid species. Various albino strains of the corn snake (*Elaphe g. guttata*) are raised in captivity. Melanism is found in colubrids, and is also frequent in European vipers. Markings may also be affected, although this is rarer. Transversal dorsal lines may be replaced by a longitudinal line (*Boa constrictor, Lampropeltis getulus californiae*). *Naja naja* has a marking on the back of its neck that looks like a pair of glasses, but it may be absent, or there may be two of them, or it can be replaced by a monocle.

Some cephalic or preanal scales are often split. The scaleless mutation in *Thamnophis, Lampropeltis caligaster, Elaphe guttata*, and *E. obsoleta lindheimeri* means that some individuals have no dorsal or cephalic scales except the labial ones.

Malformations of the head are common in snakes: shortening or absence of the mandible, fissures in the jaws or palate, hydroencephalia*, microphtalmia*, or exophtalmia*, anophtalmia*, whether single or bilateral. The body can exhibit spinal deformations that can include alternate cyphosis-lordosis. The deformation of the rachis can be so extreme as to exhibit elbows, with various fusions of parts of the body and tegument, ventral scales in particular. The most common lethal monstrosities are acephalia, the lack of a ventral closure, or, the most spectacular, axial duplication.

△ ABOVE: *Albino asp viper* (Vipera aspis) *in a terrarium*

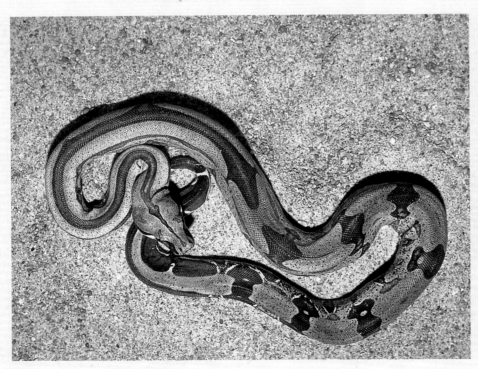

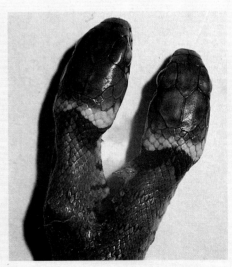

△ ABOVE: *Bicephalic smooth snake* (Natrix natrix)

◁ LEFT: *Anomalous coloration in a* Boa constrictor. *This individual exhibits a continuous dorsal line rather than transverse bands on the anterior part of its body.*

About 400 cases of bicephalic, or, even rarer, two-tailed, snakes have been inventoried. Most of the time the heads alone are duplicated, but there may also be two necks; in those cases, a longer part of the spine is forked. These individuals usually die at birth or soon after, but in some exceptional cases they have been known to survive for over ten years.

An embryo's development is the expression of its genome. Albinism and scalelessness are the result of recessive autosomal genes. But in most cases, anomalies are due to the presence of unfavorable factors during development. The fact that such anomalies occur so frequently in artificial incubators has taught us that an inappropriate temperature, sometimes too low but most often too high, can be quite harmful. Eggs that are found in nature and put into an incubator are often subject to both too-low and too-high temperatures. Pressure or dryness may also have a teratogenic effect. Endogenic reasons are, of course, also present. Axial duplication is the result of the imperfect splitting of a single blastoderm in the process of regeneration, usually after an embryonic lesion. The early stages of embryonic development appear particularly sensitive to the environment's unfavorable factors.

▽ BELOW: *A cyclops viper* (Vipera xanthina), *born in captivity, which only survived for a few days.*

* Hydroencephalia: accumulation of cephalo-rachidian liquid
* Microphtalmia: eye with an unusually small volume or size
* Exophtalmia: abnormal surging of the eye outside of the orbit
* Anophtalmia: congenital absence of one or both eyeballs

PREDATION & NUTRITION

Jean-Pierre Gasc

All snakes are predators, whether their environment is aquatic or terrestrial. They take advantage of varied animal sources: "cold-blooded" vertebrates (fish, amphibians, lizards, or other reptiles), "warm-blooded" vertebrates (mammals or birds), invertebrates (snails, slugs, worms, arthropods), as well as vertebrates' eggs. Prey can be much larger than the snake. A leopard was found in the stomach of an 18-ft. (5.5 m) python. Dasypeltis, *ophiophagous African snakes measuring around 3 ft. (0.9 m), can swallow eggs larger than those of a chicken. Nonetheless, it is important not to generalize from a few spectacular and well-known examples, as snakes tend to prefer rodents. In vertebrates, the head holds the essential sensory organs and food-intake mechanisms. This concentration is even more pronounced in limbless snakes. The head must carry out all the roles leading to successful feeding, from locating prey to capturing it and sending it down the digestive tube.*

NUMEROUS & DIVERSE FOOD SOURCES

Two factors intervene in fixing a species' diet: the animal's size and the environment it lives in.

Snakes usually exploit the resources available in their biotope. Those who live on the ground or humus like minute-snakes (Typhlopidae and Leptotyphlopidae), measuring only between 6 in. (15 cm) and 3½ ft. (1 m), eat worms, slugs, termites, and soft insects. Aquatic species' diets are mostly based on fish and amphibians, but colubrids from the *Regina* genus, for example, consume dragonfly larvae when young and crawfish when adult. The link between diet and environment speaks volumes: Slugs constitute 90% of the American garter snake, *Thamnophis elegans'*, diet when the gastropods are abundant, but it otherwise feeds on fish and frogs. Newborn snakes often ingest completely different prey from adults': invertebrates or small vertebrates when they are found in the local fauna. A young fer-de-lance (*Bothrops atrox*), a pit viper from the Amazon forests measuring 10 in. (25 cm) at birth, feeds on arthropods and lizards, but it is already equipped to locate and kill mammals and birds, which are the prey of adults measuring 5 ft. (1.5 m).

If the species is small, young and adult have the same diet, mostly based on invertebrates. In Europe, Orsini's viper (*Vipera ursinii*) eats the crickets that swarm in high mountain pastures.

In the North American colubrids *Nerodia*, which eat fish, amphibians, crustaceans, and insects, sexual dimorphism is translated by size (the female is larger), and both sexes may have different diets.

Since the great divisions in classification are often based on differences in the teeth and jaw-bone, it is not surprising that a certain dietary homogeneity exists in many families, such as the Viperidae, which mostly feed on small mammals. A detailed examination nevertheless reveals different behavior within groups, depending on whether or not they select their prey.

▶ Specialists & opportunists

Specialized species are characterized by a constant and determined diet. The genus *Dipsas*, a member of the Colubridae, live in the equatorial forests of South America. Snails are not a frequent part of

▷ RIGHT: *This tree snake* (Thelotornis capensis) *has seized a bird that recklessly stopped on this branch.*

◁ LEFT: *Orsini's viper (*Vipera ursinii*) eating a cricket*

◁ LEFT: *The tentacled snake* (Erpeton tentaculum), *eating plants. Its strange aspect is due to its small mouth surrounded by two rostral appendices, or mobile "tentacles," whose use is still unknown. It lives in the fresh waters of southeast Asia, and is the only snake known for its mixed diet (animals and aquatic plants).*

◁ LEFT: *In the Kenyan savannah, this rock python* (Python sebae) *is ingesting an impala* (Aepyceros melampus).

▷ RIGHT: *The anaconda* (Eunectes murinus) *can attack impressive prey; here, a cayman.*

AN EXTRAORDINARY ATTACK

Yannick Vasse

DESPITE PRECONCEIVED IDEAS, unprovoked attacks by Boidae are quite rare. The few published stories are generally sensationalistic.

The story of a 14-year-old Malay, killed and eaten by a reticulated python measuring 17 ft. (5.17 m) is the only really credible one, along with the following story:

On a cloudy and warm afternoon in November 1979 in northern Transvaal, South Africa, two young Tswana herdsmen followed their cattle, when one of them was seized by a python measuring 15 ft. (4.5 m) that had been hiding in the tall grass.

His friend ran to get help, 550 yds. (500 m) away. When he returned with two elders, about 20 minutes later, the victim had already been entirely swallowed by the snake. One of the men dislocated his shoulder attempting to kill the snake with a pick-axe. The python managed to take the pick-axe into its jaws. Finally, it regurgitated its prey when the snake was pelted with stones.

The adolescent was dead "from suffocation and internal wounds," according to the autopsy. One of the witnesses added that the youth's head was covered in saliva.

▷ RIGHT: *This boa* (Corallus
enydris), *hunting while
suspended by its tail, has just
surprised a rodent.*

the fauna, but *Dipsas* extract them from their shells thanks to the snakes' extended hook-shaped lower jaw and then eat them.

Small African *Dasypeltis* colubrids feed solely on birds' eggs. They swallow them laboriously, with an extraordinary distention of the mouth, and then break the shells with cervical vertical prolongations in the stomach.

Cochleophagous (snail-eating) and oophagous (egg-eating) specialists are found on different continents in otherwise unrelated species.

Some prey present particular difficulties for the general organization of snakes' skulls, which favors mobility and latitudinarianism. For example, snakes that specialize in lizards (Scincidae and Gerrhosauridae) have thick teeth, diastems (spaces in the jaw that have no teeth, found on the sides), and posterior venom fangs (covered with overlapping scales and small ossifications) to finish off the lizards' cylindrical bodies. Diastems block the prey transversally, and the fangs pierce it obliquely. In the Central American *Scaphiodontophis*, the Asian *Sibynophis*, and Madagascar's *Liophidium*—species which are particularly fond of lizards—the back teeth are mobile, thanks to a "hinge" at their base, and they take in the prey while swallowing.

The big snakes (boas and pythons), whose skulls are not particularly specialized, are opportunists. When the predator reaches a certain size, the number of available prey becomes smaller, and they make do with what is available, be it other reptiles, birds, or mammals, and whether on the ground, in trees, or in water.

These big snakes are renowned for the spec-

▷ RIGHT: *Rodent predation by a
young* Boa constrictor

STRICTLY OOPHAGOUS SNAKES are found in the genera *Dasypeltis* in Africa, and *Elachistodon* in India. *Dasypeltis* is the more common of the two, and lives in the woody Saharan savannah.

Elachistodon westermanni is a much rarer Indian egg eater. It is a small snake measuring 25 to 35 in. (60 to 90 cm), arboreal but not particularly agile, and it feeds exclusively on bird eggs.

Dasypeltis are small colubrids that can swallow an egg two and a half times the snakes' diameter without cracking the egg. When absorbed, the egg passes under the ventral prolongations (hypapophases) carried by the first cervical vertebrae.

The first 17 or 18 hypapophases following the atlas and the axis are straight and longitudinal. Then the egg arrives under the last thirty or so, which are constituted by six or nine pairs of forward-oriented spines covered with an enamel-like substance, and which penetrate the esophagus' dorsal wall.

Once the egg has reached the esophagus, the snake raises the front of its body to use gravity and curves until the hypapo-

physes break the egg shell. The snake straightens its neck, and the muscular bundles on each side of the back's median contract; the egg is thus crushed against the rounded hypapophyses.

The shell is split on the dorsal line and crushed. This takes about 15 minutes, and the egg's contents are pushed towards the back while the shell is regurgitated. A circular muscle that surrounds the esophagus' posterior area and acts like a sphincter keeps the egg itself from being regurgitated and the shell fragments from entering the stomach.

SNAKES

1	2	3
4		5
6	7	

Egg-eating snake (Dasypeltis inornata).
1. recognizing the egg; 2. taking the egg into the mouth; 3. swallowing; 4. egg being opened by the hypapophyses; 5. crushing the egg; 6. expelling the egg; 7. regurgitated shell. This sequence lasts 15 to 20 minutes.

tacular size of some of their prey. The anaconda (*Eunectes murinus*), from the Amazon basin, which can occasionally reach 33 ft. (10 m), but whose average length is 20 ft. (6 m), for a diameter of 10 in. (27 cm) and a circumference of 33½ in. (85 cm), attack the giant rodent cavy, which weighs 65 lbs. (30 kg). The largest Pythoninae weigh over 220 lbs. (100 kg) and swallow pigs and goats. The largest prey ever described was a 130-lb. (59 kg) impala swallowed by a rock python (*P. sebae*). The story of a 14-year-old Indonesian swallowed by a python appears authentic. But for the most part, pythons' and boas' catch is composed of smaller prey like bird broods or mammal litters. The *Boa constrictor* also seems to find an important source of food in bat colonies. The North American pit viper (*Agkistrodon piscivorus*), a moccasin with aquatic tendencies, is the only snake that occasionally eats carrion.

▶ *A few cases of "cannibalism"*
Many species have other snakes as part of their diet, whether habitually or occasionally. Tube snakes, coral snakes, and mole snakes, all more or less fossorial, include other snakes in their diet. The royal cobra (*Ophiophagus hannah*), from southeast Asia, measuring 20 ft. (6 m), is a great snake-eater, as indicated by its Linnaean name.

A large colubrid from the Amazon forest, known as mussurana (*Clelia clelia*), can neutralize and swallow the formidable fer-de-lance (*Bothrops*), as the former is immune to the latter's venom.

In the United States, the common king snake (*Lampropeltis getulus*) attacks rattlesnakes. In Europe, the Montpellier snake (*Malpolon monspessulanus*) and the smooth snake (*Coronella austriaca*) are the vipers' predators.

Sometimes a snake swallows another one accidentally, as when they have both chosen the same prey. Two captive Boidae were observed coveting the same rat; one snake was swallowed along with the prey.

PREDATION

Snakes hunt in two ways: Some, like vipers, am-

△ ▷ *ABOVE AND RIGHT: Smooth snake (**Natrix natrix**) eating a toad (Bufo bufo). The toad was seized by a hind leg during the attack. The whole ingestion process lasts around 10 minutes.*

bush their prey, while others, numerous colubrids among them, are prowlers. In both cases, they must locate their prey before seizing it and they use one of their senses: vision, hearing, smell, or thermosensitivity.

▶ Locating prey

The environment is often littered with herbaceous vegetation, dirt mounds, rocks, etc., which obviously limits the field of vision for an animal gliding along the ground. This is why some snakes, like the African colubrid *Psammophis*, raise the upper part of their bodies when hunting, although this forces them to expend much energy. Many snakes prefer cleared areas, often using routes and roads opened by man.

Arboreal species, which hunt by hanging from a branch (like the arboreal python), have a larger field of vision. They have big eyes and sometimes even binocular vision, namely *Oxybelis*, a diurnal tree snake. Vision is primarily important in the location of an animal and its movements and is not the dominating sense for most snakes. Since Ophidians are missing the eardrum and the middle ear, they are sensitive only to low-frequency vibrations transmitted by the ground, which are rarely useful during predation.

Smell, on the other hand, is always a dominant sense. Snakes do not just "sniff" air inhaled through the nasal cavity. The vomeronasal organ, found in the palate, analyzes the odoriferous particles collected by the tongue outside the mouth. Some snakes (Boidae and Viperidae) also have another teledetector, which is sensitive to infrared rays. These snakes can thus perceive infinitesimal variations in temperature. They have a thermic image of the warm-blooded prey or predator. The intensity of the stimulus and the comparison between left and right receptors allows them to appreciate the distance and locate the animal emitting the stimulus (see the chapter on the nervous system and sensory organs).

▶ Approach & contact with prey

In most cases, once the prey has been located, the snake orients itself and gets ready to catch it. A slow approach, during which the tongue is quite active, is the most frequent procedure, wrongly interpreted as the fascination of the prey. In fact, the latter remains immobile either because it has not seen the snake move or in order to blend in with the environment. The snake stops at a certain distance from the prey, which distance it will then cover extremely quickly, the front part of its body in an "S."

Some arboreal snakes, like mambas, fall onto their prey; prey and predator then sometimes fall to the ground. Other snakes hang on to a branch by their tail or by using many points of their bodies as supports. Tree snakes, those of the *Oxybelis* genus in particular, let a large part of their body hang from a branch, their heads close to the ground, flicking their tongues and catching lizards in the leaf litter below them.

The head plays an extremely important role during the attack. It is truly a prehensile organ, like a pair of pliers whose jaws are notched by a row of teeth curving backwards. It is carried at the end of a relatively long portion of the spine which corresponds to the neck in other reptiles. This cervical area allows for the "spurting" of the head precisely when the prey is seized. The "neck," usually folded into an "S," slightly oblique in relation to the body, and carrying the body above ground, propels the head in a straight line. This movement is accompanied by the opening of the jaws to catch the prey. In the long-nosed viper (*Vipera ammodytes*) this attack phase lasts 45 milliseconds; the head immediately reaches a speed of 33 ft/s (10 m/s), or 22 mph (36 km/hr). So it is with considerable kinetic energy that the prey is hit. If an attack fails, the entire body of the snake, especially a small snake like the African viper (*Bitis caudalis*), is sometimes taken along in a type of jump.

▶ Constriction or envenomization: the kill

Following the often-violent first contact, Ophidians have a number of behaviors available to them to immobilize their prey.

There are four types of kill: Constrictors suffocate their prey in their rings, other species inject them with their venom, minute-snakes ingest them directly, and most colubrids have a toxic saliva that is more or less venomous but they also tend towards constriction.

Death by constriction is probably the most archaic situation, since it only uses the muscular system along a regular progression. Boas, pythons, and many colubrids hold the prey in their jaws and wrap their body around it, compressing. The process is so quick that a small animal can be killed in a few seconds by suffocation and cardiac arrest.

The fight can last longer if the prey is large or if the snake's rings are badly positioned, and this constitutes a real danger for the snake when the victim has the possibility to defend itself.

In the species that use constriction, the jaws close immediately, while the head remains low, under the action of the subvertebral muscles.

The scenario is somewhat different if the prey is

◁ ▷ ▽ *LEFT, RIGHT, AND BELOW: This Arizona king snake* (Lampropeltis pyromelana) *is about to seize a collared lizard* (Crotaphytus collarus)*. It will ingest it in 15 minutes.*

a frog or toad. These animals are not very sensitive to constriction, since their respiratory movements are carried out by the lower buccal wall rather than by the thoracic cage. They also react to seizure by an extraordinary swelling of the pulmonary sacs, which makes them elastic and even more voluminous. In such a case, snakes must laboriously move to the next phase: ingesting the live animal.

Envenomization is the result of a complex process and lets the snake quickly inoculate venom into the prey's body, which either immobilizes such prey or at least keeps it from going very far.

Species with posterior hooks, like the Montpellier snake (*Malpolon monspessulanus*), envenomize their prey when these pass through the snake's mouth. Vipers and Crotalinae bite their prey and then stay away, waiting until the prey dies before swallowing safely (see the chapter on the nervous system and sensory organs).

INGESTION

Due to prey's generally large size in relation to snakes' heads, the first part of the seizure requires a maximal opening of the mouth. Rapid cinematography, which allows us to analyze movements, shows that this opening occurs both by the lowering of the mandible and the raising of the skull, immediately followed by the palate bones coming forward. This way, the teeth point towards the prey. Opening the mouth requires little effort; the lowering of the mandible is carried out by a depressor muscle joining its back part towards the back of the skull, and raising the skull depends on the action of the muscles that link it to the spine (see Illus. 3 on page 119).

On the other hand, closing the jaws on the prey and the preceding shock are the result of the action of a whole mandibular system, composed of two masses: the mandibular adductor, between the skull and mandible, and the palate's mobilizing muscles.

▶ The skull: a complex machine

Snakes' skulls are composed of a number of me-

chanical units, each having great mobility: a reinforced cranial box, an anterior region, the palate and jawbones, the mandibles, and a specialized dentition. The various parts of this skeletal whole are reinforced by a complex ligament system which ensures their general cohesion while allowing for mobility. The strength and speed of movements while food is being taken, and the transport of prey into the buccal cavity, are made possible by the jaws' mobilizing musculature. Compared to other reptiles, the muscles' general organization has undergone profound changes having to do with the specialization of cranial mechanisms.

In-depth observation of a venomous snake attacking its prey lets us detail this machinery. Viperidae have a fold in their gums that forms a sheath into which the venom fang is hidden when at rest. When the fang is deployed by the maxillary's tip, the sheath's edges near each other and form a joint that forces the venom into the orifice at the bottom of the fang. It is the palate's protraction movement that leads to the fang's movement. Indeed, the pterygoid's forward movement leads the ectopterygoid, a bony stick that sits on the maxillary's ventral abutment. The ectopterygoid pivots on its dorsal articulation until the ligament linking it to the orbital region is completely extended. The fang is thus oriented at a perpendicular angle and solidly immobilized by the joined action of the ectopterygoid and the ligament's tension. All of these movements occur in the very short time of the head's "spurt" by the spine's cervical portion.

The skull's raising, due to a dorsal flexion in relation to the vertebral axis, prevents the snake from keeping the prey within its field of vision; once the movement is started, no repositioning is possible, which is why the prey must be precisely located in space. The incredible violence of the shock may appear incompatible with the skull's disjointed composition, but, in fact, the masticating muscles contract at the moment of contact, turning this system of levers into a rigid block thanks to their insertion into the cranial box.

In vipers and pit vipers, the fangs are pushed deep into the prey by the head's ventral flexion, but since the jaws remain wide open the mandibles form a sort of basket. Usually, one of the muscular bundles compresses the venom gland during the bite. Then a dorsal flexion helps to disengage the fangs, and the head is led backwards by the spine. This lasts only a fraction of a second and the human eye cannot see the entire sequence.

▶ Specialized cranial architecture

The further one looks into the details of snake biology, the more tempting it is to see specialization.

For example, *Dasypeltis*, which feed exclusively on eggs, are difficult to integrate within the colubrid family.

Precise measurements of the various areas of the skull let us isolate particularities, such as an increased oral opening or greater mobility in the palate's bones.

The best-known specializations are those that are linked to envenomization. Vipers are an exemplary case of this: The proportionally important

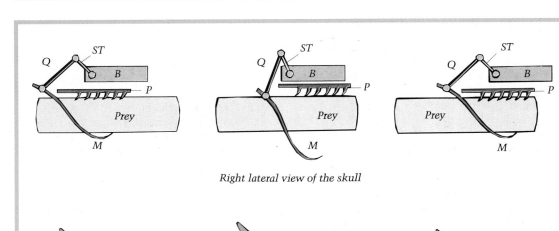

Right lateral view of the skull

Dorsal view of the palate bones' alternate movements

pa: *palatine;* **mx:** *maxillary;* **ec:** *ectopterygoid;* **pt:** *pterygoid*

ILLUS. 5. Prey-transport mechanism in the mouth: three moments in the transport. These movements have often been described as a "pterygoidian walk"; it appears, indeed, as if the head is moving forward in relation to the prey.
B: *cranial box*
Q: *quadrate bone*
P: *palate*
ST: *supratemporal bone*
M: *mandible*

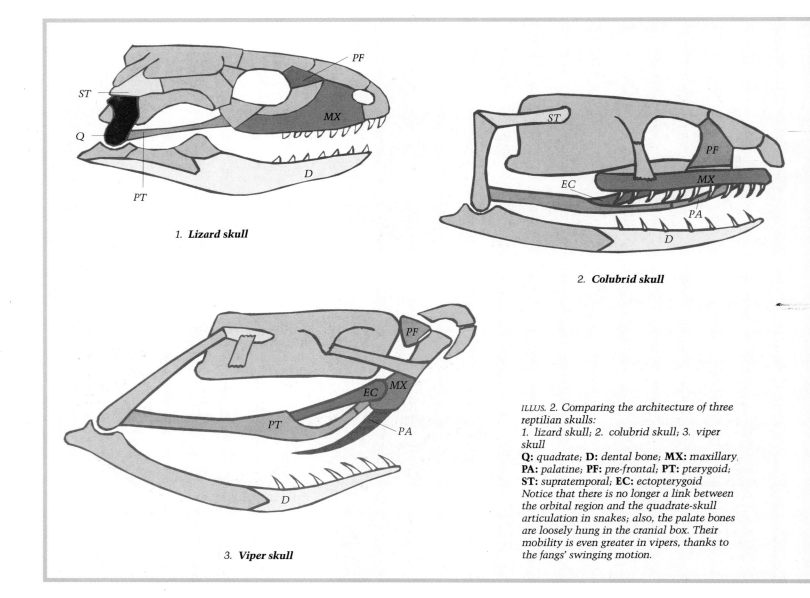

1. **Lizard skull**

2. **Colubrid skull**

3. **Viper skull**

ILLUS. 2. Comparing the architecture of three reptilian skulls:
1. lizard skull; 2. colubrid skull; 3. viper skull
Q: *quadrate;* **D:** *dental bone;* **MX:** *maxillary;*
PA: *palatine;* **PF:** *pre-frontal;* **PT:** *pterygoid;*
ST: *supratemporal;* **EC:** *ectopterygoid*
Notice that there is no longer a link between the orbital region and the quadrate-skull articulation in snakes; also, the palate bones are loosely hung in the cranial box. Their mobility is even greater in vipers, thanks to the fangs' swinging motion.

SKULL BLUEPRINT

THE REINFORCED CRANIAL BOX, which is ventrally closed by the prolongation of the parietal bones (in lizards it's only covered by a membrane), is constructed to ensure the brain's protection and to anchor the jaws' articulated levers and their muscles.

The cranial box's posterior area is directly linked to the muscles of the vertebral axis, disposed in long bundles which mobilize various vertebrae. The head can take advantage of the body's great mobility and replace hind limbs with precise movements. These limbs play an important role in holding prey in other reptiles.

Mobility & specialization

The skull's anterior area, composed of the bones surrounding the nasal cavity, is articulated onto the posterior area and can therefore move independently.

The palate and jawbones as a whole are only suspended from the cranial boxes in a few points. A system of ligaments keeps the group solid while allowing for great mobility thanks to a number of articulations and the division of the masticating muscles into specialized bundles.

Teeth are found on the palate bones (palatine, pterygoid), the upper jaw (maxillary), and the mandible (dental); they are tapered, recurved, and implanted into the bone by the bottom. Teeth are replaced throughout the animal's life from buds found on the jaw's internal wall. Tooth size often decreases towards the back of the jaw.

The left and right mandibles are not fused to the jaw, but they are joined, usually by an extremely elastic ligament, which lets them spread apart to a considerable width.

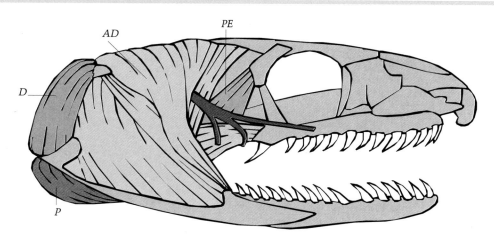

1. *Lateral view of a colubrid*

ILLUS. *3. Main head muscles*
AD: *Adductor muscles, responsible for keeping the jaws closed;* **D:** *Depressor muscle, to a great extent responsible for the jaws' opening;* **VG:** *Venom gland;* **PE:** *Pterygoid elevator muscle, one of the many responsible for the palate bones' movements;* **GC:** *Venom gland compressor muscle, derived from the adductor muscle;* **P:** *Pterygoid muscle.*

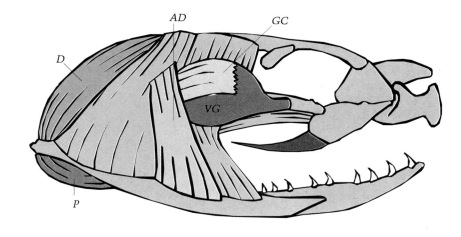

2. *Lateral view of a viper*

width of their head results from the lengthening of the quadrates, the bones linking the cranial box, the palate bones, and the mandible. The snout is shorter, the maxillary having been reduced to a short mobile piece carrying the fang and being linked to the cranial box only by a ligament. Parts of the salivary glands are transformed into a sort of laboratory, fabricating substances which, when inoculated into the prey, lead to its death and the beginning of the prey's digestion by the snake. The masticating muscles have been modified and some of them are implicated in the process of injecting the venom under pressure.

Having an efficient tool of death and strong capacities for distention of the jaw let vipers swallow prey representing 36.6% of their own mass, as opposed to 18.4% in other snakes. Their efficiency is seen in the few movements needed for swallowing their prey: One hundred palato-maxillary movements let vipers swallow 28% of their mass, while other snakes may only absorb 9% by expending the same effort. Vipers thus require less energy to feed themselves, which may help explain their relatively sedentary life-style and the long intervals between feedings. In a single ingestion, a viper consumes 2.6 times more nutritive mass than do colubrids, boas, or pythons.

▶ *Swallowing slowly*
Once neutralized by the snake, the prey is carried inside the oral cavity, usually headfirst, but frogs, toads, and other small prey may be swallowed backwards or even sideways. This transport puts a

certain mechanism specific to snakes into play: the mandibles' mobility with regard to the palate. The alternate movement of these dental elements progressively pushes the prey to the back of the mouth, while the mandibles spread under the pressure, forming a funnel. The head in effect advances on the prey, the mandibles progressing around it, like someone crawling on his elbows.

Once the anterior part of the prey has come to the pharyngeal opening, the snake's spine begins to undulate, which ensures passage of the prey into the esophagus. By propagating from front to rear, this contraction pushes the saliva-covered prey through the esophagus working exactly like the locomotive contractions that create the skin's push on the ground. In order to avoid a parasitic pressure on the ground and to let gravity intervene, the snake raises the front part of its body as much as possible.

Once the prey has reached the posterior portion of the esophagus, the snake yawns a few times to return the various parts of the skull to their original positions. It can seize and swallow a number of prey in a row. In contrast to the speed at which prey is caught, the long phase of transportation in the mouth requires a sustained effort during which the snake is vulnerable. This is why the snake prefers to regurgitate if disturbed.

▶ *Feeding rhythms*
Except for the reproductive period, a large part of snake behavior is conditioned by feeding rhythms.

Unlike lizards, which often feed on a large

DIGESTIVE APPARATUS & DIGESTION

SNAKES' DIGESTIVE tubes have various stages and are marked by the body's elongated shape as well as by their ability to ingest large prey.

The cylindrical tongue with its bifid tip does not help bring food into the mouth as it does in lizards; it is a strictly sensory organ, associated with the vomeronasal sense.

Salivary glands play an important role in lubricating the prey; some are differentiated into venom glands and have a groove for venom excretion which opens near a specialized tooth.

The esophagus is heavily longitudinally pleated, which allows for its dilation during the ingestion of prey. There is no shrinking between esophagus and stomach. The latter is rectilinear, with very muscular walls and extremely powerful acids, which can attack any tissue (including teeth) except for keratin (claws, hair) and chitin, which makes up arthropods' shells. These exceptions are expelled in the feces.

The stomach ends in an annular valve leading to the intestine, which is also rectilinear and which is surrounded by greasy lobules whose volume depends on the snake's physiological state.

The terminal intestine, or coprodeum, serves as an accumulating chamber for feces, and opens into the cloaca. The liver is tapered and extends over a large part of the body; it is reduced to the right lobe.

Digestive processes depend on temperature: They are inhibited below 50°F (10°C), and the snake must regurgitate its prey. The main problem caused by the ingestion of whole prey is its rotting, which would give off lethal toxins.

Snakes must steer the right path between enzymic processes and bacterial action. Digestive enzymes reach their optimal level of efficiency around 86°F (30°C), and the snake tries to reach this temperature by active thermoregulation, heating itself in the sun.

number of small prey, snakes absorb large quantities of food at one time and can stand lengthy fasting periods. This is often the case for the royal python (*Python regius*) when it is in captivity and the food supply is inadequate. One reticulated python (*Python reticulatus*) survived for two and a half years before dying of starvation. A cascabel (*Crotalus durissus*) fasted for 26 months, a rock python (*Python sebae*) for 29 months.

Nonetheless, important variations exist as to climate, prey size, age, and physiological condition of the predator. Snakes do not generally feed in the period preceding molting, and females, which usually consume more than males, abstain when they are gravid. Small-size species and young snakes have important metabolic needs and must feed often. Young rainbow boas raised in terrariums get a living mouse every three to four days. During an active season in a temperate zone, snakes consume one, two, or three times their weight, which is little compared to other vertebrates, and especially small homeothermic mammals.

The snakes' singular shape is the origin of their feeding mode, but a diversity of food sources seems to be the rule, with a marked preference for mammals, not so much the biggest ones as the most prolific: the rodents. This has led to the hypothesis that the mammalian expansion of the Tertiary Era had a positive effect on snakes' evolution: The two main methods of killing, constriction and envenomization, are most efficient on mammals.

Snakes' obvious success in terms of geographic distribution is probably due to a number of causes. Their ability to feed on a variety of prey and to ingest a large quantity of food in a single feeding has probably been a big advantage in expansion. Present-day populations do not seem particularly sensitive to the richness of food resources of their biotopes and often make do with constraining conditions, such as those imposed by man.

ECOLOGY OF SNAKES

HABITATS & LIFE-STYLES

Patrick David–Guy Naulleau–Yannick Vasse

Snakes may be found on dry land almost anywhere on earth—some are even marine—and they have adapted to a number of biotopes. Their habitats represent the range of natural environments at practically every latitude, including some extreme climates. The only places where snakes are not found are the polar regions, a few large islands (Ireland, New Zealand), and many small islands of the Atlantic and central Pacific. The presence of a species is not actually linked to a particular vegetal environment or type of soil. Strictly carnivorous, snakes may be found even in largely vegetarian environments, the essential being for them to find an adequate diet. Snakes can be grouped into five main categories: terrestrial, burrowing, arboreal, freshwater, and saltwater. Every species in a subfamily may have the same life-style, like the Hydrophinae, the most specialized of aquatic snakes and the only ones to have conquered the seas. On the other hand, in large families like the Colubridae, all five adaptations are present.

RAIN FORESTS

Snakes from rain forests include a number of native species, the subterranean and arboreal forms in particular. This abundance is explained by the particularly favorable life conditions offered by a tropical climate: a relatively stable temperature of 83°F (28°C), mild daytime thermic variations, and significant precipitation (over 6½ ft. [2000 mm] per year) which, spread out over the year, ensures constant humidity.

Under very tall arborescent cover, the vegetation is lush, full of ligneous vines, huge herbaceous plants, epiphytes, branches, dead trunks, and bamboo, forming inextricable undergrowth on spongy ground.

Snakes, found at each level of this vegetation, present a great diversity of shapes, more or less linked to different ecological niches. Burrowing and semi-burrowing snakes are numerous. The burrowing ones are usually dark, like the species of the *Anomapelis* genus in tropical America, many

◁ *LEFT: The river jack (*Bitis nasicornis) *is a terrestrial species from wet African forests.*

△ ABOVE: *The South American
anaconda* (Eunectes murinus) *from
the wet South American forests, is
semiarboreal and semiaquatic. It
often spends time on branches
above water.*

▽ BELOW: *The mangrove snake*
(Boiga dendrophila) *in an Asian
mangrove*

Typhlops or *Leptotyphlops* species in Africa, South
America, and Asia, and the Calabarian pythons
(*Calabaria reinhardti*) in Africa.

Many relatively nonspecialized species frequent
the ground vegetation: the Colubridae (*Geodipsas
depressiseps* and *Lamprophis olivaceus*) and the vipers (*Bitis gabonica* and *B. nasicornis*) in Africa,
the false coral snakes (*Anilius scytale*, *Atractus
elaps*, and *Oxyrhophus formosus*), the mussurana
(*Clelia clelia*) and the fer-de-lance (*Bothrops atrox*)
in South America, as well as the reticulated python (*Python reticulatus*), the rainbow snake (*Xenopeltis unicolor*), and the Malaysian moccasin
(*Calloselasma rhodostoma*) in tropical Asia. The
more mobile and rapid terrestrial forms (like the
Colubrid *Zaocys carinatus* in Asia) are less prevalent in forests.

The arboreal forms are numerous, with colorings and, often, cryptic markings (see the chapter
on coloration).

Among the most characteristic are the tree boa
(*Corallus caninus*), the tree snake (*Oxybelis fulgidus*), and the palm viper (*Bothriopsis bilineata*) in
tropical America; the emerald snake (*Gastropyxis
smaragdina*) in Africa; the long-nosed tree snake
(*Ahaetulla prasina*), the flying snake (*Chrysopelea
paradisii*) and the bamboo pit viper (*Trimeresurus
sumatranus*) in Asia; and the green python (*Morelia*—once *Chondropython*—*viridis*) in Australasia.

Marshes and flooded forest regions are very rich
in snake species, which are often dark, whether or
not they are aquatic. In the heart of rainy areas,
flooded zones and rivers shelter many species such
as *Natriceteres olivacea* in Africa, *Helicops angulatus* and the giant anaconda (*Eunectes murinus*)
in South America, as well as *Macropisthodon rho-
domelas* in tropical Asia.

On the other hand, many snakes are tied to the
mangrove—coastal marshes with aerial roots.
Riverbanks and mangroves in tropical Asia are
mostly inhabited by the semiaquatic blood python
(*Python curtus*), the strictly aquatic Javanese acro-
chord (*Acrochordus javanicus*), and *Boiga den-*

LIVING IN TREES

Guy Naulleau

SOME SPECIES are more or less pledged to a life in the heights, among them, semiarboreal species which, without being perfectly adapted to this way of life, nonetheless climb trees and bushes.

In tropical environments, man-made buildings also serve as climbing places for snakes.

Arboreal snakes can be strictly differentiated according to their favorite height. Some prefer "high altitudes" and climb to the top of trees, like the emerald tree boa (*Corallus caninus*) from South America, the green python (*Morelia viridis*) from Australia, the green mamba (*Dendroaspis viridis*) from tropical Africa, or the silver tree snake (*Oxybelis argenteus*) from tropical America, or finally *Chrysopelea ornata*, the golden tree snake from the bushy savannahs of tropical Asia.

Others are little specialized arboreals, generally found in medium-high branches, like *Philodryas olfersii*, a green colubrid from Brazil. Green mambas (*Dendroaspis*)

are found at a similar height in the African savannah, and *Boiga* is found in the rain forests and mangroves of Asia.

Many species stay in low branches, and even in bushes, such as the common African arboreal viper (*Atheris squamigera*), *Bothriechis schlegelii* in tropical America, and the cotton-mouthed *Trimeresurus albolabris* in tropical Asia, as well as *Opheodrys aestivus* in North America, *Philothamnus semivariegatus* in tropical Africa, or *Leptophis mexicanus* in tropical America.

Semiarboreal species not only live in trees and bushes, but can sometimes climb quite high, like *Elaphe*, which eat eggs and birds found in trees. The Aesculapian snake (*Elaphe longissima*) and the pilot blacksnake (*E. obsoleta*) from North America, as well as the aquatic African (*Philothamnus hoplogaster*) and the *Dasypeltis* genus, from the tropical savannahs of Africa, are all semiarboreal.

The straight and relatively smooth trunks are only conquered by adapted species;

they are not strictly arboreal. *Elaphe guttata*, *E. obsoleta*, and *E. longissima* climb tree trunks.

"Real" arboreals, which are long and thin, often use vines, branches and leaves. *Atheris* and *Trimeresurus*, which are both Viperidae, only go from branch to branch, and their progress is quite slow.

Many arboreals exhibit adaptations. Two forms are very specialized. One consists of diurnal animals with thin or very thin and long bodies, elongated heads, and lateral carina fornicis between their ventral scales and those of their flanks, keeping them from falling. They sometimes have a prehensile tail. Some of these snakes are *Ahaetulla*, *Oxybelis*, *Dendrelaphis*, *Chrysopelea*, *Leptophis*, and *Uromacer*.

Others are nocturnal animals with stocky but long bodies, massive heads and round eyes, prehensile tails and flanks lacking car-

▽ *BELOW: Equatorial Africa's green mamba* (Dendroaspis jamesoni)

less massive head and a prehensile tail (*Atheris, Trimeresurus, Bothriechis*).

"Generalists," which are not very specialized morphologically, may still be arboreals. They have long and thin bodies and are quick and agile (*Dendroaspis, Thrasops, Philothamnus, Chironius, Dispholidus*). ina fornicis. A rather specialized type forms a third category: These are nocturnal snakes, which are small and stocky, with a more or

Some species live in both trees and water, such as certain boas. This is also true of the anaconda (*Eunectes murinus*) from South America. It often stays on branches above water; when disturbed, it hides in the water. It is the largest snake of the New World, and can occasionally measure up to 33 ft. (10 m). Small Boinae, like *Candoia*, with their prehensile tails, from the wet forests of the Pacific, and the Round Island

Bolyeridae, which are on the verge of extinction, live very similarly.

Two arboreal pythons that tend to be green and have a prehensile tail are members of the Boidae family: the green python (*Morelia viridis*), from New Guinea and northern Australia, and the green tree boa (*Corallus caninus*), from South America, thus illustrating a perfect example of convergence.

△ *ABOVE LEFT :* Morelia viridis, *from New Guinea.*   △ *ABOVE RIGHT :*
Corallus caninus, *the tree boa.*   △ *ABOVE :* Oxybelis argenteus; *its long thin body with its "anti-skidding" carina fornicis makes it a particularly well-adapted tree snake.*
    ▷ *RIGHT :* Trimeresurus purpureomaculatus; *this mangrove pit viper is arboreal with a prehensile tail.*

drophila, which is arboreal and lives on branches near the water. *Acrochordus arafurae*, found in Australia and New Guinea, lives in mangroves and estuaries.

HUMID MOUNTAIN FORESTS

In the tropical zone, humid mountain forests shelter many native species. Arboreal species are predominant, like *Atheris nitschei* in Africa, the green python (*Morelia viridis*) in New Guinea, the green-and-black palm viper (*Bothriechis nigroviridis*) and Schlegel's palm viper (*Bothriechis schlegelii*) in Central America. The sharp-nosed moccasin (*Deinagkistrodon acutus*), from China, and the mountain pit viper (*Ovophis monticola*) are terrestrial, while *Atractus crassicaudatus*, from South America, is more or less burrowing.

SAVANNAH & DRY TROPICAL FORESTS

In tropical climates with marked dry seasons, vast areas are occupied by savannahs, dense herbaceous formations composed of hardy and relatively high grasses, studded with trees.

These are taxonomically rich environments, getting progressively more so when moving from dry savannahs to wet ones, and then on to gallery forests. On one hand, heavy snakes with cryptic coloring, such as the puff adder (*Bitis arietans*), which is darker in the humid savannah than in the Sahel's dry savannah, the cascavel (*Crotalus durissus*), Russell's viper (*Daboia*—previously *Vipera*—*russelli*) and *Naja kaouthia* are found in Asia; in Australia are found various Pythoninae from the *Morelia* genius (i.e., *Morelia variegata*) and Elapidae like *Acanthophis antarcticus*, known as

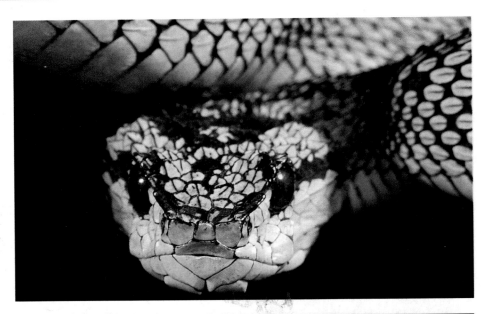

△ *ABOVE, TOP:* Atheris nitschei, *an arboreal viper*

△ *ABOVE, BOTTOM: Schlegel's palm viper* (Bothriechis schlegeli)

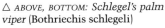

▷ *RIGHT, ABOVE: Green mamba* (Dendroaspis angusticeps), *an arboreal snake from the African savannah*

◁ *LEFT: The pointy-nosed moccasin* (Deinagkistrodon acutus), *originally from China*

△ ABOVE: *The amethyst python* (Morelia amethystina), *from Australia*

the death adder since it resembles Viperidae. There are also some very thin and swift species, which are sometimes striped (*Psammophis sibilans* in Africa, *Ptyas mucosus* in Asia, and *Liophis miliaris* and *Mastigodryas boddaerti* in South America).

True burrowing species are often dark, as are the terrestrials, whether stocky (*Lamprophis lineatus*) or camouflaged (nocturnal vipers from the *Causus* genus) and egg-eating (*Dasypeltis*) snakes. The latter, as well as the black mamba (*Den-*

droaspis polylepis), the royal python (*Python regius*), and the rock python (*Python sebae*) frequent the vegetation and bushes of the more-or-less shrubby African savannah.

Arboreal species are usually thin (*Thelotornis capensis*, for example), or rather robust except for swift species, like the green mamba (*Dendroaspis angusticeps*). In Asia, the flying snake (*Chrysopelea ornata*) is known for living in the tops of scattered trees. The colubrid *Psammophis condanarus* is semiarboreal.

The blind snake (*Rhamphotyphlops australis*), a burrowing snake, the terrestrial *Demansia atra*, and the amethyst python (*Morelia amethystina*) are found in the Australian eucalyptus savannah.

In Central and South America, the cascavel (*Crotalus durissus*) is found in wide-open spaces (campos); the tree snake (*Oxybelis aeneus*) climbs the branches of the scattered trees.

Few Elapinae live aquatic life-styles. We must mention the aquatic cobra (*Boulengerina annulata*) from the rivers of tropical Africa, which can reach 8.25 ft. (2.5 m) in length. Hidden in the river-bank's crevices, it feeds on fish.

Some other more or less aquatic species are *Afronatrix anoscopus*, from the marshes and humid African savannahs, or *Rhabdophis subminiatus*, a highly venomous Asian colubrid living in marshes and rice fields. Coloring may be dark on the back (*Afronatrix anoscopus*, *Helicops leopardinus*), and these snakes' nostrils are often found on top of the face (*Helicops*, for example).

◁ *LEFT: The horned viper* (Cerastes cerastes) *burrowing in sand. This species also frequents rocky areas.*

Truly aquatic snakes have particular adaptations. The ventral scales are reduced, the eyes are small, and since the nostrils are on top of the head, they can breathe while staying mostly submerged. A valvula seals the nostrils, and there are mechanisms to close the rostral groove, which lets the tongue pass.

Many ophidians live in drier, thorny savannahs, bordering semiarid zones and deserts. The average maximal annual temperature is often over 86°F (30°C) and the rainy season is short. Vegetation is a broken expanse of twisted trees and grasses that shade the hissing snake (*Psammophis sibilans*), the Egyptian cobra (*Naja haje*), and certain vipers like *Echis leucogaster* in the Sahel, the Elapidae *Pseudonaja modesta* in Australia, and the black-and-red fer-de-lance (*Bothrops erythromelas*) in northeastern Brazil. In the semiarid vegetal formations of Mexico and the southwestern U.S. many terrestrial *Crotalus* (rattlesnakes) are found, as well as the particularly rapid and sun-loving colubrids, such as the striped whipsnake (*Masticophis lateralis*). The diversity of snakes in these varied and more-or-less favorable environments is due to climatic conditions and the abundance of available prey.

DESERTS & ARID ZONES

In dry tropical climates, huge arid territories found in tropical and subtropical zones are characterized by irregular or light precipitation and by thermic gaps of up to 104°F (40°C). Furthermore, the ground is brutally hot during the day (up to 158°F [70°C]), and there is a considerable loss of heat at night. The air is lacking in water, the winds are constant and often violent, and the ground, subject to intense erosion, is composed of scree or sand mounds.

Snakes are rather well represented among the vertebrates living in such harsh conditions, although the number of species living in true deserts

▷ *RIGHT: The woma* (Aspidites ramsayi), *an Australian desert-dwelling Pythoninae*

is relatively low.

Desert-dwelling species, few in number and highly specialized, are often crepuscular. They avoid extremes in temperatures by burrowing into the ground.

The sandy regions of the Middle East have many burrowing snakes: the glossy snake (*Leptotyphlops macrorhynchus*), or the sand boa (*Eryx jayakari*), or sand snakes like *Lytorhynchus diadema*), or the sand viper (*Cerastes vipera*), or the horned viper (*Cerastes cerastes*), also found in rocky regions. *Lytorhynchus ridgewayi* and *Echis carinatus* live in the arid and sandy regions of south Asia.

In Mexico, the rocky deserts shelter *Salvadora mexicana*, while the horned rattlesnake (*Crotalus cerastes*), also found in the United States, spends its time in the sandy regions. Many species are sand-colored—horned viper, sand viper, MacMahon's snake (*Eristicophis macmahoni*), and the horned rattlesnake.

Sabulicole species—living in the sand rather than on it—have a modified head, either truncated as in *Lytorhynchus maynardi*, or covered with a heavily reinforced nasal scale, while the body scales are smooth. The scales of Viperidae—which burrow by undulating their bodies—are keeled.

Rupicolous snakes are ochre or grey, like the horned viper (*Cerastes cerastes*) or the species *Pseudocerastes persicus* and *Coluber rogersi*.

Many species are massive in shape (*Crotalus* and *Cerastes* genera); Viperidae are strongly represented in arid zones and practically the only family found in deserts. There also exist desert-dwelling snakes whose slender bodies let them multiply support points in the sand (*Lytorhynchus diadema*, *Chionactis polarostris*, *Chilomeniscus cinctus*).

The colubrid *Alsophis elegans* is only found in the foggy littoral deserts of the southwestern coast of South America.

In Australian deserts the woma (*Aspidites ramsayi*), a Pythoninae, and an Elapidae *Acanthophis pyrrhus* are most prevalent.

A few species are found in cold deserts (Tibetan plateau, foggy coastal deserts of Chile and Namibia), such as the *Philodryas chamissonis* in Chile, although it only lives on the desert's periphery. The colubrid *Thermophis baileyo* lives in a few Tibetan valleys and streams.

SEMIARID ZONES

These are intermediary between arid zones and savannahs. Large subtropical regions in a dry climate offer snakes a poor, herbaceous and shrubby vegetation, which they exploit at best according to the ground's type, which is usually rocky, although sometimes looser.

These areas are rich in snakes, a large proportion of which are heavy and camouflaged: *Crotalus atrox*, *Crotalus ruber*, *Echis carinatus*, *Echis leucogaster*, *Eryx jayakari*, *Phimophis guianensis* (in the llanos of Venezuela), *Bothrops pictus*, *Bothrops erythromelas*, *Heterodon nasicus*, and *Acanthophis pyrrhus*.

The thin and swift active forms are even more numerous: whether terrestrial or semiarboreal,

▽ *BELOW:* **Acanthophis pyrrhus**, *an Australian Elapidae from arid zones*

they are often longitudinally striped. Species like *Masticophis taeniatus* or *Salvadora mexicana* can thus openly hunt for lizards and try to avoid birds of prey.

Among those that are not striped, some are camouflaged by broken patterns (dark spots on a grey or sand-colored background) like *Malpolon moilensis*, *Coluber florulentus*, or *Spalerosophis dolichospilus*).

Some homocryptic species live in shrubs in these semiarid areas, like the tree snake (*Oxybelis aeneus*), as well as truly burrowing species (*Leptotyphlops macrorhynchus*, *Atractaspis microlepidota*), and some semi-burrowing ones (*Eryx johni*, *Eryx colubinus*).

Hypsiglena torquata, *Boiga trigonata*, and *Telescopus dhara*, nocturnal or crepuscular, are usually transversally striped or spotted, and spend most of their time in rocky areas. In central and western Africa, the rupicolous flower colubrid (*Coluber florulentus*) lives under stones; the Indian sand boa (*Eryx conicus*), from the more-or-less arid areas of south Asia, is a desert dweller.

Some species from semiarid zones are also found in arid zones. In North America, secondary formations known as chaparrals, with a Mediterranean-type climate, shelter *Leptotyphlops humilis*, a burrowing species, the whipsnake (*Masticophis flagellum*), and the diamond rattlesnake (*Crotalus atrox*). The latter two are both terrestrial.

Finally, in the Middle East are species such as the false Arab cobra (*Malpolon moilensis*) and *Daboia*—previously *Vipera*—*lebetina*.

MEDITERRANEAN-TYPE VEGETATION

Snakes are moderately represented in Mediterranean-type vegetation, found in the same type of climate, with mild, humid winters and dry sum-

△ *ABOVE: Diamondback rattlesnake (*Crotalus atrox*) in a chaparral*

▷ *RIGHT: Cottonmouth pit viper (*Trimeresurus albolabris*)*

△ *ABOVE: Smooth snake*
(Natrix natrix)

△ *ABOVE LEFT: Asp viper* (Vipera
aspis) *in a hedge*

▷ *RIGHT: Copperhead* (Agkistrodon
contortrix) *in the leaf litter of a
temperate American forest*

◁ *LEFT: Smooth snake* (Natrix
natrix) *hidden in aquatic vegetation*

mers. They are more numerous in Australia and Asia Minor, where they are essentially terrestrial, sometimes arboreal. The ladder snake (*Elaphe scalaris*) is found in Europe in oak forests and secondary formations like scrub, the result of thousands of years of human exploitation: deforestation, fires, and livestock grazing.

The terrestrial red-throated colubrid (*Hierophis jugularis*) and *Vipera xanthina* are found in eastern Europe. The Montpellier snake (*Malpolon monspessulanus*) is found around most of the Mediterranean.

In California, with its similar climatic conditions, the king snake (*Lampropeltis zonata*) lives on the ground in oak, coniferous, and succulent plant forests.

In Australia, the python *Morelia spilota* glides through the brush in sparse forests or more open herbaceous grounds. It can also be found in low branches, whereas the death adder (*Acanthophis antarcticus*), living in the same biotope, is strictly terrestrial, sometimes even sand-dwelling.

Gradated vegetal formations in southern Africa shelter the mole snake (*Pseudaspis cana*), which is terrestrial and has burrowing tendencies—it explores rodents' burrows—and the terrestrial *Psammophylax rhombeatus*.

Many species are found in both Mediterranean-type and semiarid zones, like *Daboia*—formerly *Vipera*—*mauritanica* and *Coluber algirus*. Although their characteristics are due to the biotope rather than to the climate, these snakes tend to be larger and more colorful than temperate species.

HUMID SUBTROPICAL FORMATIONS

In humid subtropical regions, winters may be harsher than in Mediterranean-type zones, but the wet, hot summers are favorable to vegetation. Snake species are numerous and many live with fauna from tropical areas.

Burrowers are rare, terrestrial and aquatic species more numerous, and there are some arboreal species.

In Asia, the arboreal bamboo pit viper (*Trimeresurus stejnegeri*) hides in deciduous bushes and trees, tropical hardwoods, vines and flowers. *Dinodon rufozonatum*, which is terrestrial and aquatic, enjoys fallow lands, marshes and rice fields. These areas are also full of aquatic species from the *Sinonatrix* and *Amphiesma* genera.

In the southeastern United States, where palm trees, tulip trees, and various hardwoods, as well as sandy pinewoods, are found, the more prevalent snakes include the harlequin snake (*Micrurus fulvius*) and the diamondback rattlesnake (*Crotalus adamanteus*), which are both terrestrial, as well as the chicken snake (*Elaphe obsoleta quadrivittata*), with its arboreal tendencies.

The black marsh snake (*Seminatrix pygaea*) lies in ambush in the water hyacinths in the marshes, which are full of cypress, from which hang long branches of epiphytes.

In South America, one can also cite the Colubridae *Clieia rustica* and *Tomodon ocellatus*, both terrestrial.

TEMPERATE FORESTS & AGRICULTURAL BIOMES

Snakes' taxonomic richness is lessened in climates with longer winters, where the warm season is too brief to satisfy most species' vital needs. The species found are little specialized, and most of them are terrestrial, whether swift members of the *Coluber* and *Hierophis* genera, or slower ones like *Elaphe*, *Vipera*, *Crotalus*, *Agkistrodon*, and some semiaquatic snakes (*Thamnophis sirtalis*, *Natrix natrix*, *Rhabdophis tigrinus*).

Snakes are not usually found in the coniferous forests or in very developed European clusters of deciduous trees since there isn't enough sun to heat the ground and almost no herbaceous vegetation. Nonetheless, the Aesculapian snake (*Elaphe longissima*) can live in forests. Important environmental changes have occurred in large regions, which have been transformed into fields and pastures. These areas, mixed woodlands and clearings favor the asp viper (*Vipera aspis*) and the common grass snake (*Natrix natrix*), which spend time in areas surrounding water.

If some regions are too deforested, oak forests can turn into moors (deforestation, fires, grazing). One can then find the peliad viper (*Vipera berus*) and the smooth snake (*Coronella austriaca*) in the dense vegetation, and, in warmer regions, the asp viper and the green and yellow grass snake (*Hierophis viridiflavus*).

The terrestrial copperhead (*Agkistrodon contortrix*) is found in the clearings and underbrush of North America's temperate forests.

The Great Lakes region, with its cold winters and hot, humid summers, as well as the Pacific coast of the United States, have mixed forests with a varied arrangement of vegetation suitable for snakes, as well as a rich underbrush. The bull snake (*Pituophis melanoleucus*), the blue racer (*Coluber constrictor foxi*), and the scarlet snake (*Cemophora coccinea*) are all found there. There are many more species in warmer temperate areas.

In the Far East, the mixed forests have lush flora, which gives them the look of tropical forests, with vines and epiphytes. There one can find the Chinese green snake (*Entechinus major*) and some snakes like *Elaphe taeniuria* in China and *E. climacophora* in Japan. *Rhabdophis tigrinus* is found in marshes, rice fields, and the edges of forests.

BOREAL & AUSTRAL FORESTS

Although neither snakes nor any other reptiles are found in the polar regions, snakes are found in northernmost Eurasia, where the common viper (*Vipera berus*) spreads above the Arctic Circle in Scandinavia. Ophidia are the only ones who confront the rigorous boreal climate, the common viper and smooth snake (*Coronella austriaca*) in Eurasia, the Siberian moccasin (*Agkistrodon intermedius*) in north Asia, and the garter snake in Canada, which is restricted to the forest zones (taiga) and avoids the tundra, with its sparse vegetation and especially its cold weather.

▷ *RIGHT: Wied's fer-de-lance (*Bothrops neuwiedii*) in the Argentine pampas*

In the Southern Hemisphere, *Tachymenis chilensis* and *Bothrops ammodytoides* live in the austral regions.

These snakes have adapted in much the same way as mountain species, especially in terms of ovoviviparity.

HIGH MOUNTAINS

Snakes living in cold mountain areas have adapted in many different ways. They are dark (*Vipera aspis* is melanic), measure less than 31½″ (80 cm), and are generally ovoviviparous, which lets embryos benefit from their mother's thermoregulation (see the chapter on reproduction). There are few species, one or two per region, and many are endemic (*Bothrops andianus*, *Thamnophis fulvus*, *Atheris hindii*).

The montane levels (European mountainous regions with high humidity) shelter in their prairies or screes the peliad viper and the asp viper.

Medium-sized mountains in tropical and subtropical zones can be semiarid (Central Asia), temperate, or Mediterranean. There are numerous species, which are somewhat specialized and quite varied, from burrowing to arboreal.

In Mexico, *Conopsis biserialis*, *Toluca lineata*, and *Lampropeltis ruthveni* are found on the ground and in the clearings of scattered high altitude forests, which are mostly full of fir trees.

STEPPES

Continental areas are characterized by steppes: areas of extreme weather with cold winters, hot summers, and little rain, thereby rendered treeless. The ground is covered with grasses and there is a large burrowing fauna.

Nonetheless, there are few species, both because of the climate and the bare vegetation, which leave the environment open and without shelter, comparable to that of semiarid zones. Both swift (*Hierophis spinalis*, *Psammophis linoleatum*) and more massive snakes (*Vipera ursinii renardi*, *Agkistrodon blomhoffi*, *Bothrops ammodytoides*, *Elaphe dione*) are found in steppes.

These are obviously burrowing or semiburrowing (using rodent burrows); a few are aquatic or semiaquatic (*Thamnophis radix*, *Natrix tessellata*). Many of these species are also common to temperate zones. In the Great Plains (prairies) of the United States, the bull snake (*Pituophis melanoleucus*) is found in rodent burrows, and the prairie snake (*Crotalus viridis*) in short grass.

Grasses predominate in northern Eurasia, where the central Asian *Hierophis spinalis* and *Elaphe dione* hide, whereas the steppe is sparse in the southern region, where *Vipera ursinii renardi* is found.

Maximilian's viper (*Bothrops neuwiedi*) and *Bothrops ammodytoides*, which lives all the way down into Patagonia, are found on the pampas and plains of Argentina. In the high-altitude South African prairies, *Pseudaspis cana* lives in rodent burrows and bushes. The same biotope, but in South America, is where the coral snake (*Micrurus frontalis pyrrhocryptus*) is found.

◁ *LEFT: European adder* (Vipera berus), *whose distribution reaches the Arctic Circle*

OCEANS

Aquatic species are both freshwater and saltwater. The Elapidae *Laticauda colubrina* is little specialized and swims in the shallow coastal waters of the Pacific, regularly climbing onto beaches for thermoregulation and prey digestion. Before mating, members of these species get into groups of thousands, in the winter, on sandy islets. Females lay their eggs in the humid sand during the summer. Other marine snakes are strictly aquatic. They also frequent freshwater areas such as estuaries and large rivers. They are ovoviviparous and give birth in the water. *Hydrophis cyanocinctus* and *Enhydrina schistosa* live in the warm coastal waters of Asia. The giant of the group, *Hydrophis spiralis*, can measure as much as 9 ft. (2.75 m). Only one species, the yellow-bellied sea snake (*Pelamis platurus*), which lives in the Indian and Pacific oceans, is truly pelagic.

Adaptations to marine life are maximal in the Hydrophinae subfamily. The body is laterally compressed, particularly in the tail. The nostrils and rostral groove are closed by special mechanisms. The lungs are elongated and hold a large volume of air, allowing for prolonged immersion.

Most of these are found on the intertropical coasts of the eastern Indian ocean and the western Pacific. Most feed on fish. Some, like *Emydocephalus annulatus* live in coral reefs and eat fish eggs.

Since these species live in warm waters, they aren't faced with thermoregulation problems.

UNDERGROUND LIFE

Guy Naulleau

SNAKES LIVING underground are burrowing or semi-burrowing. They dig underground tunnels and move in the vegetal litter or compost. Snakes that spend time in rodent burrows or glide in loose soil—sand, mud—are considered semifossorial. The ophidian branch is believed to have evolved from burrowing lizards, and it is assumed that snakes' ancestors lived in the mud (see the chapter on the origin of snakes).

The adaptation to underground life is shown in a cylindrical body covered with smooth scales, a head that is not really distinct from the body, small eyes and a powerful tail, often sporting a cone-shaped scale which serves as a support while the animal is digging.

Typhlopidae, found throughout the world, and Leptotyphlopidae, from the tropical regions of America, Africa, and western Asia, appear to be the best-adapted burrowers. They are found in the compost of wet forests, where termites and ants, their dietary mainstay, are plentiful, as well as in arid or sandy zones, savannahs and cultivated areas. They only surface at night. Their long and thin bodies and their general appearance often lead to their being called two-headed snakes, and their regressed or hidden eyes earn them the nickname "blind snakes." The head is angular and cuneiform. They are small (usually 4–12 in. [10 to 30 cm]), agile and hard to catch. The biggest, *Typhlops punctatus*,

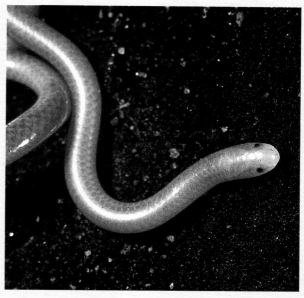

△ *ABOVE: A typical burrowing snake,* Leptotyphlops sp.

from tropical Africa, measures up to 31 in. (80 cm). Central and South American Anomalepididae seem to have a similar lifestyle.

Atractaspis snakes, long classified among Viperidae and called mole-vipers, spend time not only in compost but also in the harder savannah soil. Like all burrowers, they have a barely distinguished head and a short and powerful tail.

Among Colubridae, African species like *Scaphiophis*, with their hard and sharp snouts can burrow into relatively compact ground. Another type is represented by small vermiform snakes living in the forest humus, like the coral snakes *Cemaphora* from the southeastern U.S., *Calamaria* from southeast Asia, or *Achalinus*, from the Far East.

Anilius scytale (false coral snake from South America, which feeds on apodal amphibians, lizards and snakes), Cylindrophiinae and *Xenopeltis unicolor*, as well as the dwarf Mexican python (*Loxocemus bicolor*), are also burrowing or semi-burrowing. They are found on the surface, but occasionally burrow. They also frequent rice fields.

Sand-dwelling snakes are semi-burrowing, and often small and cylindrical (*Chilomeniscus cinctus* or *Chionactis palarostris*). There are also large agile colubrids (*Spalerosophis*), or stockier Viperidae (*Cerastes vipera, Eristicophis macmahoni*).

Uropeltinae have extremely specialized tails. These are small snakes from forests in the south of India and in Ceylon that feed mostly on worms and insect larvae. Their terminal scales are covered with spines or crests. In the genus *Rhinophis*, the cylindrical tail abruptly ends in an oblique, ovoid shield which obstructs tunnels.

Snakes are not usually found in caves except, sometimes, during dormancy. Some tropical cave-dwelling species do exist, the best known being *Elaphe taeniuria ridleyi*, known in Thailand and Malaysia as the cave colubrid. It lives close to, and feeds on, bats. There are also cave-dwelling snakes in the Philippines and in Madagascar.

△ *ABOVE: The sand-dwelling viper* Eristicophis macmahoni

WORLD DISTRIBUTION OF SNAKE SPECIES

Relative to vegetation (see the double page following)

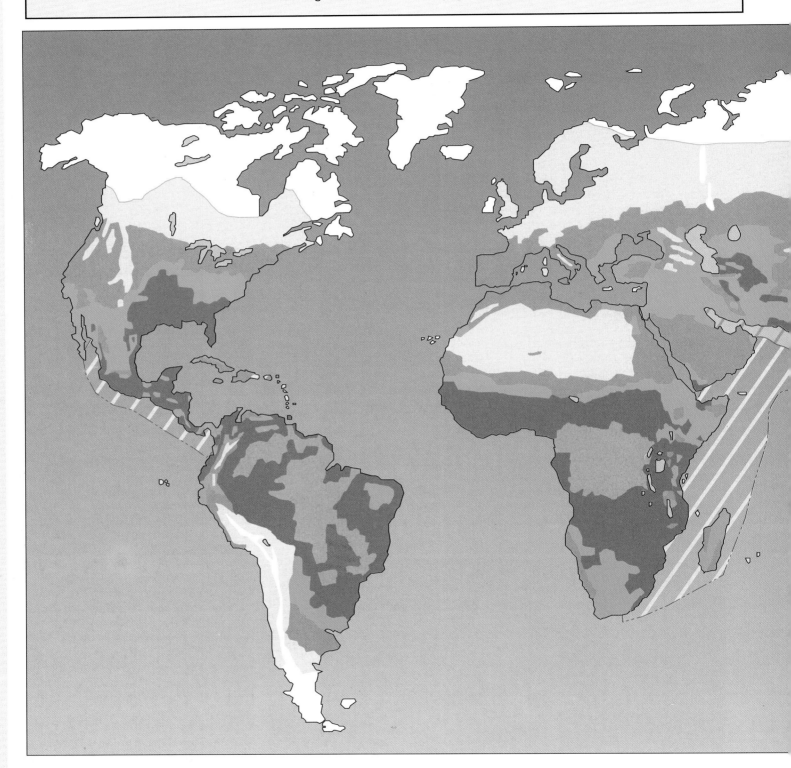

This map (with a 90–95% accuracy) gives the number of snake species for any given geographic zone, including all biotopes. The numbers given should not be read as the number of species that share any given biotope: the number of truly sympatric species never exceeds about thirty, according to Vitt (1987).

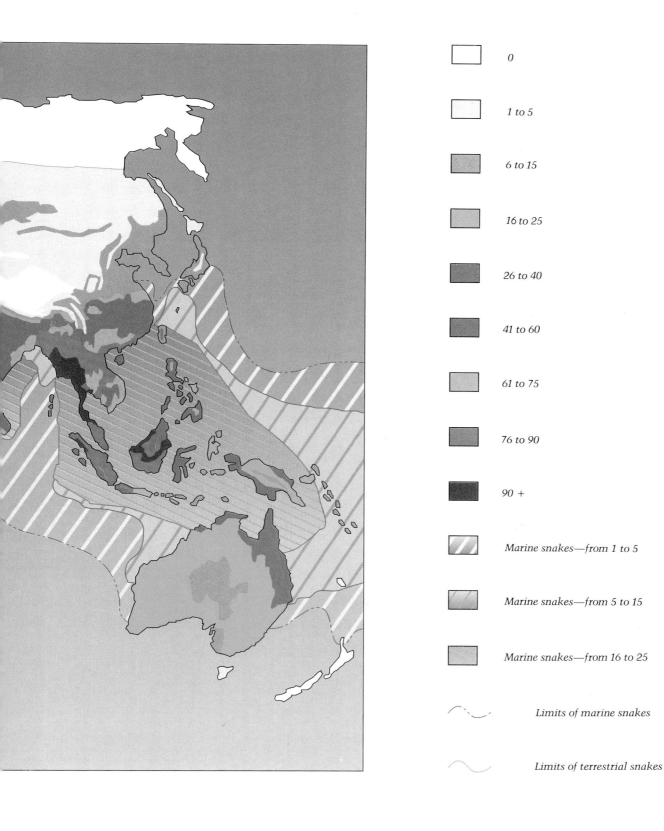

	0
	1 to 5
	6 to 15
	16 to 25
	26 to 40
	41 to 60
	61 to 75
	76 to 90
	90 +
	Marine snakes—from 1 to 5
	Marine snakes—from 5 to 15
	Marine snakes—from 16 to 25
	Limits of marine snakes
	Limits of terrestrial snakes

WORLD DISTRIBUTION OF VEGETATION

Compare this with the distribution of snake species (see the preceding pages)

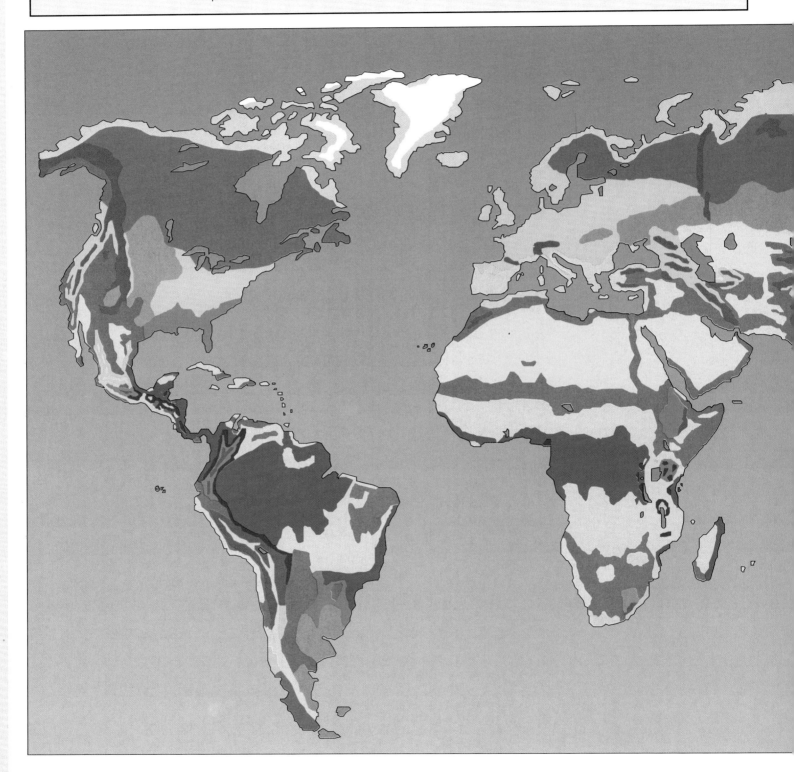

The world's numerous types of vegetation are classified here in twelve large categories. In certain cases, different vegetation have been grouped under one name, for example, boreal forests are made up of conifers and deciduous trees.
High-altitude mountain zones, nearly bare of vegetation, are grouped with the tundras.

Tundra & polar vegetation

Mountain vegetation

Boreal forests

Forests, farmland & woodlands of
temperate regions

Subtropical forests & vegetation

Humid forests of tropical &
subtropical mountains

Tropical forests & savannahs

Rain forests

Steppes & prairies

Mediterranean vegetation

Semi-arid zones vegetation

Desert & arid-zone vegetation

ENVIRONMENT & POPULATION DYNAMICS

Guy Naulleau

Social behavior is not very developed in snakes, considered the least social of reptiles. They are generally individualistic and, although they don't show any intolerance to it, they avoid closeness and seek isolation. Furthermore, interactions between snakes are difficult to observe in natural conditions outside those related to mating and daily (thermoregulation or feeding) or seasonal (wintering or reproduction) reunions.

ENVIRONMENT

▶ Reunions

One form of social behavior exhibited by snakes is that of reunions in precise locations.

Daily reunions

These are generally ecological in nature. In temperate regions, thermoregulation may bring snakes to group in an area with the right microclimate (sun, little wind). This behavior is particularly prevalent in temperate-region males after wintering.

Some winter reunions have been observed in certain pythons and the boa constrictor; these are also for reasons of thermoregulation. A study (see Illus. 1) has shown that these Boidae warm up faster and cool down more slowly when in groups.

Snakes sometimes congregate where a high density of prey may be found at a particular moment. This is typical in *Thamnophis*, or garter snakes, which converge in areas where amphibians metamorphose. A number of grass snakes (*Natrix*) have been observed hunting in an area with a high density of carp alevins. Four hours after all of these snakes were taken out of the water, more appeared. Water moccasins (*Agkistrodon piscivorus*) behave similarly: They assemble beneath cormorant and heron colonies to feed on the fish that these birds hunt and to feed on young birds that occasionally fall out of their nests.

Another feeding reunion has been observed with some marine snakes (*Pelamis platurus*), which join in groups of a few hundred in specific areas in the sea. Captured individuals from this group had full stomachs while none of those taken in other places had eaten. Such groupings show that snakes are willing to crowd at feeding time.

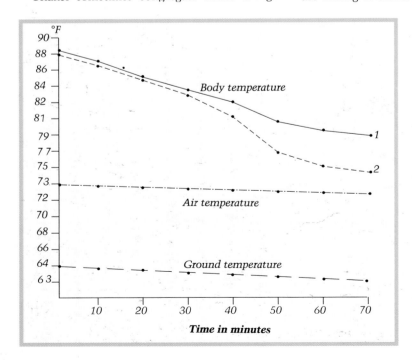

◁ *ILLUS. 1: Variation in the cooling-down rate as observed in the boa constrictor in accord with grouping (from Myres & Ells, 1968): 1–4 boas cooling in a group; 2–4 boas cooling individually*

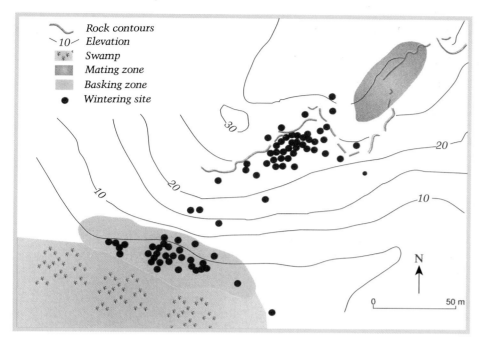

ILLUS. 2: *Dormancy, insulation, and mating sites in European adder* (**Vipera berus**) *as studied by Vitanien (1967) in Finland*

Legend:
- Rock contours
- 10 Elevation
- Swamp
- Mating zone
- Basking zone
- ● Wintering site

Seasonal reunions

Wintering reunions are relatively frequent. Individuals of a species, such as the asp viper (*Vipera aspis*), tend to winter alone on the plains, but in groups in mountains, where there are less suitable burrows available. The European adder (*Vipera berus*) even takes over wintering places in Finland (see Illus. 2). The number of individuals in the same place increases with latitude and cooling temperatures. The greatest number ever observed (800) was in Finland, at 63° latitude. In Canada,

the wintering reunions of garter snakes (*Thamnophis sirtalis*) are well known (see the table); up to 10,000 individuals have been found in certain areas.

Different species may group together for wintering. The Aesculapian snake (*Elaphe longissima*) and the green-and-yellow grass snake (*Hierophis viridiflavus*) are often found together. Snakes may also winter with amphibians or other vertebrates. In Finland, two types of amphibians—the common toad (*Bufo bufo*) and the russet frog (*Rana temporia*)—three other types of reptiles—the slow worm (*Anguis fragilis*), the viviparous lizard (*Lacerta vivipara*), and the grass snake (*Natrix natrix*)—as well as a bat (*Eptesicus nilssonii*) were found wintering with adders.

In Utah, the prairie snake (*Crotalus viridis*) has been seen wintering with two other snakes—the black racer (*Coluber constrictor*) and the bull snake (*Pituophis melanoleucus*)—and in Michigan, seven snake species and three types of amphibians were found wintering together.

Other snake reunions, usually having to do with reproduction, have been observed. In the asp viper (*Vipera aspis*), these groups, generally composed of a reproducing female and many males, are called balls or vipers' nests. Garter snakes (*Thamnophis sirtalis*) mate at the end of the wintering season and on the same grounds where there are high concentrations of snakes. One of this species' characteristics is that a large number of males will surround a receptive female (see the table).

Females may also group together when gravid, especially to enjoy a microclimate favorable to embryonic development or to protect themselves

▷ RIGHT: *green-and-yellow snake* (Hierophis viridiflavus)

GARTER SNAKES' SPECTACULAR GROUPINGS

Yannick Vasse

GARTER SNAKES (*Thamnophis sirtalis*) live in the United States and Canada. They are small colubrids, around 20 in. (50 cm) long, and owe their name to the stripes on their body.

In the fall, garter snakes go to their wintering sites to spend the bad season—in Canada, the temperature can go down to −40°F/C in the crevices of a Manitoba limestone plateau. Males emerge in April and form groups of thousands while waiting for the females, who finish dormancy a few days later, as the females have greater thermic needs. The males form mounds of intertwined bodies at the bottom of small depressions in the ground. Such a sight always surprises tourists.

Females then appear, arriving for around a month. They emit pheromones, the chemical substances which attract tens of males per female.

No sexual or territorial battle is even hinted at: Males rub their chins on the female's head and neck. When she is ready to mate, she raises her tail and the nearest male penetrates her. The other males lose interest, and the fertilized female leaves. When all the females have left the group, the males also leave. Not having eaten since fall, they begin feeding on worms and insects while travelling to the watery areas, where, during the summer, they will hunt for tadpoles and frogs.

Females are viviparous: They incubate their eggs until they hatch, usually about three months later.

▽ *BELOW: Garter snake* (Thamnophis sirtalis) *grouping when emerging from dormancy sites. These mounds of snakes attract tourists, who are stunned by the show.*

▷ RIGHT: *Desert species, like the horned viper* (Cerastes cerastes), *move randomly over large areas.*

against predators. There are also places where they group to lay their eggs. Some see this behavior as a tendency towards social behavior. Two hundred sixteen grass snake (*Natrix natrix*) eggs were found in some manure by a river in France. Different species can also lay eggs together: 1200 eggs were once found, some of them from the grass snake and some from *Natrix maura*.

Vision and chemoreceptive organs play an important role in these groupings, with pheromones being involved even when reproduction is not the goal. American rattlesnakes (*Crotalus*) appear to find their *hibernaculum* through celestial indications and topographic markers, while the young find them by following the marks left by adults.

Pheromone traces also facilitate reunions for snakes that could lessen their water- and thus weight loss; snakes find a thermic advantage to these groupings.

▶ Spatial occupation

Snakes' spatial occupation is linked to both ecological (biotopes, alimentary resources) and ethological requirements (territories, competition for food). Snakes rarely engage in territorial behavior, but African mambas do defend their territory during reproduction.

Snakes tend to isolate or to maintain a certain distance (which varies with circumstances) from each other. Active competition for food, involving battles between individuals, is rare in nature, but occurs under certain conditions in captivity. Dominating behavior has been observed in four families (Boidae, Colubridae, Elapidae, and Viperidae).

If two males are stimulated by the same prey (which is extremely rare in nature), a real fight may take place, similar to the ritualized fights that happen during mating season. This behavior occurs in both sexes. The fighting ends when one protagonist escapes and the other seizes the prey.

▶ Displacements

Three types of displacement are common in snakes: erratic, migratory, and sedentary. Erratic migration, characterized by arbitrary displacements over a large area, is found in desert-dwellers: sidewinders (*Crotalus cerastes*) and the horned vi-

per (*Cerastes cerastes*), as well as the Avicenna viper (*Cerastes vipera*). What determines this behavior is unknown, but it seems linked to external conditions. During the summer the Avicenna viper spends most of the day burrowed in the sand to avoid excessive heat and it wanders aimlessly at night. Daily displacements may be over 0.62 mile (1 km). As the cold season approaches, these movements become more restricted, and the animal ends up spending months burrowed at the foot of a bush.

Snake migrations are much more limited than those of birds, but snakes can move from wintering ground to active summering ground; in Manitoba, this distance can exceed 2 miles (3.6 km) in the garter snakes (*Thamnophis sirtalis*). Migrations usually occur along a north-south axis. The European adder (*Vipera berus*) can migrate up to ¾ mile (1.2 km) in Finland and 1.2 miles (1.9 km) in Great Britain. Seasonal displacements correlate with group wintering. The asp viper, which usually winters alone in the plains, sometimes migrates to deep shelters for group wintering, especially in the mountains. Movements of dispersion related to population density do occur, as in the black racer (*Coluber constrictor*), which moves farther in years with high populations, which probably helps to decrease competition for food.

Sedentary displacement is characterized by movements over short distances, linked to the individual's domain.

POPULATION DYNAMICS

Populations are characterized by a number of criteria, such as the age, growth, structure, density, maturity, fertility, mortality, and survival rate of individuals. Our knowledge of snake populations of variable densities allows us to determine age, growth, and sex ratio.

▶ Age & growth

Two main methods are used to determine a snake's age. The first is to capture, mark, release, and recapture young snakes whose age is already known. The animals are marked by the partial

◁ *LEFT: Aesculapian snake (Elaphe longissima) during a migration. Males move faster and have larger domains than females.*

removal of ventral or subcaudal scales, by tattoos, banding, paint markings, or thanks to the scales' natural anomalies.

The second method is skeletochronology, which involves killing the animal, and consists in examining its bones *in toto*, or in crosscuts. This is usually done to the skull bones, and examines the seasonal growth marks naturally left on the bones.

These marks are usually made in a circannual period. They include an annual zone of important bone growth occurring during the snake's active period and a stop line corresponding to the slower parts of the year (winter in temperature zones). Counting these marks leads to a good estimate of

the snake's age; the marks are most accurate when the snakes are young.

Small snakes (Colubridae and Elapidae) do not grow very much, except for ovoviviparous colubrids and Viperidae. Growth begins at a rapid rate, slows down with sexual maturity, and continues, although at an increasingly slower rate, until death (see Illus. 5).

Growth reproduces environmental conditions: In temperate regions, growth is slow in winter and rapid in summer.

This annual intermittence is what gives rise to the skeletal markings.

The sex differences in growth rates vary from

ORIENTATION

SNAKE MIGRATIONS between seasonal habitats and their return to areas from which they have been moved or captured show that they can orient themselves in nature. Their aptitude in returning to their shelter depends upon the species and the environment. After having been moved 3½ miles (5.6 km), two bull snakes (*Pituophis melanoleucus sayi*) were recaptured in the same place two years later. For the water snake (*Nerodia sipedon*), the chances of returning to the shelter are better the bigger the snake, at least when they are moved about 870 yds. (800 m). When striped whipsnakes (*Masticophis taeniatus*) are moved from their wintering site in the fall, the return to the shelter takes place in 100% of the cases for distances of 325 yds. (300 m) or less; but a single male came back after a 435-yd. (400 m) displacement.

Which mechanisms and sensory organs help the snake direct itself? Vision is probably important, at least for small displacement, but it does

not operate alone, as has been observed in the asp viper and in the striped whipsnake. A male striped whipsnake was temporarily blinded and moved 255 yds. (235 m) and

found its way back. Chemoreception probably plays an important role, but it has not been clearly determined for long distances.

△ *ABOVE:* **Masticophis lateralis**

△ *ABOVE: The female bull snake* (Pituophis melanoleucus sayi) *has a larger domain than the male.*

species to species (see Illus. 5). There is a correlation between the size of newborns and adult females, with larger females giving birth to larger offspring (see Illus. 6).

▶ Longevity

Temperate-region colubrids, with their precocious sexual maturity, do not live very long. In Kansas, longevity in two types of *Heterodon* varied from 5 years for *H. platirhinos* to eight years for *H. nasicus*.

In temperate-region colubrids with a later sexual maturity, the minimum longevity is ten years in the black racer (*Coluber constrictor*), and the maximum is thirty years in the black ratsnake (*Elaphe obsoleta*).

In temperate-region Viperidae with late sexual maturity, longevity ranges from eight years in the prairie snake (*Crotalus viridis*) to twenty years in the asp viper (*Vipera aspis*). Longevity within a single species is affected by the geographic milieu. The prairie snake lives to eight in Kansas and twenty-one in Canada.

▶ Domain

The domain is concretely represented by a polygon within which the snake's movements are marked and delimited by the most extreme observations. It varies from 97 square feet to 1.2 square miles (9 m^2 to $345,000$ m^2), depending upon the species. Its area often depends on the snake's sex. In

both the asp viper (*Vipera aspis*) and the Aesculapian snake (*Elaphe longissima*), males have larger domains than females have.

The asp viper, living in the mixed woodlands of western France, has a domain that varies from ¼ acre to 1⅓ acre (990 to $5,280$ m^2) for males and from ¹⁄₁₄ acre to 1 acre (300 to $4,320$ m^2) for females. The Aesculapian snake, living just a little to the south, has an average domain of 3 acres ($12,450$ m^2) for males and 2 acres ($7,980$ m^2) for females. In other snakes, females have the largest domain. This is true of the grass snake (*Natrix natrix*) in southern Sweden, where females' domain is 34 acres ($136,000$ m^2) and that of males is 24.5 acres ($99,000$ m^2). The female bull snake (*Pituophis melanoleucus*), in Utah, has a 5-acre ($20,900$ m^2) domain, while the male's is 2.5 acres ($10,500$ m^2). This area can be independent of sex and also varies from one year to the next, both in size and location. A male Aesculapian snake followed by telemetry for three years in the Deux-Sèvres region of France had a domain of 5.3 acres, ($21,629$ m^2), 3.8 acres ($15,543$ m^2), and ¾ acre ($2,944$ m^2) with some overlaps.

Various opinions exist as to the influence of age and size on snakes' displacements, as well as on the dimensions and shape of the domain. But it is undeniable that the structure of the habitat and available resources play an important role.

Human intervention, when it destroys a biotope and eliminates snakes' prey, can be the cause of strange displacements, and sometimes of spe-

◁ LEFT: *Male and female Massasaugas (Sistrurus catenatus), North American Crotalinae, are equally active.*

cies' extinction (see the chapter on commerce, legislation, and protection).

▶ Activity

Activity follows nycthemeral (day and night) and annual (spring and summer in temperate regions) rhythms. This activity can be linked to thermoregulation in temperate regions, as well as to feeding and reproduction.

Daily activity

Daily activity is diurnal or nocturnal, depending upon the species, or, within a species, on seasons and climatic conditions. In temperate regions, activity often depends on temperature. The asp viper (*Vipera aspis*), which is active during the day in spring and fall, becomes crepuscular—or even nocturnal—in the summer. The diamondback rattlesnake (*Crotalus atrox*) is active in the middle of the day in winter, early in the morning, and late at night in the spring and fall, and is nocturnal in the summer.

Some species have an endogenous activity

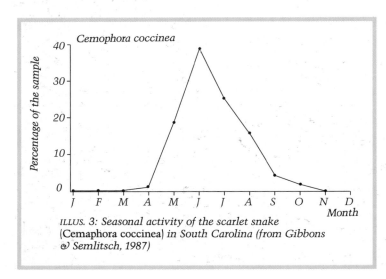

ILLUS. 3: *Seasonal activity of the scarlet snake (*Cemaphora coccinea*) in South Carolina (from Gibbons & Semlitsch, 1987)*

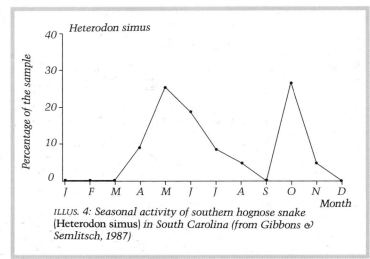

ILLUS. 4: *Seasonal activity of southern hognose snake (*Heterodon simus*) in South Carolina (from Gibbons & Semlitsch, 1987)*

rhythm that is independent of seasons and temperature. Most Australian Elapidae are diurnal, with some crepuscular activity. The European adder is diurnal only in England. In France, *Coronella girondica* is strictly crepuscular, no matter what the climatic conditions.

Sexually related activities

In temperate regions where snakes winter, males often have a lengthier active period than females: Males begin wintering later and they emerge earlier in the spring. This is true of the asp viper (*Vipera aspis*) in France; males are also more active during mating and experience larger displacements. On the other hand, the Massasauga (*Sistrurus catenatus*), a North American pit viper, shows no difference between males and females. Gravid females are, nonetheless, more sedentary than the others. During the vernal reproductive season, the common grass snake (*Natrix natrix*) males are more active than females, while they are less so during the summer. Gestating females in ovoviviparous species are not very active, particularly towards the end of the gestation period, when their activity is basically limited to thermoregulation.

▽ BELOW: *The scarlet snake* (Cemophora coccinea)*, a false coral snake, is active from May to August.*

Seasonal activity

Temperate-region snakes are especially active from spring to fall, and not very during the winter. Activity may hit a peak during the summer months, as in the scarlet snake (*Cemophora coccinea*) (see Illus. 3). There can also be two peaks, in the spring and fall, as Illus. 4 shows. A certain locomotive activity may exist during the winter, as snakes can move at low temperatures. Winter displacements are usually linked to thermoregulation. Snakes may either come out during sunny days, or move to warmer microsites within their underground hibernaculum. Sometimes, underground moves have nothing to do with thermoregulation, as has been observed in the Aesculapian snake in the Deux-Sèvres region of France.

► *Population structure*

Structuring a population by age groups depends mostly on birth and mortality rates. If the first is easy to discover, the second is more problematic. In nature, the number of unfertilized ovocytes and nonviable embryos is much lower than it is in captivity.

The percentage of eggs destroyed by predators is unknown. Embryos of ovoviviparous species are much better protected, and although gestating females appear more vulnerable than other adults, their birth-success rate is high. Mortality rates run high for the first few weeks of life—in the American *Coluber constrictor*, it comes close to 0.50% per day. Youth mortality decreases, but stays high for the first year, even during wintering. In the same snake, mortality has been estimated at 0.24% per day from the beginning of wintering to the end of the first year. Although the data we have is approximate, it suggests that first-year mortality rates are much higher in the Colubridae (around 77%) than in Viperidae (less than 50%) in temperate zones. Unfortunately, we do not know whether this lower mortality rate for young snakes is a characteristic of venomous snakes in

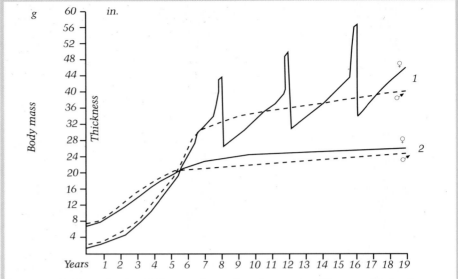

ILLUS. 5: (1) ponderal and (2) statural growth in the asp viper (**Vipera aspis**). As of seven years, the females' ponderal growth is subject to the sexual cycle. The peaks correspond to the maximal corporal mass during gestation, while the minimums correspond to births (from Saint-Girons, 1952).

general, or if it applies to temperate-region Viperidae alone.

In order to understand a population's structure by age groups, one must realize that the same amount of elapsed time does not have the same significance in a small tropical colubrid, which matures at nine months, reproduces every two or three months, and has a short life span, than in a cool-temperate-region viper, which is mature at five, reproduces every three years, and can live to twenty. In fact, it is impossible to differentiate age groups in the first case, as it would involve the marking and recapture of a large number of individuals for over a year, which has never been done. Most studies come from temperate regions, and three demographic strategies have been perceived. The first concerns itself with Colubridae that become sexually mature early (two years) and have a high adult mortality (approximately 50% per year), high fertility rates (12.2 young per year), and a relatively short life span (6.7 years). The second group of Colubridae attain sexual maturity later (three years), have a lower mortality rate (approximately 30%), a lower fertility rate (six young), and a longer life span (14.3 years).

Finally, the third strategy concerns Viperidae, which attain sexual maturity much later (three to seven years), have a lower mortality rate (23%), a lower fertility rate (six young every two years), and a longer life span (15.5 years). These averages mask the many variations that exist between species, and many parameters are estimated with a high margin of error. Still, the general tendencies are clear.

Tropical-region snakes often reproduce more or less continuously. When climatic conditions impose a seasonal (usually annual) reproduction, population numbers represent age groups separated by a year, and the structure of these populations varies with the age at the onset of sexual maturity and the longevity of these species.

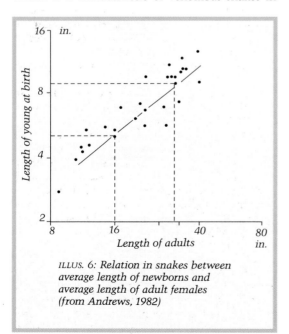

ILLUS. 6: Relation in snakes between average length of newborns and average length of adult females (from Andrews, 1982)

◁ LEFT: The regression line shows that there is a good correlation (0.89) in snakes between the average newborn and the mother's length. For example, a female measuring 16 in. (40 cm) gives birth to 5-in. (13 cm) long young, while a female measuring 30 in. (77.5 cm) gives birth to 9-in. (23 cm) long young.

Some snakes, like the Plains garter snake (*Thamnophis radix*), reach sexual maturity during their second year. Individuals can thus be classified as newborns, young immatures who will reproduce the following year, and adults over two years of age, according to size. Growth rates are high for the young in spring; 18-month-olds mate and soon join the adult groups. In July, the bigger immatures (ten months old) are almost the same size as adults (see Illus. 7). Of 384 such snakes captured, 52.7% were in their first year, 34.6% were second-year subadults and young adults, and 12.6% were older adults.

Many snakes reach sexual maturity in their third year, such as *Laticauda colubrina*. Females can be classified by age groups due to their size (see Illus. 8). In New Caledonia, in July (the austral winter) 33% are six-month-old young (12 to 18 in. [30 to 45 cm]), 20% are immatures of less than 18 months (1½ to 2 ft. [50 to 65 cm]), and 47% are mature individuals; 18% are young adults 2½ years old (2 to 2½ ft. [65 to 81 cm]), and 29% are older adults (2½ to 4 ft. [80 to 120 cm]) belonging to different age groups. In temperate-region Viperidae, and some big tropical snakes with a slow growth rate and advanced longevity, age groups are not as well marked. Collecting a representative sample is quite difficult, and their population structures remain hypothetical. In the sample of prairie snakes, 22.5% were year-old young, 9.4% were two years old, 13.4% were three to four, and 54.7% were adults and subadults. Age groups decrease numerically in the asp viper (*Vipera aspis*), as calculated by the bony age-marks (see Illus. 9).

▶ Sex ratio

The sex ratio is usually 1:1 at birth. It can then change, illustrating the population structure. Different behavior along sex lines may affect the proportion. In a springtime sample of the asp viper, males may predominate due to sexual activity or thermoregulation, which is observed at the end of wintering and in the mating period that follows. During summer, gravid females, which are more sedentary and have greater thermic needs, are

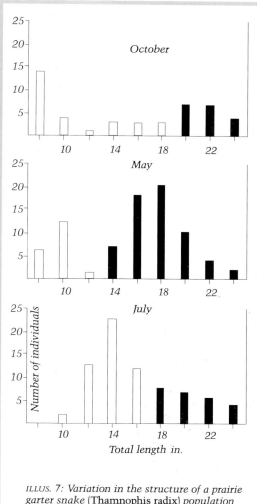

ILLUS. 7: *Variation in the structure of a prairie garter snake* (Thamnophis radix) *population by height, in October, May, and July (from Seibert & Heigen, 1947, modified by Saint-Girons, 1965). Mature individuals are shown in black.*

more visible: A sample at this time of year is unbalanced in favor of females. A long-term study of a population is necessary to get a clear idea of the sex ratio. A synthesis of these results shows that the sex ratio remains close to 1:1 in the asp viper (*Vipera aspis*).

Many Colubridae and Viperidae species have an unbalanced sex ratio. For example, males dominate in the common viper in Finland (1.55:1); but the ratio is 1:1 in England. Females are more numerous in the Plains garter snake (*Thamnophis radix*), where there are 75 males for 100 females. The striped whipsnake (*Masticophis taeniatus*) has more males than females in one population, and the opposite situation in another. The sex that has a fast growth rate and reaches adult size earliest usually dominates the population.

▶ Population density

Various abundance indices are used to measure snake density, such as the number of captures per hour, of specimens trapped, or of individuals per 2½ acres (hectare). If high densities are often

▽ BELOW: *Some marine snakes, like* Laticauda laticauda, *are sexually mature within their third year.*

observed in wintering sites, they are usually low in certain areas for marine snakes, and on some islands (other than special cases). Density also varies considerably by species, from less than one individual per 2½ acres (hectare) in certain Colubridae (*Crotalus tessellata*) to over 1800 per 2½ acres (hectare) for *Diadophis punctatus*. Geographic variations also exist from species to species. Garter snake (*Thamnophis sirtalis*) densities vary from 2–8 to 16–34 individuals per 2½ acres (hectare).

▶ Mortality & survival

Snake mortality can vary from year to year. Studies done on North American wintering sites have shown that mortality rates were different during three consecutive years: 7.7%, 21.1%, and 12.5% in *Masticophis taeniatus*, and 25%, 33.3%, and 12.5% in the prairie rattlesnake (*Crotalus viridis*). Correlations between mortality and environmental factors are difficult to establish. Too-hot summers, too-cold winters probably lead to increased mortality. Drought years often have important repercussions on aquatic populations. Winter mortality varies from 34 to 40% in garter snakes (*Thamnophis sirtalis*), while it only accounts for 4.5% of annual mortality in prairie rattlesnakes. Color variations may play a great role. Melanic individuals of a colored species are often hunted in greater proportion, as in the European adder (*Vipera berus*).

Experiments carried out in nature in Sweden with lures painted in the species' regular color and in black have shown that predation was almost twice as high for melanic forms. Mortality is maximal during the first year and decreases with age. Ninety-two percent of black racers (*Coluber constrictor*) survive at birth, 72% between birth and wintering, 45 days later, and 17% up to a year. Survival at birth increases with birth weight. After the first year, survival varies from 50 to 75%. Mortality may also be different according to sex. A prairie rattlesnake population followed over ten years showed that females disappear from wintering sites faster than males. Their proportion went

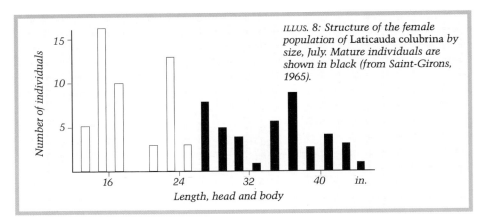

ILLUS. 8: *Structure of the female population of* Laticauda colubrina *by size, July. Mature individuals are shown in black (from Saint-Girons, 1965).*

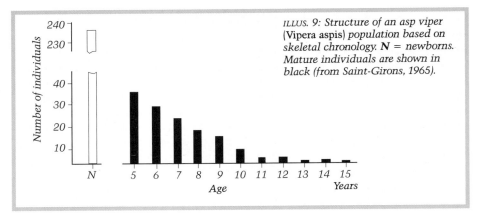

ILLUS. 9: *Structure of an asp viper* (Vipera aspis) *population based on skeletal chronology.* **N** = *newborns. Mature individuals are shown in black (from Saint-Girons, 1965).*

from approximately 45% to less than 20% in ten years.

Human intervention (commerce, purposeful destruction, etc.) may also affect snake populations. In large asp viper (*Vipera aspis*) adults, annual mortality is of 20 to 25% in various populations, but it decreases to 11 to 17% when man's influence is discounted. The impact is even more obvious in the Canadian garter snake (*Thamnophis sirtalis*), often caught on its wintering grounds, and whose numbers in such grounds has gone from 10,000 to approximately 1000 in 1989 (see the chapter on commerce, legislation and protection).

◁ LEFT: *Female asp viper with some of its young. This species is victim to man's interventions (biotope destruction, gratuitous elimination).*

▷ *RIGHT: Psammophis schokari, sand snake*

▽ *BELOW: Melanic European adder (Vipera berus). Melanic individuals are more often the object of predation than are normally colored individuals.*

COLORATION

Patrick David–Yannick Vasse

Snakes have all sorts of color patterns that appeal to man's esthetic sensibility. From off-white to black, going through copper and bright green, they also have different patterns: orange stripes, zigzags, yellow flecks. These splendid colors are rarely gratuitous. Nuptial colorations do not exist, but the various tints are often quite useful to snakes in their attempts to avoid their enemies.

CONCEALMENT

Concealment is the best way to avoid conflict, although snakes have a number of intimidation and dissuasion tactics in their arsenals. Concealment is one of the techniques most often used in the animal world: Colors, shapes, and attitudes let the animal blend into its environment. Camouflage also facilitates prowling.

Concealment works in many different ways. "Cryptic" coloring, which is homochromatic with the environment, may be uniform. This is true of the common sand viper (*Cerastes vipera*), which is yellow ochre, grey, or pinkish, depending on the color of the sand, and of many arboreal species. In the *Ahaetulla, Oxybelis, Morelia, Trimeresurus,* or *Boiga* genera, some species' green is the same as that of vegetation (*Ahaetulla prasina, Oxybelis fulgidus, Morelia*—previously *Chondropython—viridis, Dendroaspis angusticeps,* etc.), while the greyish-brown of others blends with branches (*Oxybelis aeneus, Trimeresurus puniceus, Boiga cynodon,* etc.). Many marine snakes (Hydrophinae), the pelagic species *Pelamis platurus* in particular, like many marine vertebrates (seals, fish, cetaceans), have a dark back, which is difficult to see from above, and a light stomach which, seen from below, looks like the sky.

Ahaetulla and *Oxybelis* are also surprisingly homotypical. Rather than just hiding, they look exactly like a branch or vine. Their very slender bodies (usually longer than 3 ft. [1 m] but with the diameter of a big pencil) make them look like plant stems or the small branches on which they are found. *Thelotornis* excels at this camouflage.

The green night viper (*Causus resimus*), which, despite its name, tends to be diurnal, is green, flecked with black. It lives in swamps in central and eastern Africa, where, unseen, it clears a passage through the lush vegetation. Some burrowing and semi-burrowing snakes that glide along the loose and dark grounds of temperate or humid and tropical forests are dark grey and brown, as is the case for *Atractaspis* in tropical Africa, of *Carphophis amoenus* in the United States, or of *Atractus* in South America. Snakes' spots may also have a homochromatic function when no single color dominates the environment. European vipers (*Vipera*), which move about in brush, have a dark zigzag along their back. The puff adder (*Bitis arietans*), which is found in Africa south of the Sahara desert, merges with the brush and dried grass thanks to its brown and straw-yellow markings. The *Coluber nummifer*, spotted grey, lives in the rock formations in Middle Eastern mountains. *Hierophis viridiflavus*, in Europe, manages to stay hidden in hedges and bushes thanks to its yellow spots on a black or dark green background.

The best examples are of snakes with interrupted patterns. The patterns are large and colorful, and highly visible outside the biotope. They resemble the various irregularities of the substratum (leaves, rocks), and they help camouflage the body by coming into random contact with the animal's contours. The Gaboon viper (*Bitis gabonica*) from tropical Africa has beige, bluish, red,

◁ *LEFT: Horned viper* (Cerastes cerastes) *in its environment*

▷ RIGHT: Dendroaspis angusticeps, *the green mamba, a homochromatic arboreal*

▽ BELOW: *The brown tree snake* Oxybelis aeneus, *which is homotypic and homochromatic*

▷ RIGHT: Bothriechis schlegelii, *cryptic coloration (lichen, moss)*

and brown markings. Russell's viper (*Daboia russelli*), from tropical Asia, has large brown oval spots on a lighter background, and the North American copperhead (*Agkistrodon contortrix*) is a grey-beige with pinkish stripes. The copperhead glides on dead leaves on the forest floor, and it is a real champion at this type of camouflage.

WARNING COLORS

Not all snakes seek to hide. Many are ready to fight the enemy, backed up by their venom. Many of these announce their presence loudly with their colors. All human populations have noticed that venomous plants or animals are often showy, with black, yellow, and red being their usual code.

Obviously this observation must be qualified, but it appears to contain a large grain of truth. Many animals that emit or contain venomous or toxic substances have bright and varied color markings: black, white, red and yellow, which are called warning colors and which are found in some marine invertebrates, insects, fish, amphibians, and, of course, snakes.

This is typical in coral snakes, which are small or medium-size animals—the largest, *Maticora bivirgata*, can reach 6½ ft. (2 m). The appellation

"coral snake" applies to terrestrial snakes ringed with three successive categories of colors: red or orange (whence their name), a dark color—black, grey, or brown—and a light color—white, off-white, or yellow. These are either very venomous Elapidae (*Micrurus* and *Micruroides*), or harmless or only slightly venomous American Colubridae. Other snakes, living in warmer regions, are called coral snakes by extension: *Aspidelaps* in Africa, *Maticora* and *Calliophis* in Asia, *Brachyurophis* in Australia, some *Micrurus* species in America. These do not have the tricolor markings, but are black, brown, or dark blue with whitish or red stripes. The usual interpretation is that predators are dissuaded by these colorations (fear of the contrast, surprise, innate avoidance, or learned caution?) and recognize venomous snakes by this code. It is difficult to see these patterns as warning signals in nocturnal and unobtrusive animals living in vegetal ground cover. And of course, the predators to whom these colors are directed must be diurnal to see them.

MIMETISM

Many species of coral snakes—harmless because they are aglyphous or only mildly venomous because they are opisthoglyphous, the false coral snakes—resemble the real, and dangerous, coral snakes by their coloring, marks, and behavior to the extent that it is sometimes difficult to tell them apart (see the table on the venom system on pages 22–23).

American coral snakes, both real and false, have been studied extensively. The real coral snakes (*Micrurus* and *Micruroides*) are Elapidae with powerful venom, usually ringed with variable two- or three-color sequences, and the false coral snakes are Colubridae, which include harmless

HOW TO TELL REAL FROM FALSE

IN THE UNITED STATES, the harlequin snake (*Micrurus fulvius*), a venomous coral snake member of the Elapidae, has thick black and white stripes separated by thin yellow ones, forming circles, while the colubrid *Lampropeltis triangulum* only has incomplete stripes, which do not go around onto the stomach, and where the succession of colors is different (see the drawing at right).

The drawings are practically identical in some tropical species. *Simophis rhinostoma*, which is perfectly harmless, imitates the dangerous *Micrurus frontalis* by its coloration and by its behavior (see the chapter on posture and behavior). The only difference is in the shape of the head, and in the animal's speed.

Pliocercus elapoides, a false coral snake, and *Micrurus hippocrepis*, a real coral snake, live in Central American forests and exhibit almost identical colorings.

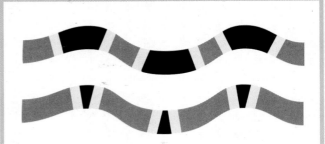

ILLUS. 1: Markings of two coral snakes, with bands of yellow, red, and black. Above, a true venomous coral snake, Micrurus fulvius; *below, a false coral snake,* Lampropeltis triangulum annulata

▷ *RIGHT:*
A true coral snake,
Micrurus frontalis brasiliensis

◁ *LEFT:*
A false coral snake,
Simpohis rhinostoma

△ *ABOVE: Gaboon viper* (Bitis gabonica)*, hidden in the humus*

▷ *RIGHT: A river Jack* (Bitis nasicornis)*. The broken coloration is even found in the iris.*

species, as well as opistoglyphous and mildly venomous species, and *Anilius scytale*, a member of the Aniliidae. Although their coloring is similar to that of the first group, false coral snakes rarely have the same tricolor combinations. Subtle differences in striping usually help experts identify them.

This characteristic is called mimetism, from the Greek *mimos*, "imitator." It is attributed to the close similarities between living organisms that may be quite separate in classification. Mimetism is characterized by three factors: an emitting organism (the model or mimetic), a receiving organism (usually a predator, sometimes a prey), and the symbol's generalization by the receptor.

There have been many attempts to explain the numerous cases of mimetism throughout the natural world.

The physical resemblance between real and false coral snakes is generally astonishing, and has been interpreted as a case of mimetism since 1861; it is called Bates' mimetism, and usually applies to a harmless or edible species with warning color markings. Bates considered a number of criteria: Mimetic factors are limited to exterior characteristics, mimetics are less apt to defend themselves than models, and both occupy the same hunting territory as their predator (this is not an absolute rule).

Faced with a harmless coral snake, the predator believes it is dealing with a dangerous animal and doesn't attack.

According to Bates, using warning colors is an effective technique that requires little or no energy and was thus copied by usurpers.

In 1878, Müller studied the resemblance between dangerous or bad-tasting species. A predator that has had a bad experience remembers it, and all the lookalikes benefit. Although many examples exist in plants and arthropods, it is rarer in vertebrates.

When it comes to real coral snakes, one can ask what the chances are of the predator remembering the "lesson" after having been mortally bit!

These theories have been contested since the beginning of the twentieth century, when it was observed that the coral snake's color markings were sometimes cryptic with interrupted patterns.

In 1956 a synthetic hypothesis was formulated suggesting the patterns' primal function was warning, but which took into account sympatry (sharing the same territory) with a common predator, rather than between model and mimetic. Müller's version has been adopted.

Mertens (1956, 1957) believed that opistoglyphous snakes were models, able to inflict painful but not lethal bites on their predators. The mimetics would be both the *Micrurus* (Elapidae) and aglyphous, nonvenomous species.

This controversial interpretation has been discounted because opistoglyphs rarely have the opportunity to bite an agile mammal or bird, which are further protected by feathers and fur. A behavior of innate avoidance is possible in predators, and

is seen in birds, although for others, response to this type of coloration is clearly learned.

In 1981, Green and McDiarmid felt that even if the coral snake's coloring has a warning function, it also plays a cryptic role in many species. Campbell has said that it is difficult to pick out a *Micrurus*, a real coral snake, when it is immobile and hidden in a sunny spot of the vegetal litter. The cryptic effect of its pattern and rings hide it well. Many *Micrurus* and false coral snakes live in the litter, are often hidden, and most are crepuscular, nocturnal, and sometimes diurnal depending on climatic factors and their geographic distribution. A bird of prey can find a crepuscular king snake (a false coral snake of the *Lampropeltis* genus) during the day. We do not have enough data on color perception at night, whether for animals with chromatic or achromatic vision, as red appears grey at night.

Whatever the reasons, potential predators are discouraged by the patterns and bright colors of *Micrurus* and *Micruroides*, which have adapted to dealing with danger; and sympatric coral snakes, whether venomous or not, benefit by adopting the same color.

▽ BELOW: *Copperhead* (Agkistrodon contortrix). *Cryptic coloration and broken patterns*

IS THE HYPOTHESIS OF SYMPATRIC MIMETISM PLAUSIBLE?

IF WE ADMIT that false coral snakes "copy" the real ones, in order to benefit from the effect that their colors have on predators—and this is the founding principle of Bates' mimicry—then we must expect that they occupy the same hunting grounds as their predators, which means the same biotopes and distribution areas.

This is the case in the American inter-tropical zone, where biotopes are always inhabited by both one or more species of *Micrurus* and one or more species of false coral snakes belonging to different genera, but the situation is often more complex, especially in the more extreme zones of their distribution area, such as in the United States.

In the southeastern coastal states, a real coral snake (*Micrurus fulvius*) and some false ones—the scarlet snake (*Cemophora coccinea*) as well as four subspecies of *Lampropeltis triangulum* that all look alike—are found in the same light forest biotope. However, the false coral snakes have greater distribution areas and thus include areas without any *Micrurus fulvius*. In Arizona, the true coral snake, *Micruroides euryxanthus*, partially cohabits with a small and totally harmless snake that resembles it, *Chionactis palarostris*, which has a much smaller distribution area. Another false coral snake lives in this region, which is the northernmost limit of its distribution, the Arizona king snake, *Lampropeltis pyromelana*, but it doesn't frequent the same biotopes. The first lives in semiarid zones, steppes, and rocky areas, and the second lives in coniferous forests and high-altitude prairies. There is little chance for them to meet, but they can be observed together in common border areas. Except for *Micruroides euryxanthus* in those areas, *Lampropeltis pyromelana* doesn't share its distribution area with any other coral snake, real or false.

Mexico's climatic conditions are more favorable. *Micruroides euryxanthus* can reach higher altitudes and wetter biotopes, where they can run into the *Lampropeltis pyromelana*. The number of coral snake species, both real and false, increases towards the south.

However, the California mountain king snake, *Lampropeltis zonata*, a false coral snake living in the coastal California moun-

tains, is the only coral snake (real or false) in its distribution area.

It seems difficult to write about mimicry in such cases, when the so-called models and mimics are not sympatric. Perhaps this sympatry* existed during the Pleistocene in animals that are now allopatric.**

Sympatry: cohabitation of two different species

**Allopatry: The opposite of sympatry. Is said of species occupying different zones, living close to each other but with no contact.*

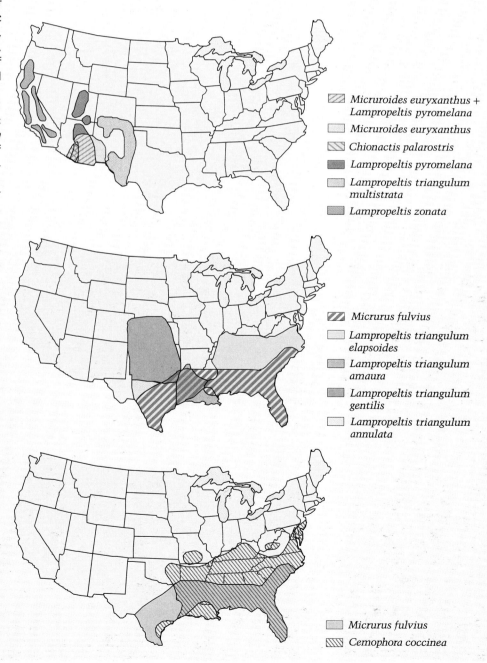

☒ *Micruroides euryxanthus + Lampropeltis pyromelana*
☐ *Micruroides euryxanthus*
▨ *Chionactis palarostris*
■ *Lampropeltis pyromelana*
▨ *Lampropeltis triangulum multistrata*
▨ *Lampropeltis zonata*

☒ *Micrurus fulvius*
☐ *Lampropeltis triangulum elapsoides*
▨ *Lampropeltis triangulum amaura*
■ *Lampropeltis triangulum gentilis*
☐ *Lampropeltis triangulum annulata*

☐ *Micrurus fulvius*
▨ *Cemophora coccinea*

POSTURES & BEHAVIOR: DEFENSE OR INTIMIDATION

Marie-Charlotte Saint-Girons

Like all animals, snakes have various methods of defending themselves that can be used as warranted by circumstances. Flight is the most common reaction, although many species first trust their ability to blend into their surroundings. Warning or intimidation postures follow, more or less easily depending on the species. Some wait until they are "cornered," while others, usually less agile and/or venomous snakes, assume these postures quickly. Warning sounds go along with menacing postures. When caught, some snakes struggle (some more than others) and bite, while others use chemical means of defense. Some colubrids play dead as a last resort. Most snakes only defend themselves passively.

HIDING THE HEAD

Certain postures are only for defense purposes. This is the case of snakes that coil themselves, their heads hidden, and their tails out, a behavior that is common to small semi-burrowing Boidae like the African *Calabaria*, and the royal python (*Python regius*).

The rubber boa (*Charina bottae*), which is prey to small mammals searching for food under rocks and vegetal litter, hides its head, raises it tail while shaking it, and uses it to hit its aggressor. Thus it calls attention to a nonvital part. Its tail often bears bite marks.

Burrowing snakes, such as the tube snakes (*Anilius*), the cylindrical snakes (*Cylindrophis*), Uropeltinae and coral snakes (*Micrurus* and *Maticora* [sic]), often defend themselves by hiding their heads under their bodies and raising their tails instead. Some species have brightly colored undersides, such as the small colubrid *Oligodon taeniatus*, and *Diadophis punctatus*. Some populations of the latter, the American ring-necked snake, have a yellow or orange ventral area and simply turn the posterior part of their body upside down, while others, whose ventral area is striped, raise their tail in a spiral. The striped version is seen as a warning coat.

ON THE DEFENSIVE

Colubrids, which are quite agile, flee as soon as they see a predator, while the heavier vipers count on their cryptic coloration and wait until the last minute to flee, or, sometimes, immediately take a defensive position without trying to escape. Some not-very-nimble vipers turn around and adopt a defensive posture when they have reached their hiding place, thus avoiding an attack to the head or body.

Nonetheless, it is often difficult to differentiate between defense and intimidation. Many "cornered" snakes adopt the same posture, trying to impress or discourage the predator: The body is more or less coiled in on itself, the front forming an "S" so as to extend quickly, the head slightly raised and directed towards the adversary. This classic

▽ *BELOW: Royal python (*Python regius*) in a defensive position, its head hidden in its coils*

▷ RIGHT: *When it is disturbed, the semi-burrowing* Cylindrophis rufus *from southeast Asia tries to hide its head while showing its enemy its raised tail.*

position is found both in venomous species getting ready to bite and harmless species, who hit with their head, mouth closed. Other species, especially arboreal colubrids, as well as the North American water moccasin (*Agkistrodon piscivorus*), a very dangerous species, open their mouths wide before trying to bite. Since this snake's mouth is white, it contrasts greatly with the dark color of its skin, giving rise to its nickname "cottonmouth." In general, nonvenomous snakes tend to exagge-

rate their intimidation methods and to "bluff" more than truly dangerous species do.

A snake, once disturbed, may bite an intruder placed between it and its shelter. Many human bites by African black mambas (*Dendroaspis polylepis*) occur under such conditions.

When escape is impossible, the most common response is rapid aggression, the body curled into an "S," and followed by a bite. The green-and-yellow grass snake (*Hierophis viridiflavus*) first faces

▷ RIGHT: *The small American colubrid* Diadophis punctatus *flips the ventral part of its body when it is disturbed, showing its bright colors (yellow or red). It is only later, if the adversary continues, that it attempts other defensive methods, especially chemical ones.*

the aggressor folded onto itself, the front part of the body raised, before throwing itself with its mouth wide open to bite. When caught, it bites hard, all the while beating its aggressor with its tail, which has led to the nickname "whip."

APPEARING LARGER

A certain number of intimidating or aggressive postures precede the bite or a simulation thereof. Appearing larger is a real advantage when faced with a predator. The tiger snake (*Notechis scutatus*), the South American false coral snake *Erythrolamptus*, and the Asian colubrid *Rhabdophis subminiatus* all flatten their necks for this very reason. Many snakes also raise the upper part of their body, which is a much more impressive sight. The most famous and spectacular examples are, of course, cobras (*Naja* genus), which, when threatened, adopt a famous posture: The front third of the body is raised and they spread their hoods. Their cervical vertebrae, which are long and inclined backwards, make them seem larger and intimidate their enemies. Their mouths open, they breathe out and hit.

The Egyptian cobra (*Naja haje*) only hits, mouth open, when the intruder gets too close. It can only throw its head to the front and bottom, and generally really bites only after a few false attacks.

The hood is more or less developed according to different species. African cobras usually have

◁ *TOP LEFT: A water moccasin* (Agkistrodon piscivorus) *in an aggressive posture, its body in an "S" and its white mouth open, which has led to its nickname "cottonmouth"*

▷ *RIGHT:* Cobra (Naja kaouthia) *in an intimidation posture, with hood spread*

smaller ones; that of *Naja nivea* is quite small. That of *Naja naja*, the Asiatic cobra, is quite developed, reaching 6 in. (15 cm) in an individual measuring 7¼ ft. (2.2 m).

Some Colubridae imitate cobras, with which they share a biotope, such as the *Pseudoxenodon* genus in Asia, or *Malpolon moilensis* in Africa and the Middle East. In South America, *Hydrodynastes gigas* resembles cobras, although cobras don't live in that region. This may be an example of convergence rather than behavioral mimetism.

Another way of looking bigger is to blow the

▷ *RIGHT:* Cobra (Naja naja) *shown from behind and showing its eyeglass-like markings*

◁ *LEFT: The harmless* Heterodon platyrhinos *blows very hard and spreads its neck and the back of its head to intimidate its adversaries.*

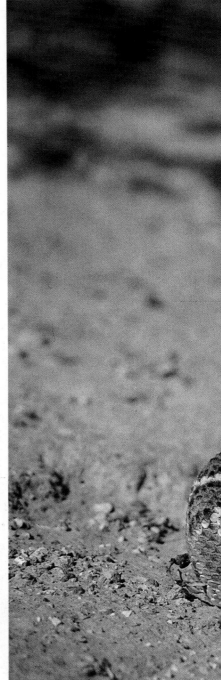

◁ *LEFT: Like many other colubrids,* Pseustes sulphureus *inflates its neck when disturbed, giving the appearance of greater body volume.*

▽ *BELOW LEFT:* Boiga pulverulenta, *an arboreal colubrid from equatorial Africa, in intimidation position, mouth open*

body up with air. With its body in an "S," the boomslang (*Dispholidus typus*) and the black arboreal snake, *Thrasops jacksonii*, enlarge their necks with air. *Malpolon monspessulanus* raises the front part of its body, blows it up with air, and flattens its neck. It breathes noisily and bites if caught. Some Colubridae that blow up their bodies to almost twice their volume also flatten their heads, which makes them look flat and triangular, and they then resemble vipers; they also breathe noisily like vipers. They hit with their body in an "S," but with their mouth closed. This is true of the South American *Xenodon*, which then looks like *Bothrops*, and of the African *Crotaphopeltis hotamboeia*, which, when angry, looks like a *Causus* viper. The

members of the *Heterodon* genus, which are harmless, also act aggressively if they cannot escape. Swollen with air, head and body flattened, cervical vertebrae spread out, they breathe noisily and pretend to bite while throwing themselves forward.

Many other species also have a coloration similar to that of the vipers in their area, such as the viperine snake (*Natrix maura*) and the asp viper (*Vipera aspis*), or the *Lystrophis dorbignyi* and *Bothrops alternatus* in South America. When faced with an ophiophagous snake, some species blow up and raise the middle part of their body in an arc, and try to hit their adversary with it, thus keeping the predator from seizing their head. The water moccasin (*Agkistrodon piscivorus*) and the rattle-

snakes, *Crotalus*, do this when faced with a king snake, for example. The Australian bandy-bandy (*Vermicella annulata*), a ringed black-and-white Elapidae, can raise its body up to 6 in. (15 cm) off the ground, in one or more arcs. If nothing else works, snakes sometimes play dead, as some predators only attack live prey. Members of the *Heterodon* genus can writhe around, flip over, mouth open and tongue hanging, for a number of minutes. If turned over, they immediately return to their "death" pose.

CHEMICAL DEFENSE

Although the use of toxic products emitted by exocrine glands is less common in snakes than it is in amphibians, there are some instances of such use. All snakes have glands in the anal region that

▽ *BELOW: The diamondback rattlesnake* (Crotalus atrox) *in a warning position. While it shakes its rattle to announce its presence, its body is shaped in an "S" and it's ready to attack if the threat should become more precise.*

emit a strong and disagreeable-smelling substance. When a *Leptotyphlops* is attacked, especially by ants, it coils up and empties these glands; the substance is then spread out over its entire body. When a predator seizes a grass snake (*Natrix natrix*), the latter passes its cloaca over the former's body and spreads the foul-smelling liquid over it. Many Colubridae, Natricinae in particular, act this way, but the quantity of liquid as well as its repulsive character vary from species to species. The ringneck snake (*Diadophis punctatus*), a ground dweller from southern Canada to Mexico, empties its intestine when it is seized, and the truly foul-smelling contents of its anal glands have a great chance of discouraging any predator which had not taken note of its colored tail. This chemical method of protection, which is frequent in colubrids, is rarely used by venomous snakes. Nonetheless, the water moccasin (*Agkistrodon piscivorus*) can spray an 11-square-foot (1 m^2) surface with the contents of its anal glands mixed with its fishy-odored excrement, giving strong blows to the right and left with its tail. Some Colubridae have subcutaneous upper dorsal glands secreting an irritating product that spreads on their skin when their back is stimulated. Surprisingly, this gland is missing from the southern populations of *Rhabdophis subminiatus*, while it is quite developed in northern populations.

VENOMOUS FANGS

Venomous fangs are one of the most effective defense mechanisms among vertebrates. Their first function is to attack prey, but they are also useful against aggressors, since, in some cases, a single bite is enough to discourage the attacker.

SPITTING VENOM

Some cobras, like the African *Naja nigricollis* and *Naja mossambica*, as well as some Asian populations, are spitting cobras. They can project their venom several yards or metres, thanks to a slight specialization of the fangs. The snake abruptly expels air from its lungs, while a muscular contraction makes the venom gush forth at the bottom of the fangs. It is then blown in small drops. When projected onto the skin it has a minor effect, but the snake generally aims precisely for the eyes. This is quite painful and leads to severe irritation. If the eye is not immediately rinsed out, the cornea may be destroyed by a severe inflammation, and blindness can result within ten or so hours.

Harmless snakes appear to benefit from the fear inspired by venomous species: It has been observed that predators take the same amount of care, whether or not their prey is venomous.

Snakes' defense mechanisms are varied, and most species use a number of them successively: flight at first—if the cryptic colorations have not done their job—or warning, followed by intimidating postures, and finally the closer defense methods: bites or emissions of chemical substances, the two being mixed in venomous snakes. Some colubrids, like the Eastern hognose snake (*Heterodon platirhinos*) or the grass snake (*Natrix natrix*), simulate death as a last recourse.

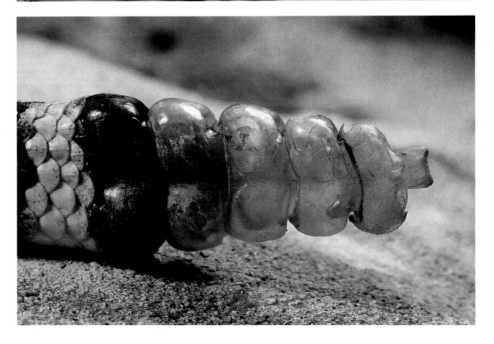

RATTLESNAKES WITHOUT RATTLES

Yannick Vasse

THERE IS A HYPOTHESIS that the rattlesnake's rattle evolved along with the great North American herds of ungulates. The rattle would let bison know that the snake was around and, wanting to avoid an uncomfortable, if not lethal, bite, the bison would be careful not to step on the snake.

It is also said that rattlesnakes have lost their rattle on islands without ungulates, citing especially the case of *Crotalus catalensis*, which lives on the Catalina islands, and which has no rattle.

But this species is the only one, among nine that live in the region's islands that has totally lost its rattle. And Santa Catalina, formed about two million years ago, is one of the oldest of these islands.

The red diamondback rattlesnake, *Crotalus ruber*, which was geographically isolated, underwent a number of morpho-logical and ecological modifications. It has become smaller, thinner, and semi-arboreal.

On the island of San Lorenzo del Sur, the subspecies of the diamondback rattlesnake, *Crotalus ruber lorenzoenzis*, includes populations with and without rattles. Other *Crotalus ruber* island subspecies have kept their rattles. Thus, the absence of ungulates does not seem to be a convincing explanation for the loss of the rattle.

RIGHT: ▷
Crotalus catalinensis

The grass snake, which lives in Europe, Asia Minor, and North Africa, has a number of options available. When surprised by an intruder, it first tries to flee. If that proves impossible, it widens the back of its head and blows menacingly, and then hits with its head, without biting. If seized, it generally does not bite, but emits a foul-smelling liquid from its anal glands. If this is not enough to discourage the enemy, it can simulate death by flipping onto its back, mouth open, keeping this position until it is freed, at which time it "comes back to life" and flees.

SONOROUS WARNINGS

Most snakes, when in a defensive position, either breathe loudly or hiss, more or less violently and rhythmically; the sound is produced by both inspiration and expiration of air. The hissing is loudest, the larger and more excited the snake is. Its pitch varies according to the species: Some colubrids from the *Pituophis* and *Heterodon* genera emit a hoarse hiss from the trachea, which is why members of the *Pituophis* genus are called bull snakes. The European Montpellier colubrid *Malpolon monspessulanus*, the North American *Heterodon* genus, the South American genus *Pseustes*, and *Vipera* vipers all emit a lengthy hiss. The colubrid (*Coluber nummifer*) and the large *Bitis* vipers (the puff adder, *Bitis arietans*, and the Gaboon viper, *Bitis gabonica*) emit a powerful and deep breath which is as impressive as their appearance. The vibrating tail is also used by many animals (the bull snake and *Lachesis muta*), but the best-known case is that of the American rattlesnakes, *Crotalus* and *Sistrurus*. These have a noise-making organ on the end of their tail, formed of keratinized seg-

△ ABOVE: Some "spitting" cobras first defend themselves not by threatening to bite, but by projecting their venom into the adversary's eyes with surprising precision and up to a few yards (metres) away. This is true of Naja nigricollis, shown here.

◁ LEFT: The grass snake (Natrix natrix) simulating death

▷ RIGHT: The dice snake (Natrix tessellata) simulating death. This simulation can vary: The animal in the photograph is immobile, but it has not flipped over, and its mouth is only partly open.

A FEW ORIGINALS

Yannick Vasse

Flat as a pancake

An aquatic colubrid living in South American marshes (members of the *Helicops* genus, *Helicops angulatus* in particular) flattens completely on the ground when faced with an intruder. If provoked, it surges into an "S" and bites energetically, while jumping.

The board snake

Erpeton tentaculatum, a strictly aquatic snake measuring 2 to 3 ft. (60 to 90 cm), is sometimes called the board snake because of its strange reaction when caught: It becomes totally rigid and holds itself straight, like a stick. It is found in Indochina.

Spitting blood

In the Antilles, small *Tropidophis* snakes (from the Tropidophiidae family, related to the Boidae) measuring about 3 ft. (1 m) can spit blood when they are excited. Unfortunately, we still don't understand the mechanism or reasons for this behavior.

ments that fit into each other, making up the rattle. When the tail is shaken, these segments produce a dry, characteristic sound by hitting into each other, which signals the snake's presence. A new segment is formed with each molting, but their number is only rarely more than eight in the wild (although it exceeds 15 in captivity), as the back segments fall off. The distance from which the sound is perceived varies with the wind's direction and, especially, with the snake's size.

Another type of sound can be made by the rubbing of scales. This is mostly used by arboreal vipers like *Cerastes* or *Echis*, with their keel-shaped scales; their body flat on the ground, they glide in place, rubbing their flanks against each other. The noise resembles that of steam under pressure. Each species uses only one sound, but all are apparently warning signals and supplement intimidation postures.

A rattle spreads over dozens of yards (tens of metres) and is more efficient than a whistle. Rattlesnakes alert others of their presence more often than other Viperidae and from a greater distance. The sound is immediately perceived by mammals.

Another sound is made by pushing air out of the cloaca. It is a dry, repeated sound accompanied by excrement expulsion, used by some venomous and nonvenomous species, such as the Arizona coral snake (*Micruroides euryxanthus*) and the American hook-nosed snake (*Gyalopion canum*). It is probably an intimidation sound to surprise, rather than a warning sound. A second of hesitation or a step back on the aggressor's part may also give the snake an extra chance to escape.

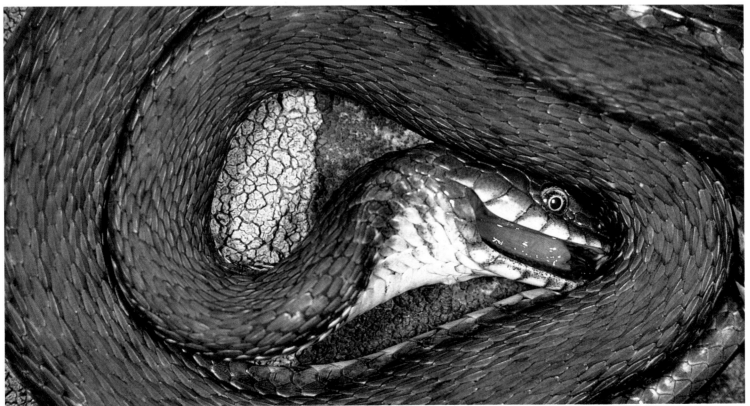

SNAKES' ENEMIES

Marie-Charlotte Saint-Girons

All snakes are carnivores and thus predators. They are also prey for other animals, thus occupying an intermediate place on the food chain. Other than direct predators, snakes' potential enemies include microorganisms and multicellular parasites, as well as animals with which they may be in competition for food, or even territory. Man's actions, unfortunately, are not limited to simple predation, but include the senseless destruction of animals and their biotopes (see the chapter on commerce, legislation, and protection). Potential predators are found in each class of vertebrates—mammals, birds, reptiles, amphibians, fish—and even among invertebrates.

MAMMALS

There are no strictly ophiophagous mammals, but many eat snakes with some regularity.

▶ Carnivores

Small carnivores catch snakes by circling around them, trying to bite any part of the body. The snake keeps its head raised and tries to bite its predator, which avoids it with some ease. The carnivore's agility and energy are superior to those of the snake, which tires more easily. The carnivore bites the snake's neck and shakes it before swallowing.

Small Felidae, like Europe's wildcat (*Felis silvestris*) and the Asian marbled cat (*Felis marmorata*), occasionally capture snakes. Domestic cats (*Felis catus*) are sometimes seen hitting snakes with their front paws.

Larger snakes may be caught by larger carnivores. Panthers (*Panthera pardus*) can attack rock pythons (*Python sebae*) measuring 13 ft. (4 m), and vice versa.

Among the Canidae, the jackal (*Canis* sp.) and the fennec (*Fennecus zerda*), a small desert-dwelling fox from North America and Arabia, eat various reptiles.

Some carnivorous Mustelidae—stone martens, weasels, and skunks—occasionally eat vipers and other snakes. The Canadian otter (*Lutra canadensis*) catches aquatic racers of the *Nerodia* and *Regina* genera; it bites them repeatedly and carries them to the shore to eat them, starting with the tail. Badgers and the ratel (*Mellivora capensis*), omnivorous Mustelidae, can eat snakes. The American badger (*Taxidea taxus*) sometimes eats rattlesnakes (*Crotalus*).

Some Viverridae also eat snakes, like the African civet (*Civetticus civetta*) and the genet (*Genetta*), which even attacks mambas (*Dendroaspis*). The suricate (*Suricata suricata*), from the west African savannahs, eats snake species from open, grassy areas in particular (*Psammophis, Ramphiophis*).

Skunks and other mammals that look for food in vegetal debris or beneath rocks can find burrowing or semi-burrowing species.

The mongoose remains the best known of snakes' enemies. The *Herpestes* genus is known for attacking cobras. The battle between the cobra and the mongoose Riki-Tiki-Tavi, as told by Kipling in *The Jungle Book*, has given Eastern mongooses a reputation for avid snake consumption. There are too few snakes in the mongoose's distribution areas for this to be its main source of food.

In fact, mongooses are opportunistic and feed on various small vertebrates, insects, and other invertebrates, as well as on fruit. Both the marsh-dwelling mongoose (*Atilax paludinosus*), which lives by the water in Africa (south of the Sahara), and the white-tailed mongoose (*Ichneumia albicauda*), which lives in the African and Arabian brush, occasionally capture snakes.

If the Asian mongoose can be a real enemy to snakes, these animals are most often confronted in fights organized by man, within an enclosure. During three- to six-second rounds, the mongoose jumps around the cobra (*Naja naja*), and tries to bite its neck. It bites it from top to bottom to pin the snake to the ground, since the snake cannot bite upwards. During such a fight, the mongoose counts on its agility and its long, downy fur, which gives it some protection against bites. It also has some natural resistance to cobra venom. But mongooses and suricates are almost as sensitive to Viperidae venom as are other mammals of the same size.

▶ Other mammals

The mulgara (*Dasycerus cristicauda*), a carnivorous marsupial that looks like a shrew, sometimes eats snakes that it immediately bites on the head, as opposed to its other prey, which it first bites on other parts of the body.

The omnivorous Suidae attack both venomous and nonvenomous snakes. They appear to be pro-

▽ *BELOW: A panther* (Panthera pardus)*, a dangerous predator, even for a 13 ft. (4 m) long python*

▷ *RIGHT: An organized fight between a cobra* (Naja naja) *and a mongoose (held on a leash, because cobras are expensive)*

tected from venom, not by any specific antibodies, but by a thick layer of fat.

Wild Australian pigs destroy large numbers of snakes. The warthog attacks every snake it meets, including species as venomous and lively as the black mamba (*Dendroaspis polylepsis*), or as large as the rock python (*Python sebae*). In Europe, pigs and boars in the wild eat racers and vipers. The Asian Suidae, especially the semiwild Indochinese hogs, can attack cobras.

Most ungulates kill snakes inadvertently, by stepping on them, which happens often. They may also destroy snakes to protect their own young, using their forelimbs.

Primates such as the carnivorous African baboon occasionally eat the small snakes they find under rocks.

Many insectivores actually have more varied diets consisting of various small animals, both invertebrates and vertebrates. Shrews may eat newborn Colubridae. The European hedgehog (*Erinaceus europaeus*) kills the reptiles it finds, including vipers. Since the hedgehog is nocturnal, these occurrences are rare. With the quills on its forehead raised to avoid retaliation, it bites the snake until it dies. Hedgehogs usually resist the venom of snakes and hymenopterans well. When bitten by a viper, they do not necessarily die, but may do so a few days later. Moles, which can eat any animal smaller than themselves that they find in their tunnels, can attack racers. Some golden moles, living in the dunes of the Namibian desert, in southwest Africa, eat many apodal lizards living underground and the mole snake (*Pseudaspis cana*).

Some bats also eat snakes. These bats from the Megadermatidae family, called false vampires, live in the tropics and eat insects and small vertebrates, including reptiles.

BIRDS

▶ Birds of prey

Snake-eating birds are mostly diurnal birds of prey, who sight-hunt. Birds of prey eat snakes in all parts of the world, from African savannahs (*Psammophis*, *Dasypeltis*, *Python*, *Dendroaspis*) to the North American marshes (*Agkistrodon*, *Nerodia*) or in the Central Asian steppes (*Elaphe*). Some, like eagles and falcons, immobilize the prey in their claws, usually seizing them by the neck and breaking it with a brutal twist.

The king cobra (*Naja haje*) is prey to eagles, buzzards, kites, and falcons. Asiatic colubrids from the genera *Ptyas* may be captured by diurnal birds of prey. Bald eagles, buzzards, and eagles catch climbing snakes (*Thelotornis*, *Oxybelis*, *Ahaetulla*), when they are at the top of trees.

In Brazil, the sparrow hawk (*Herpetotheres corchiinans*) is revered as a sacred animal by the native Indians because it eats reptiles, and it is invoked to cure snakebites.

The snake-eater, or secretary bird (*Sagittarius serpentarius*), a large ratite bird of prey 3 ft. (1 m) tall, lives in the savannahs and open spaces of southern and eastern Africa. It is renowned as an enemy of both venomous and nonvenomous snakes—cobras (*Naja*), grass snakes (*Ramphiophis*, *Psammophis*)—which it attacks by "dancing" around them, wings open wide, long scaly legs protecting it against bites, and throwing the snakes up in the air until they die. The snake-eating bird is not strictly ophiophagous, it also feeds on small birds and insects, and many different prey (frogs, lizards, birds, and even terrestrial turtles) have been found it its stomach.

Bald eagles are well known as snake consumers throughout Europe and Africa. After a characteristic flight, they drop themselves on their prey from a height of 22–55 yds. (20 to 50 m). The short-toed bald eagle, a migrator that spends time in Europe, mostly catches racers, which are larger and more plentiful than vipers. African eagle species eat both venomous and nonvenomous species: racers, vipers (*Daboia*, *Vipera*, *Bitis*), cobras (*Naja*), pythons (*Python*), and mambas (*Dendroaspis*).

These birds bring prey measuring up to 5½ ft. (1.70 m) back to the nest after having started to swallow them, letting some of the tail hang from their beaks to facilitate regurgitation and feed their single offspring. These are the only birds for which snakes constitute the essential part of their diet.

▶ Wading birds

Wading birds are occasional snake predators, usually eating more-or-less aquatic species like members of the Natricinae. European storks (*Ciconia ciconia*) and herons (*Ardea cinerea*) can eat species like *Natrix maura* or *N. tessellata*. In Colombia, the "colubrero guacabo" are used by man to hunt young snakes.

▶ Corvidae, roadrunners, rheas & kookaburras

In Australia, the kookaburra (*Dacelo*) occa-

△ *ABOVE: A hedgehog eating an asp viper* (Vipera aspis) *begins by grinding its head.*

sionally catch snakes. Some of the larger passerine birds feed on small snakes. This is true of Corvidae, such as crows (*Corvus*), or the magpie (*Pica pica*), which eats them quite regularly.

Rollers (*Corarias*) and various magpies (*Laniinae*) can eat arboreal snakes. Similarly, some species of carnivorous hornbills (*Tockus camurus*, *Bucorvus abyssinicus*) living in Africa eat snakes, among other vertebrates.

The roadrunner of cartoon fame (*Geococcyx californianus*), from the southwest North American chaparrals, enjoys lizards. Some fantastic accounts say that it provokes snakes with a cactus thorn until the snakes hit and impale themselves, thus offering themselves to the bird.

In the Americas, the rheas (*Pteronecmia*), which are mostly vegetarian, sometimes eat reptiles.

▶ Galliformes

The greatest snake eaters are the Galliformes: roosters, pheasants, guinea-fowl, and turkeys, which eat an unbelievable number of young and small-size snake species. Fowl thus get rid of racers and vipers around farms. The impact of wild Galliformes in nature is much smaller. Although many birds eat snakes seemingly without worry, they do not appear to enjoy a natural immunity to venom, but they are protected instead by their feathers, the scales on their legs, as well as by their hooked beaks and claws.

REPTILES

▶ Alligators & crocodiles

These reptiles can eat all sorts of snakes, like the kartung (*Acrochordus javanicus*), the water moccasin (*Agkistrodon piscivorus*), American racers like *Nerodia*, the tentacled snake (*Erpeton tentaculatum*), or pythons (*Python*) crossing water. Despite their armored skin, crocodilians seem to fear venomous snake species.

Carnivorous freshwater turtles, especially those with soft shells like *Trionyx*, which are very active and quite voracious, swallow aquatic snakes when hunting for food. *Nerodia* and *Agkistrodon piscivorus* can also become prey to North American snapping turtles (*Chelydra serpentina*, *Macroclemys temminckei*).

The big carnivorous lizards fight with snakes, even venomous ones. The desert monitor, *Varanus griseus*, eats *Cerastes* vipers, and is probably immune to their venom. It seizes them by the head or tail and shakes them violently to break their spine.

Cobras (*Naja*), pythons (*Python*), and egg-

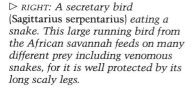
▷ RIGHT: *A secretary bird* (Sagittarius serpentarius) *eating a snake. This large running bird from the African savannah feeds on many different prey including venomous snakes, for it is well protected by its long scaly legs.*

◁ *LEFT: A short-toed bald eagle* (Circaetus gallicus) *bringing a colubrid to its young. These birds are probably the only strictly ophiophagous raptors. They are particularly fond of colubrids, although they can easily battle venomous snakes.*

eating snakes (*Dasypeltis*) may also be prey to the *Varanus*. These reptiles also eat eggs, snake eggs in particular.

Large European lizards like the glass lizard (*Ophisaurus apodus*) and the eyed lizard (*Lacerta lepida*) may eat young snakes.

OCCASIONALLY OPHIOPHAGOUS SNAKES

Some snakes without a strictly defined diet may eat other snakes; this is mostly the case with terrestrial species. The ringnecked snake (*Diadophis punctatus*) often preys on the genera *Virginia*, *Sonora*, and *Tantilla* and is often prey to a number of species, like the harlequin snake (*Micrurus fulvius*), the black racer (*Coluber constrictor*), or various common king snakes (*Lampropeltis*).

The smooth snake (*Coronella austriaca*), the green-and-yellow grass snake (*Hierophis viridiflavus*), and the Montpellier snake (*Malpolon monspessulanus*) are often ophiophagous, with the latter even eating members of its own species.

The Asian krait (*Bungarus fasciatus*), whose diet includes lizards and amphibians, also eats snakes.

The king cobra (*Naja haje*) and the rubber boas (*Charina bottae*, etc.) are also ophiophagous on occasion. Venomous snakes do not escape: Colubridae and Elapidae can attack king cobras. A black mamba (*Dendroaspis polylepsis*) measuring

9½ ft. (2.9 m) has been seen eating a black-and-white cobra (*Naja melanoleuca*) measuring 7½ ft. (2.25 m). These mambas, when young, are eaten by *Psammophis sibilans*, a racer, thus completing the circle. Among arboreal snakes, *Thelotornis kirtlandi* can eat grass snakes (*Psammophis* and *Psammophylax*), young boomslangs (*Disphodilus typus*), or other members of the *Thelotornis* genus.

TRUE OPHIOPHAGOUS SNAKES

Ophiophagous snakes are far from rare. It is a characteristic of many burrowing species, such as the pipe snake (*Cylindrophis rufus*), a southeast Asian semi-burrowing type, which feeds mostly on strictly burrowing species like *Typhlops*, or on terrestrial forms found in their burrows. The prey is seized between the jaws and killed by a twist of the prey's spine. Although the pipe snake is generally small, it can be larger than its predator. *Cylindrophis* can also be eaten by other snakes, especially those of the *Bungarus* genus.

The American common king snake (*Lampropeltis getulus*) eats rattlesnakes and racers. When the stomach contents of 58 king snakes were recently analyzed, every prey was a snake, most of them bitten around the head. The attacker coils around its victim while the predator's mouth advances by alternating jaw movements, without worrying about possible bites: It is immune to its prey's venom and can survive an amount that would kill a thousand mammals weighing the same.

The harlequin snake (*Micrurus fulvius*), a venomous Elapidae from the south and southeast United States, feeds essentially on lizards and burrowing snakes. Other small venomous Elapidae (*Micruroides*, *Micrurus*, *Calliophis*, *Vermicella*), the bandy-bandy (*Vermicella annulata*), which itself becomes the prey to other snakes, and the burrowing "viper" *Atractaspis* are also ophiophagous.

The royal cobra (*Ophiophagus hannah*) eats large racers (*Ptyas*, *Elaphe radiata*) and pythons (*Python reticulatus*, *P. molurus*, etc.).

The South American mussurana (*Clelia clelia*) feeds mostly on snakes, venomous or not. Snake eggs are also fed on by certain predators, like the North American scarlet snake (*Cemophora coccinea*), which lives in hedges and eats these eggs almost exclusively.

The foliated snake (*Phyllorhynchus browni*), living in the semiarid zones of the western United States, and *Oligodon*, from the grassy regions of Asia, eat snake and lizard eggs.

▶ Cannibalism

Snakes are sometimes cannibals, particularly in captivity. The young are usually eaten by adults, who seem not to make any difference between the young of their own and other species. In nature, cannibalism is particularly prevalent in species from the genera *Clelia*, *Bungarus*, *Ophiophagus*, and *Malpolon*. If circumstances warrant it, snakes of any species may eat their own.

▶ Resistance to venom

In general, venomous species are quite resistant to their own venom, and to that of individuals of their species.

A young captive male asp viper (*Vipera aspis*), which had been bitten by a female over the eye, recuperated the next day, although the eye had first been swollen and bloodshot. But this immunity is not absolute, and contradictory cases exist. The moccasin (*Agkistrodon*) is more sensitive to its own species' venom than to that of other Crotalinae. A rattlesnake that had accidentally bitten its tail died 27 hours later.

An experimental injection of high doses of venom into a rattlesnake leads to its death. On the other hand, it can often survive other species' venom.

The venom of ophiophagous Elapidae (*Bungarus*, *Ophiophagus hannah*) is usually quite toxic for snakes that are its usual prey.

Reptiles seem to be more immune to venom than are warm-blooded animals.

AMPHIBIANS

Amphibians catch snakes, but rarely, and these are usually young snakes. For example, a very young *Boa constrictor* measuring 12 in. (30 cm) was found in the stomach of an Antillian toad, which (in turn) figures on boas' menus. This toad sight-

▽ BELOW: *A savannah varan (*Varan exanthematicus*) attacking a cobra (*Naja nigricollis*), which will bite itself during the fight*

◁ LEFT: *Two phases of predation by a Nile varan* (Varan niloticus) *and a hissing adder* (Psammophis sibilans)

▽ BELOW: *A green-and-yellow grass snake* (Hierophis viridiflavus) *ingesting an asp viper* (Vipera aspis)

COMMENSALISM

Yannick Vasse

ALTHOUGH SNAKES are remarkable predators, some animals can cohabit with them. Snakes do not eat every day, and their metabolic requirements sometimes lead them to enter other animals' shelters (see the chapter on physiology).

A rodent's burrow can shelter and can occasionally serve as a pantry for *Pituophis m. melanoleucus*, which is not equipped for burrowing. This is not really an example of commensalism.

In Alabama, the long underground tunnels burrowed by turtles may also be inhab- ited by spiders and frogs feeding on in- sects, field mice, pine snakes, and copro- phagous coleopters, which feed on the ejected matter.

Snakes may also be commensal with man, whose activities favor the proliferation of prey. The reticulated python (*Python reti- culatus*) is often found in rat-infested Asian ports. The Indian cobra (*Naja naja*) is often found in villages and cities where rats and toads are found, who are themselves linked to man's presence and activities.

hunts and does not use its tongue to catch this type of prey, but takes the snakes directly into its excep- tionally large mouth.

The adult common European toad (*Bufo bufo*) and green frogs (*Rana esculenta, R. lessonae, R. ridibunda*) can catch young racers measuring 8 in. (20 cm). The horned frog (*Ceratophrys cor- nuta*), which lives in the humid and sandy marshes of South America and measures up to 6 in. (15 cm), catches any animal measuring up to 20 in. (50 cm), particularly marsh snakes like *Lio- phis, Helicops,* and *Hydrodynastes*.

FISH

All carnivorous fish, whether freshwater or saltwa- ter, can eat the aquatic snakes they encounter. They may catch young Acrochords (*Acrochordus*), water moccasins (*Agkistrodon piscivorus*), tentacled snakes (*Erpeton*), and snakes that are only tempo- rarily in the water, like the African genera *Natriciteres* and *Afronatrix*, or the Asian *Xeno- chrophis*, and some Homalopsinae. Perch, pike, and eels sometimes eat semiaquatic racers, and larger marine fish, sharks in particular, may catch marine snakes.

INVERTEBRATES

Some arthropods are snake predators. They usu- ally attack small species and young snakes, whose size is close to their own. Arachnids, such as

▷ *RIGHT:* Mussurana (Clelia clelia), *a large South American ophiophagous colubrid*

SNAKE DISEASES

Laurence Gravier

THE FOLLOWING TEXT only attempts to present ophidian pathology in general (infections and parasites), and to give an idea of its diversity.

Infections

Viral diseases that fell snakes are still not well known. Bacterial diseases are more common. Snakes are quite resistant to germs: They can harbor bacteria that are pathogenic to other animals without suffering any ill effects. Important environmental or physiological modifications (molting, dormancy) may favor these microorganisms' resurgence and lead to infection in their hosts. Snakes are very sensitive to cold, which may be translated into diarrhea or pneumonia.

In natural conditions, the most common bacterial diseases are those that contaminate wounds. Abscesses and skin infections often appear after parasites' or predators' bites and scratches, or wounds coming from other members of the species or prey. Rodents, when battling for their lives, occasionally bite the inside of the snake's mouth, leading to a stomatitis, an infection of the mouth that is always quite dangerous for snakes.

Parasites

Under natural conditions, snakes are host to internal and external parasites, without suffering any adverse consequences. The most visible parasites are far from being the most pathogenic.

Skin parasites

Ticks and other acarians can fix onto the skin of any snake, but leeches and flatworms (platyhelminths) are more common on aquatic ophidians.

These small parasites attach in areas where the skin is thin, on the head or near the cloaca.

They all feed on their host's blood, but there are rarely enough of them to lead to anemia. They can transmit diseases when biting (filaria, hemogregarinosis), and disrupt molting by their sole presence. Once it has gorged on blood, the parasite often spontaneously abandons its host. Flies sometimes lay their eggs on open wounds; the larvae feed on the tissues, keeping them from healing. These are cutaneous myiasis.

Subcutaneous and visceral parasitic nodules

Ophidian skin is sometimes deformed by parasitic nodules lodged in its thickness and containing larvae. There are identical nodules on their viscera. When the host snake is eaten by another animal, these larvae will become adult parasites in that predator.

Digestive-system parasites

Snakes' digestive tube may shelter protozoa (amoebas and coccidia) which are particularly aggressive. Symptoms appear as anorexia or apathy, followed by violent diarrhea and death. Various worms may also live in ophidians' digestive tracts.

The roundworms Ascaridae are the most pathogenic. They lead to vomiting and intestinal blockage or perforation. The adult parasites lay their eggs in the snakes' intestinal tract; they come out with feces. This explains how a microscopic examination of excrement can help identify the snake's parasitosis.

Respiratory apparatus parasites

Rhabditidae, which are roundworms (nemathelminths), sometimes wreak havoc with lung tissue: Both adults and larvae can cause pneumonias that are reinfected by bacteria and can lead to the snake's death from respiratory distress.

Some wormlike parasites, the tongue worms, may be seen hanging from their host's pharynx; they are also known to lodge in the snake's lungs.

Circulatory apparatus parasites

Some filaria (nematodes) can live in snakes' cardiac cavities; their larvae, the microfilaria, circulate in blood vessels, from which they can be captured by a tick drawing blood. By biting another animal later, the tick will transmit the larvae. Other parasites, protozoa like hemogregarine and flagellates, can also be transmitted in this way.

Hemogregarines can provoke anemia in snakes.

One remarkable trait in snakes is their precise adaptation to their biotope, which leads to their great fragility when it is modified or degraded.

Ticks on the head of a member of the genus Chironius

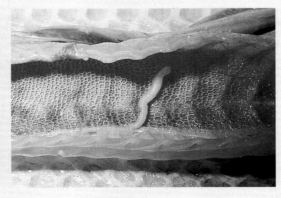

Parasitic worm in the lung of a puff adder (Bitis arietans)

△ *ABOVE: Python is on sale in this market in the Philippines.*

scorpions, solpugids, and large spiders as well as myriapods can attack a small snake.

Grammostrala often feed on snakes. As with their other prey, they inject digestive juices when stinging, which knock the victim out without killing it. Blood circulation is required to spread the juices that digest the prey's tissues and transform them into mush. Spiders, some myriapods, and coleopterous insects sometimes feed on snakes, which cannot flee when they are surprised while wintering.

Ants marching in tight columns can take apart any animal that does not quickly escape. They can kill and eat a slow-moving snake (even big pythons and vipers may be immobilized during digestion) leaving behind only its skeleton.

So snakes, which are predators with varied and efficient arms, are not invincible. They are an occasional, if appreciated, prey for many kinds of predators.

Their position in the food chain places them at the top of the pyramid, which means they are sensitive to any modification in the population they feed on, while they are not irreplaceable for their predators. Only a few snakes and birds of prey are fundamentally and sometimes even strictly ophiophagous.

MAN AS PREDATOR

In many areas of the world, man acts as snakes' direct predator, meaning that man kills them for food. In southern Africa and Asia, snakes are eaten regularly. The large Boidae are eaten by the South African Bushmen, while *Python molurus* and *Elaphe taenuria* are popular dishes in Hong Kong, Canton, and, more rarely, Shanghai.

Rattlesnakes (*Crotalus*) are usually only eaten when absolutely necessary, although they can still be found, canned, in the United States.

Malpolon monspessulanus was once eaten in the south of France under the name "hay eel," and this may still go on.

Aquatic species are also appreciated, especially by Cambodian fishermen, who eat the snakes they find in their nets, but do not purposefully search for them.

In the Philippines, marine snakes are smoked and sent to Japan. The karung (*Acrochordus javanicus*), a nonvenomous and relatively indolent snake, is eaten in Indonesia.

Man predates on snakes in other ways, not for culinary tradition, but under the guise of folklore and tourism. In the United States, yearly rattlesnake roundups (when the snakes emerge from their wintering areas) end with barbecues. Some restaurants serve snake for snob appeal, as is the case in Rio de Janeiro and other cities throughout the world. It is difficult to evaluate the impact of this consumption on the worldwide snake population, but it is thought to be minor, other than in China, where tens of thousands of snakes are eaten each year. It is probably less harmful to snakes than is the hunt for their skin, their gratuitous destruction, or, worst of all, the destruction of their biotopes, which drives species to certain extinction (see the chapter on commerce, legislation, and protection).

SNAKES
& MAN

MYTHOLOGY

Patricia Fourcade

As man observed snakes' morphological and biological peculiarities, he attributed to them a supernatural character. Moving quickly without limbs, found on the ground, in trees, and in water, appearing suddenly out of underground hiding places, fixing the world with its ever-open eyes, swallowing its prey in one piece, able to inflict venomous bites, and occasionally changing skin, the snake appears quite different from other animals and from man. There has been a tendency to classify snakes among the strange and supernatural in societies around the world; everywhere, in fact, where snakes are part of the local fauna. They have been seen either as demons, monsters, gods, ancestors, or sacred protectors, according to the civilization in question. Through the mythologies of various societies, or even within those of a single one, one discovers that there is an ambiguity and plurality of the snake's image, which represents opposite values, or serves as a link between them. Some themes recur frequently: good/evil, knowledge/lie, health/sickness, fertility, immortality, eternity/death, man/woman, earth/water, earth/sky, etc.

CREATION & DESTRUCTION MYTHS

Snake gods or monsters are found in various creation myths.

Mesopotamia: Apsoo, the primal god, created Tiamat, a feminine deity looking like a snake or dragon, and the two of them conceived other gods. One of them, Marduk, organized the world and took Tiamat apart, using half of her body to create the sky.

Canaanite mythology: The Leviathan, a monster sometimes represented as a seven-headed snake, living in the depths and representing primitive chaos, was vanquished by Baal, god of the sky, generating rain and fertility.

India: After a deluge a number of vital elements, divinities, and precious objects had disappeared from the sea of milk and from its cream, the Amrita, from which gods drew their strength. To find what had been lost, and to re-create the world, the gods beat the sea with the snake of eternity, Vasuki.

Greece: Many Greek cities include a snake in their original myths. Cecrops, Athens' founding king, was half-man and half-snake. According to Greek legend, Thebes was founded after a battle between Cadmos, a Phoenician king, and a snake or dragon guarding a sacred spring. Helped by Athena, Cadmos killed the monster and sowed its teeth. An army grew out of the ground; they fought with each other and the few survivors helped build Thebes. At the end of his life, Cadmos, king of Thebes, and Harmony, his wife, left the city and changed into snakes.

Africa: The snake has a preponderant role in creation myths from various parts of Africa. For the Dogons, from Mali, the god Amma created earth and surrounded it with a huge snake. The first men, the "great ancestors," were transformed into snakes upon dying.

For the Fon people of Benin (Dahomey), the world is made of earth carried by a coiled snake that floats on the sea; one day the snake will stop carrying it, and the earth will sink into the water.

The Dinka, from Sudan, present the primordial couple and give a mythical explanation of sexual

▽ *BELOW: A painting of Amenophis III, from the Egyptian New Kingdom. Paris, the Louvre.*

IN THE COBRA'S SHADE

Daniel Heuclin

THE COMMON COBRA (*Naja naja*) owes its nickname as "the spectacled cobra" to the characteristic design on its neck. An Indian legend says that one day, Buddha fell asleep in the sun while travelling in the desert. He was surprised to awaken in the shade . . . of a cobra, which shielded him from the sun's harsh rays with its open hood.

The story says that to thank it, Buddha blessed the animal by putting his two fingers on its neck.

Since then, these snakes have carried the mark of divine gratitude.

▷ *RIGHT: Jurlungur, the sacred snake of the Australian aborigines*

differences through the existence of distinct vital elements: The first man was associated with the snake and sun, the first woman with the snake and water.

Australia: For the Australian aborigines, the world was created by a huge supernatural snake, a totemic ancestor named Kurrichalpongo: Mountains, trees, and animals emerged from its eggs.

SNAKES & THE FORCES OF EVIL

Venomous, carnivorous, gliding in the shadows, the snake is generally seen as a treacherous and cruel animal: Its image has long been used by various civilizations to represent the most dangerous forces of evil.

In Jewish and Christian traditions, according to the Old Testament, the snake is first and foremost a shifty tempter who plays a great role in Genesis. Having convinced Adam and Eve to taste the fruits of the tree of knowledge of good and evil, the only tree in Eden they had been forbidden to touch, the snake pushed them to commit the original sin, exiling them from paradise, and obliging them to work, procreate, and die.

Within the Christian tradition, the snake appears as the manifestation of evil and of the devil. Medieval legends gave rise to any number of demonic snakes, many of which are sculpted on cathedrals. Two of them are the basilisk, a small crowned serpent whose strength lies in its eye, and the dragon, a huge winged snake, whose strength is concentrated in its tail.

In stories from different cultures, monstrous and evil snakes fight with gods and heroes. Many of ancient Greece's legendary monsters were

THE BEGINNING OF THE WORLD IN EGYPT

BEFORE THE WORLD BEGAN, the universe was in darkness: There was only a chaotic ocean called Nun, in which snakes and frogs lived. A great snake, Apep or Apopis, emerged from this chaos and spat out the gods and living beings. At the end of the world, all will return to the snake.

Other versions of this legend and other myths flesh out the ancient Egyptian cosmogony. One version is that an island appeared in the ocean Nun, with a sparkling egg on it. When the egg broke, the sun god (Re) emerged, and his light illuminated the entire universe. He then created the gods, men, and living creatures.

Each day Re is born in the morning and dies at night, having travelled across the ocean of the sky in his golden boat. At dusk, when he disappears from man's sight, he is transformed into a ram-headed god. He can then enter into the kingdom of the dead, a valley where the snake Apopis' river flows.

Re must pass through twelve doors, one by one, while his enemy the snake tries to stop him. Apopis lengthens as the hours pass, but he can never reach nor stop Re. The sun god always pushes the snake back into the river and Re reappears at dawn.

THE BATTLE BETWEEN INDRA & THE SNAKE VRITRA

THE BATTLE between a hero or god and a snake is found in many civilizations, especially in Asia and in the Indo-European societies.

In India, the battle between the god Indra and the snake Vritra is one of the essential myths of the Rig Veda. Indra is the god of warriors, lightning, atmosphere, seasons, and rain. His role is to establish cosmic order and to destroy the titans, who are harmful monsters.

One of these titans is the huge snake Vritra, with whom Indra fights many times. This snake's name means "he who tightens and imprisons," and Vritra was probably modelled after a constricting snake like the python.

Vritra demonstrates his harmful powers by provoking droughts: He imprisons the waters.

Thanks to his lightning (*vajra*), Indra slits the snake's stomach, and the waters emerge, letting the sun reappear. They spill onto the earth, either as rain or as seven rivers that throw themselves into the sea.

This myth has been interpreted in a number of ways: either as a myth explaining the organization of the world, or as the victory of life over death, or as an explanation of atmospheric phenomena.

◁ LEFT: *The important place held by snakes (cobras in this case) in Indian art and mythology is emphasized by this detailed and colorful painting.*

▷ RIGHT, ABOVE: *Forward corner of the Mexican feathered-snake, xo chicalco pyramid.*

▷ RIGHT, BELOW: *Painting of the feathered snake at Teotihuacan, Mexico. Unlike the Aztecs' other bellicose gods, the feathered serpent represented civilization. The symbolism represented by the snake brought it close to earth, while its feathers referred to spirituality.*

snakes, or had some ophidian attributes. Cerberus, the three-headed dog and guardian of Hell, had a snake for a tail. The Lerna hydra, fought by Hercules, had nine snake heads that grew back when cut off.

According to Hindu mythology, Vishnu vanquished the demon snake Kaliya by dancing on its many heads. In Japan, the eight-headed snake, which ate the king's daughters, was vanquished by the god Susano-o.

The Scandinavian god Thor wanted to kill his enemy, the snake of Midgard, which lived in the sea. He used a cow's head as bait and managed to

HOPI INDIANS
Daniel Heuclin

ONE OF THE MOST surprising Amerindian rituals is the Hopi snake dance, performed in northeast Arizona. The dance marks the end of a cycle of ceremonies which are generally carried out in late August, and which last nine days. These ceremonies are supposed to make it rain, and they use snakes as the messengers who will carry the Indians' prayers to the spirits.

These ceremonies are organized by two secret religious groups: that of the snake and that of the antelope.

On the fourth day, the "snake men" go to the desert to catch fifteen to sixty snakes, mostly colubrids (*Pituophis melanoleucus*) and rattlesnakes (*Crotalus viridus nuncius*, below). They are stocked in the snake society's kiva.* The "antelope men" use colored sands to create a mosaic on the floor of their own kiva, representing the clouds from which four snakelike lightning bolts emerge.

On the eighth day a dance is held representing the symbolic struggle between the young "snake man" and the virgin of the corn.

On the ninth day, during a ceremony in a kiva, the snake society chief washes the reptiles and dries them in the sand. The animals are then placed in the kisi.* The snake dance takes place at the end of that day.

Surrounded by the antelope men's chants, the snake men dance in groups of three. In each group, a dancer takes a snake in the kisi, carries it to his mouth, and holds it between his lips. Another dancer hits the reptile with his snake whip* each time it threatens to bite. Once a circle has been completed (always from the northwest to the southeast), the snake is exchanged for another.

When all of the snakes have thus "danced," they are put in a circle drawn in the soil with corn flour, and they're sprinkled with some of this flour. They are then taken by the snake men, who go towards the cardinal points and release them in the desert so that they may carry out their task as messengers.

Many theories were offered to explain the lack of accidents in these ceremonies, until, in 1932, a scientist clandestinely captured one of the snakes right after it had been released and discovered that its fangs had been removed. Twenty years later, the capture of another snake in similar conditions confirmed this observation.

Kiva: A room dug beneath ground where different religious rituals are carried out. Each society has its own kiva.
Kisi: A temporary, cone-shaped hut made out of branches and erected in the middle of the place where the ceremony occurs.
Snake whip: Made of eagle feathers (the master of snakes), it is supposed to terrify reptiles.

△ ABOVE: *The "Hopi" rattlesnake (*Crotalus viridis nuntius*), from northeast Arizona, is the snake most often used by the Hopis during their snake dances.*

catch it. In many versions of the myth, he could not kill it. According to Scandinavian mythology, Thor will kill the snake at the end of the world, but will be poisoned by its breath.

Many African societies represent snakes as messengers of death and tyrants. According to the Hausa, from Nigeria, the Ki snake guarded a well and demanded a young girl each time anyone wanted to get water. Ki was destroyed by a hero who married the queen of the people liberated from the snake's tyranny. In Australia, drinking without permission led to punishment from the mythical rainbow snakes. These snakes, which may also give beneficial rain, are represented as gigantic monsters, sometimes miles long, who devour those who break the laws.

THE SNAKE, GUARDIAN OF TREASURES AND SECRETS

Many of the snake's biological characteristics have given rise to the roles it has been given in mythology. Sloughing old skin has been interpreted as a renewal of vital forces, or as a sign of immortality. The eye, which is always open, due to the lack of a movable eyelid, has symbolized clear-sightedness and vigilance.

Various societies have given snakes a noble role: that of guarding time and of keeping the secret of immortality.

In Hindu mythology, while Vishnu rests on the snake of immortality, the reptile swallows Creation and awaits the god's awakening.

For the Toltecs, Quetzalcoatl, the feathered snake, was both a king who had once reigned and a god who left its people on a raft made of snakes to sail towards eternity. For the Aztecs, the snake was the god who had invented the calendar, and the snake symbolized both death and rebirth.

The myth of the snake stealing the secret of immortality is found in many cultures. Certain populations from Annam, Melanesia (New Britain), and Ethiopia (the Galla people) use this myth to explain both the origin of death in humans and snakes' sloughing.

The world-creating divinity (in the general sense, for this myth is common to many civilizations) wants to transmit the secret of immortality

to men, advising them to change skins to live eternally. His messenger makes a mistake and tells the snakes, instead.

The docility of some snakes and the sacred character that has been attributed to them has also made them the guardians of peace, deities, and the people.

According to a story found in both Greek and Roman mythology, Hermes (or Mercury), the god of travellers and commerce, found two sparring snakes. He separated them with a stick, around which the reconciled reptiles coiled themselves. A symbol of peace, which later became the caduceus, and then the emblem of the medical profession, was thus created.

In India, Mucilinga, the mythical king of the Nagas—deities which can show themselves in both human and snake form—protected the Buddha from a storm with his hood. Pythons venerated by the Mossi, from Burkina-Fasso, are village guardians.

The Egyptian asp goddess Ejo protected the delta of the Nile and guaranteed the sovereignty and divinity of the pharaohs, on whose crown she appeared as the raised and vigilant asp, or uraeus.

Many legends have the snake not just as the keeper but as the transmitter of knowledge.

The snake is associated with medicine and its gods in many civilizations: It's thus the guardian of healing knowledge.

The Biblical story of the bronze snake (Numbers 21:8–9) is one such an example. Wandering in the desert, the Hebrews began to doubt God's power. Snakes were sent to punish them, and God asked Moses to make a bronze snake to heal or protect anyone who looked at it and who sincerely regretted his incredulity. The snake then became a cult object until Hezekiah, king of Judaea, destroyed this idol in the 8th century B.C.E. The snake/health association already existed in Mesopotamia, where Ningishzida, the medicine god, holds a stick around which is the dual-sexed and double-headed snake Sachan. There are very similar representations in Greek and Roman civilizations. The Greeks' and Romans' god of medicine (Asklepios or Aesculapius) often appears as a snake. In his anthropomorphic representation, he carries a stick with a coiled snake around it; the snake was sent by Apollo to teach him the value of

THE OROBOUROS

RATHER THAN being the mythical snake of a particular civilization, the orobouros represents a number of ideas which are linked and found in the mythologies of many societies. It is the well known image of a snake forming a circle by biting its tail, giving the impression that it is both swal-

lowing and giving birth to itself. The name orobouros is from the Greek, and means "he who devours his tail" (*oura* means tail). It symbolizes the eternal return, life as an infinite cycle, the idea death denied. The snake's ability to renew its skin by molting is at the origin of this

idea. The circular form of this symbol leads to a vision of the world in which there is union between earth and sky, where nature is a totality. In occult science, the orobouros is used as a symbol of immortality and of the transmutation of death into life.

THE PLANT OF IMMORTALITY
STOLEN BY THE SNAKE

IN MESOPOTAMIA, *Gilga-mesh*, the Babylonian heroic epic, some versions of which are 4000 years old, deals at one point with immortality. After a number of exploits, Gilgamesh embarks on a long and perilous journey to find the herb of immortality, which grows beyond the ocean of the departed, at the bottom of the waters of the dead.

Gilgamesh is able to take the plant and bring it to the country of the living. However, being exhausted and thirsty, he falls asleep on the ground. In another version, he jumps into a river after having left the plant on the banks, where a snake takes it and becomes immortal, to the detriment of man.

A Greek myth, told by the poet Nicander of Colophon (2nd century B.C.E.), explains the origin of the immortality attributed to the snake. Prometheus, having stolen fire from the sky to give it to man, some men betrayed him and told Zeus, who decided to thank them by sending them a donkey carrying a cure against old age. While on the way, the donkey was thirsty and stopped by a river guarded by a snake, asking for permission to drink. The donkey gave the snake the remedy, which let the animal enjoy eternal youth.

medicinal plants. This snake is now identified as *Elaphe longissima*.

According to a Navajo myth, the snake people lived in an underground hell, near a lake. One of these snake-men kidnapped a young woman, and when she returned to her tribe two years later, she had the power to heal.

The Indian Nagas, snake divinities, can also transmit medical knowledge and increase humans' cognitive faculties by granting them extraordinary sight and hearing.

The snake is often thought to know secrets that can change men's lives.

In Genesis, the temptor snake is the guardian of the tree of knowledge. In Slavic, Germanic, and Scandinavian traditions, the snake or dragon is the mythical creature that informs men of the present and future.

This theme appears repeatedly in Greece. The Delphic python guarded a sacred river that gave rise to the priestess' prophecies when she drank from it or inhaled its vapors. Snakes have given legendary characters like Cassandra and Melampus the faculty to understand the language of birds or to predict the future, just by licking their ears while they were asleep. In Africa, the snake appears as an intermediary between men and gods, between the dead (ancestors) and the living. For the Dogons from Mali, the snake Lebe, born from the union of a genie and an ancestor, reveals information to his priest by licking him at night.

In other places, the snake guards treasures and brings riches.

Many myths and legends include fantastic snakes guarding treasures in caves or near water, or that allow one to amass riches. The Gaulish Druids believed in the "snake egg," a magic stone formed by a group of vipers. In France, the "vouivre" is the name of a magic flying snake with a precious stone in its forehead that it removes only when drinking in lakes. In western France, the fairy Mélusine married the lord of Lusignan and promised him riches and happiness. But he broke his promise never to try to see her on Saturdays. One day he found her in a lake and discovered that the lower half of her body was that of a snake. Betrayed, Mélusine left.

SNAKES & THE ELEMENTS

As an animal living in both aquatic and terrestrial environments, the snake serves as a link between the elements.

▶ The sun and moon

Many civilizations have looked to the snake to explain various characteristics of the solar system.

In some societies, particularly in Benin, the snake was associated with the moon. The disappearance and reappearance of the lunar disc have been identified with the snakes' sloughing, a sign of perpetual youth. During Egyptian antiquity, the raised asp, an emblem of the pharaoh's divinity, was linked to the sun god, Ra; it was called "Ra's eye" and was represented as supporting the solar disk. Quetzalcoatl, the feathered snake god of the Aztecs also had a celestial role: It was identified with the planet Venus, visible in the east in the

▽ *BELOW: The red cobra (*Naja pallida*), a close relative of* Naja nigricollis, *is also an efficient spitter found in East Africa.*

▷ RIGHT: *This bas-relief represents a cobra (*Naja haje*), a symbol of the divinity of the pharaohs. It was also called "Re's eye," for the sun god.*

▷ RIGHT: *The back of the Asian* Naja kaouthia's *hood sports a circular marking that has led to its nickname "the monocle snake."*

morning and in the west at night.

▶ Water

The relation between snakes and water is quite well developed. Water often appears as the generator of life in mythology. The snake is associated with it, either because of its resemblance to waves in water, or because the snake is itself a vital symbol.

In Mesopotamia, the Euphrates was identified as a male snake. To the Egyptians, the god living in the Nile was a snake who incited the annual fertilizing floods.

Chinese river gods were often represented as snakes, and were revered. The Yellow River god was envisioned as a golden snake with red marks beneath its eyes. Those living along the river organized representations in the snake's honor so as to enjoy its goodwill.

On the monumental frieze "The Descent of the Ganges," in the Mavalipuram sanctuary, each animal comes to pay his respects to the fertilizing Ganges, the sacred river of India, which is represented as half-man, half-snake.

The cult of sacred snakes and pythons in Africa is often linked to that of the water genies, especially around the Niger delta. Temples are often built to such cults.

▶ Earth

As an animal that glides along the ground and nests in caves, the snake, in the myths of many societies, is associated with the earth. It is seen as an agent able to capture telluric energy, able to transmit its beneficial aspects or use it to destructive ends. In the mythology of the pre-Columbian Andes, the goddess Pachamama, mother earth, often took on the shape of a dragon living underground and creating cataclysms (earthquakes, volcanic eruptions, landslides). The Aztec earth goddess, Cotlicue, wore a skirt made of snakes. For the Celts, the ram-headed snake was a symbol of earth and fertility, associated with Kernunnos, god of abundance.

In many societies, the snake has had a complex role and served as a link between various elements. It links the water of rivers and sky to the earth, the masculine to the feminine. It is part of various fertility myths, both in terms of crops and human reproduction. It has a sexual role, but, if it is often revered as the principle of masculine generation, sometimes directly in the form of a phallic cult within which it is given the power to fertilize women, it is also linked to the earth and to the mother goddess.

The Mexican feathered snake (which is equivalent to the Mayas' Kukulcan) was revered by the Aztecs. Its name reflects its dual nature: The quetzal, a green bird, linked it to the sky, while the coatl, a rattlesnake, linked it to the earth. It was known as the god of wind, but also as he who had taught farming to men and had given them corn.

In Hindu mythology, the Nagas and their wives, the Naganis, are snake deities linked to the earth and the ground. They live as kings in palaces hidden beneath the sea, or underground. They are thought to hold the power to control rain and the flow of rivers. Their role is not limited to the fertilization of the ground; women devote a cult to

△ ABOVE: A temple is dedicated to the royal python in Ouidah, Benin. This snake is the totem for the Fon ethnic group, and is considered to be the ancestor of all Fons. Many of these animals are put there by "priests," attracting both tourists and monetary offerings.

them so as to increase their fertility. A phallic cult is dedicated to the god Shiva, often called the "snake god," and he is linked to fertility and fecundity.

In Greece, Aesculapius, in the shape of the snakes kept in his sanctuaries, visited the women who slept by his temples (in their dreams) and was supposed to be the father of many famous people. In Greece and Rome, during fertility celebrations, Dionysus' adorers danced frenetically, with snakes coiled around their bodies.

Some African cults, with the same goal in mind, also have dances where the snake is handled; this is the case with the snake-god Damballah-Wedo, in Dahomey, also revered in Haitian voodoo, especially until the nineteenth century.

Damballah-Wedo is also a snake that some myths associate with the rainbow. In France, in the departments of Aude and Ariège, it was still possible in the 1940s to hear that snakes used rainbows and the sun's rays as ladders to climb up to the sky or to fly over wheat fields. In Brittany, the rainbow is identified as a snake coming down to drink. But most of these snake/rainbow myths were developed on the African continent and in Australia.

In Africa, the rainbow is shaped like a big snake, called the "sky snake" by the Nigerian Esas. It links the sky to the earth and is a sign of rain. This heralding role is also held by rainbow snakes in Australia, which sometimes appear as atmospheric rainbows, but which are mostly supernatural beings who guard and distribute water and represent human fertility.

Snakes are associated with milk and milk-producers in the legends, mythologies, and popular beliefs of many civilizations. Some authors, trying to find a rational explanation for this convergence, have posited that snakes like milk, while others have said the opposite. Snakes are morphologically incapable of drinking milk from a cow, a goat, or a wet nurse, nor can they drink the

milk in babies' throats, all of which they have often been accused of doing. This belief still exists in the French countryside and in the United States. There are also stories of complicity between the snake and the milk-producing animal. Milk has often been an offering to sacred snakes and is still practised in many countries. In India, where the beating of a sea of milk is a fundamental piece of mythology, milk was offered to the Nagas so as to obtain better crops. In central Europe, in Greece since antiquity, and until recently, milk has been left for snakes in exchange for their protection.

To the extent that the role played by snakes in fertility myths and cults is important throughout the world, the production of milk can be interpreted as a result of fertility, a sign of abundance.

▶ Duality of the symbol

Myths, legends, and beliefs involving snakes are numerous, and cannot be presented exhaustively, due to the complexity and geographic range of the theme. Beyond this diversity, often due to a multitude of local interpretations and to the existence of many versions of most myths, a few general traits are apparent. The snake's image is ambivalent rather than negative. Even in societies where it represents a destructive or evil power, the snake is given noble or beneficial roles, usually as guardian of a treasure or of vital elements (water, earth, fertility, fecundity, health, knowledge).

A rational explanation of this phenomenon can be offered. The term "snake" refers to a particular animal form, but it covers a wide range of individuals (venomous or constrictors, aggressive or harmless, oviparous or ovoviviparous, terrestrial or aquatic, differently colored), which have contributed to the elaboration of various myths. Its powerful place in the human imagination rests not only on the size and power of some large species, but on the snakes' more subtle faculties (sloughing, crawling, fixed stare, venom production), which are integral parts of its mystery.

▷ RIGHT: Pre-Columbian petroglyph from the Arawak culture. Most primitive peoples have attributed great importance to the snake as a symbol. This Guyanese petroglyph, over 2000 years old, probably represents either a bushmaster (Lachesis muta) or an anaconda (Eunectes genus).

SNAKE VENOM & PHARMACOPOEIA

Cassian Bon

Snake venom is a complex mix of proteins: toxins, which are responsible for the venom's lethal effect, other substances, which are responsible for important but nonlethal biological effects, and enzymes, which play an important role in the digestion of prey. Some of these proteins are characterized by a very particular effect on various essential biological functions (blood coagulation, blood-pressure regulation, transmission of the nervous or muscular impulse) and have turned out to be excellent pharmacological or diagnostic tools or even useful drugs. Treating ophidian envenomizations consists of symptomatic treatment, geared towards relieving the numerous ills brought on by the venom, and antivenom serotherapy—injecting the patient with antibodies that will neutralize the venom's major toxins.

Snake venom has no meaning in a biological vacuum. The venom is part of a whole—the venom apparatus—which is essentially composed of two venom glands synthesizing the venom and an injection system: fangs (modified teeth) with which to make the venom penetrate into the enemy or aggressor. This appears to be one of the most perfect mechanisms developed by any animal. Its primary function is obvious: catching prey. Venom also appears to play an important role in digestion.

A defensive snake may bite man or a domestic animal that it considers threatening and inject it with some or most of its venom. From a medical point of view, the danger represented by a venomous snake depends on the quality of the venom, especially its abundance and toxic power, but also, and maybe even especially, on the efficiency of the injecting system. This is why, except for a few rare exceptions, only snakes with a proteroglyphous (Elapidae, Hydrophidae) or solenoglyphous (Viperidae, Crotalidae) dentition are considered dangerous, because they can inject man efficiently.

CHEMICAL COMPOSITION OF SNAKE VENOM

The proteinaceous nature of snake venom was established in 1843 by Lucien Bonaparte, Napoleon's brother. Proteins are, in fact, 90 to 95% of venom's dry weight and are responsible for almost all its biological effects. Among the hundreds or thousands of proteins found in venom, there are toxins of course, neurotoxins in particular, as well as nontoxic proteins (which does not mean that they lack pharmacological properties), and numerous enzymes, especially hydrolithic ones.

To understand venom's biological effects, one must understand that snake venoms are complex mixtures of toxins, enzymes, and other proteins, which combine their effects according to their properties and levels. The compositions vary

Type	Name	Origin
1. Oxydoreductases	dehydrogenase lactate L-Amino-acid oxidase Catalase	Elapidae All species All species
2. Transferases	Alanine amino transferase	
3. Hydrolases	Phospholipase A$_2$ Lysophospholipase Acetylcholinesterase Alkaline phosphatase Acid phosphatase 5'-Nucleotidase Phosphodiesterase Deoxyribonuclease Ribonuclease 1 Adenosine triphosphatase Amylase Hyaluronidase NAD-Nucleotidase Kininogenase Factor-X activator Heparinase α-Fibrinogenase β-Fibrinogenase α-β-Fibrinogenase Fibrinolytic enzyme Prothrombin activator Collagenase Elastase	All species Elapidae, Viperidae Elapidae Bothrops atrox Deinagkistrodon acutus All species All species All species All species All species All species All species All species Viperidae Viperinae, Crotalinae Crotalinae Viperinae, Crotalinae Viperinae, Crotalinae Bitis gabonica Crotalinae Crotalinae Viperidae Viperidae
4. Lyases	Glucosamine ammonium lyase	

△ ABOVE: Illus. 1. Main enzymes present in snake venom

◁ LEFT: Gaboon viper (Bitis gabonica) with semierect fangs and a venom drop

enzymatic activity, but have been characterized by their biological actions, which can be spectacular.

As early as 1949, it was proved that an enzyme from the Bothrops venom produces an |Ë| vaso-dilatation, resulting from the production of a hypotensor neuropeptide, bradykinin, in the animal bitten. The study of this enzyme's pharmacological properties has led to the discovery of a very important system for the control of arterial pressure in man, the characterization of bradykinin, and the understanding of its in vivo production by kallikrein from an inactive precursor, kininogene.

Another very well known example is that of nerve growth factor (NGF), which indexes the differentiation of sensory neurons in sympathetic ganglia. It was discovered by Cohen and Levi-Montalchini and won them a Nobel prize. NGF is very abundant in the venom of some Elapidae and Viperidae, and in the salivary glands of some non-venomous animals, like the male mouse.

There is yet another group of proteins and enzymes in venom, important both numerically and pharmacologically, interfering with blood coagulation (see the table on hemostasis and plasmatic coagulation mechanisms). These enzymes and proteins have no enzymatic activity and function as activators or inhibitors of blood coagulation. They are characterized by specific actions in certain blood coagulation factors (Illus. 1) and many are used as therapeutic or diagnostic tools. These proteins and enzymes, which are particularly abundant in Viperidae, are responsible for the highly feared effects these venom have on hemostasis.

▶ The main toxins

Snake venoms are rich in toxins that can kill or immobilize prey. Table 2 shows the main ones. A large number of these work by disrupting the nerve-impulse transmission between nerves and muscles (see Illus. 2). In other words, many venoms are paralyzing (see also the table concerning neuromuscular transmission mechanism). Each venom does not contain all of the neurotoxins shown in Table 2, but may possess a number of them, which then act synergetically. For example, krait venom contains curarizing α-bungarotoxins, which block neuromuscular transmission at a postsynaptic level by preventing the link between acetylcholine and its muscular receptor, and of the presynaptic neurotoxins that alter the liberation of acetylcholine by the nerve endings (Illus. 2).

Many consider that the Elapidae venom's lethal power is due to its neurotoxins' paralyzing actions, while that of Viperidae venom is linked to its actions on the cardiovascular system and on hemostasis (Tables 1 and 2). There are too many exceptions for this to be considered a rule. Although certain paralyzing neurotoxins such as the curarizing α-neurotoxins are characteristic in Elapidae venom, others that are just as powerful, like the presynaptic β-neurotoxins, are found in both Viperidae and Elapidae venom.

greatly from one species to the next. The complexity and composition of snake venoms and their great variability explain the huge diversity of their biological effects.

▶ The enzymes

Snake venoms contain a large number of enzymes (see Illus. 1). They are rich in hydrolithic enzymes (A$_2$ phospholipases, nucleases, peptidases, etc.), which play an important role in digesting prey. It has often been observed that an animal killed by snakebite decomposes quite rapidly. Some venom enzymes can also contribute to the toxic effect. Certain neurotoxins in particular, like crotoxin or β-bungarotoxin, have an A$_2$ phospholipase activity, while certain enzymes increase the venom toxins' pharmacological effects.

▶ Biologically active but nontoxic proteins

Snake venoms contain proteins that are characterized by their biological properties. They can be toxic at high doses, and sometimes include an

PHARMACOLOGICAL TOOLS & MEDICINES

FROM SNAKE VENOM

Since antiquity, man has tried to use snake venom

HEMOSTASIS & PLASMATIC COAGULATION MECHANISMS

IN THE CASE OF a vascular lesion, three systems interact to stop bleeding (hemostasis): the vascular walls, the blood platelets, and the plasmatic coagulation factors.

A vascular lesion leads to a reflex contraction of the muscles, the liberation of the "tissue factor" by the endothelial cells which line the vessel walls, and to the contact between the subendothelial structures and the blood. The blood platelets adhere to the exposed structures and are activated. This is seen by their changed shape and the liberation of some substances which maintain and amplify this phenomenon. These first events, called primary hemostasis, help to seal the vascular gap by platelet aggrega-

tion and the triggering of the chain of activities that lead to plasmatic coagulation.

The subendothelial surfaces exposed at departure point are called intrinsic, for they call on factors found in the blood. The triggering of the tissue factor by the injured endothelial cells sets off the extrinsic mechanism.

The modification of the platelets' membrane while they aggregate leads to the formation of characteristic sites on which the principal factors of plasmatic coagulation are activated.

These plasmatic factors exist in an inactive form in the blood. They are activated during a chain of activations that has a con-

siderable amplification potential, as each activated factor is an enzyme able to activate a number of others. It is convenient to differentiate three stages in this avalanche of reactions:
1. The formation of activated X factor (Xa) from inactive X factor, which can be done either intrinsically or extrinsically;
2. The formation of thrombin from prothrombin by Xa;
3. Finally, the conversion of fibrinogen into fibrin by thrombin; fibrin polymerizes to form the long fibres which constitute the blood clot by shutting around the blood cells.

Illus 1: "Flow chart" showing enzymatic activation leading to plasmatic coagulation

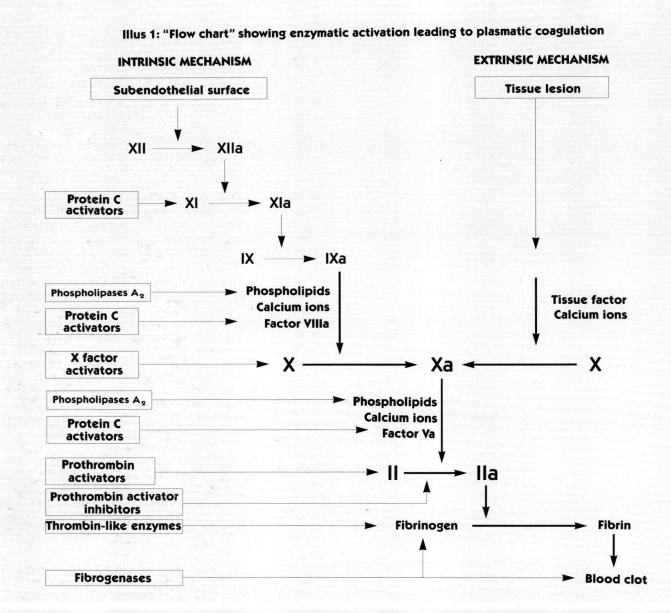

Class	Examples	Means of Action
α-Neurotoxins	α-Bungarotoxin, α-toxin, erabutoxin, cobrotoxin	Block neuromuscular transmission by linking, like curare, onto the cholinergic receptor found on the skeletal muscle fibres.
κ-Toxins	κ-Toxin	Blocks some of the central nervous system's cholinergic receptors.
β-Neurotoxins	Notexin, ammodytoxin, β-bungarotoxin, crotoxin, taipoxin	Block neuromuscular transmission by keeping nerve ends from liberating acetylcholine. Could interact with a potassium canal sensitive to voltage.
Dendrotoxins	Dendrotoxin, toxins I and K	Increase amount of acetylcholine liberated by nerve ends. Could interact with a potassium canal sensitive to voltage.
Cardiotoxins	γ-Toxin, cardiotoxin, cytotoxin	Disturb the plasma membranes of some cells (cardiac fibres, excitable cells . . .) and lead to their lysis. Lead to cardiac arrest.
Sarafotoxins	Sarafotoxins a, b, and c	Powerful vasoconstrictors affecting the cardiac system as a whole. Lead to cardiac arrest.
Myotoxins	Myotoxin-a, crotamine	Lead to muscular degeneration by interacting with a sodium canal dependent on voltage.
	Phospholipase A$_2$	Leads to muscular degeneration.
Hemorragines	Mucrotoxin A, hemorragic toxins, a, b, c . . ., HT1, HT2	Lead to very serious hemorrhages by altering the vessel walls.

△ *ABOVE: Table III: Main toxins in snake venom*

for his own good. Aristotle, Hippocrates, and Pliny wrote about the multiplicity of its effects, and Galen regularly used venoms as therapeutic agents. At the time, the totality of the venomous snake, including its venom, was used in many preparations. Whether ground or macerated, the animal was supposed to transmit the properties attributed to its venom to the liquid in which it sat. Viper alcohol, still used in some rural areas, is one such example.

Biochemical and pharmacological analysis of snake venoms performed during the past three or four decades has shown their tremendous richness in enzymes, toxins, and biologically active substances, as well as the great diversity of their actions. This has led to numerous studies attempting to use their constituent parts as biochemical or pharmacological tools or even as therapeutic or diagnostic aids.

▶ *α-neurotoxins & cholinergic receptors*
The α-neurotoxins in Elapidae venom are polypeptides that selectively link on acetylcholine's muscular receptor (Illus. 2), a remarkable factor that has been used to characterize this receptor and study its structural and functional properties. These neurotoxins have also become famous through a study of Erb-Golflam's disease (myasthenia gravis), which is characterized by a weakness of the skeletal muscles. It was first shown that the muscles of patients suffering from some forms of this disease did not fix enough α-neurotoxins, as if they had too few cholinergic receptors. It was then shown that animals immunized with purified cholinergic receptors developed a similar sickness, suggesting that myasthenia gravis was an autoimmune model and providing a model to study it.

Although there is still much work to do before the causes of this disease are really understood and prevented, the α-neurotoxins are radioactively marked and used to measure the anticholinergic receptors' antibodies in afflicted patients and to follow their evolution.

▶ *Hypotensing peptides*
Many snake venoms contain polypeptides that can cause a drop in arterial tension. These were discov-

▷ *RIGHT: Asp viper conserved in alcohol*

NEUROMUSCULAR TRANSMISSION MECHANISM

THE MUSCULAR CONTRACTION command is brought about by specialized cells, the motoneurons, whose cellular substance is found in the bone marrow. Motoneurons emit a prolongation, the axon, whose ramified extremity enters into contact with a number of specialized structures, the synapses, represented in Illus. 2, below. The group of axons constitutes the nerve, and the group of muscular fibres, the muscle.

The nerve impulse travels the cellular substance's axon to its synaptic extremity, but is not directly transmitted to the muscular fibre. The nerve signal's passage from nerve to muscle is done through a chemical substance, acetylcholine. It is synthesized by the nerve ending and stored in the synaptic vesicle. The nerve impulse which invades the nerve ending liberates a small amount of acetylcholine, which is diffused into the synaptic space between nerve ending and muscular fibre, and then links with a specific receptor, the cholinergic receptor. This interaction gives rise to a depolarization which is responsible for forming a potential muscle action that is propagated along the fibre and leads to its contraction. Acetylcholine is then hydrolized into choline and acetate by the enzyme acetylcholinesterase; both substances will be used in its resynthesis.

Snake venoms contain neurotoxins that intervene at different levels in this series of events (see Table 2 and Illus. 1). Some presynaptic toxins, the β-neurotoxins, block the neuromuscular transmission by inhibiting the liberation of acetylcholine. Others, like dendrotoxins, help transmission by increasing the amount of acetylcholine liberated at each nerve impulse. α-neurotoxins inhibit acetylcholine from linking with its muscular receptor. Finally, the acetylcholinesterase inhibitors (fasciculins) cause muscle contractions by prolonging acetylcholine's action, and the venom acetylcholinesterase hydrolizes the neurotransmitter.

▽. *BELOW: Illus 2. Schema of neuromuscular transmission (location of action of principal serpent venom neurotoxins)*

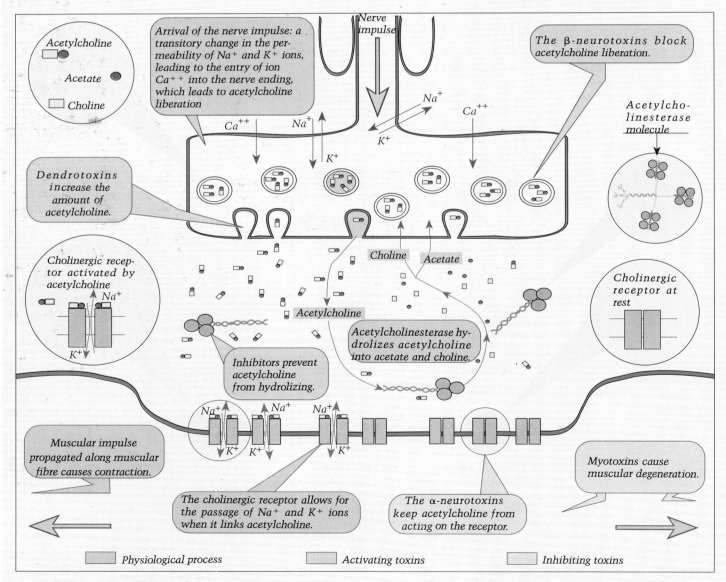

▷ RIGHT: *Fer-de-lance* (Bothrops lanceolatus)

ered in 1948 and studied throughout the 1950s and 1960s as potential adjuncts in treating hypertension. They have served as models for the synthesis of some excellent medicines which are used to treat some hypertensions. The venom peptides act by inhibiting the enzyme responsible for the conversion of angiotensin I, which is inactive, into angiotensin II, the active form, and have contributed greatly to the discovery of this physiological system.

▶ *Venom components & blood coagulation*
Snake venoms, especially those of the Viperidae, are rich in substances (often enzymes) that act specifically on certain stages of the rush of enzymatic action leading to blood coagulation. (See Illus. 1 and the table concerning hemostasis and plasmatic coagulation mechanisms.) Some of them are used as diagnostic tools to evaluate the working order of these mechanisms.

The X factor blood coagulation activator,

which is abundant in Russell's viper (*Daboia russellii*), makes it possible to measure directly the amount of X factor in a patient's blood. It is commonly used to diagnose certain hereditary troubles in coagulation and to measure the efficiency of orally taken anticoagulant drugs.

The thrombin-like enzyme of *Bothrops atrox*'s venom, batroxobine, sold under the name Reptilase®, allows for the detection and measurement of a patient's fibrinogen, even when the patient is treated with an anticoagulant like heparin.

A protein C activator has been purified from the venom of the water moccasin (*Agkistrodon piscivorus*). Sold under the name Protac®, it allows for the measurement of protein C, a deficiency of which is often associated with an abnormally high risk of vascular thrombosis.

In fact, out of three simple tests designed by hematologists to explore the good working order of blood coagulation, three are directly derived from substances with a serpentine origin.

TREATING ENVENOMIZATIONS, & ANTIVENOM SERUMS

Venomous snake bites are a medical, social, and economic problem in many tropical countries, especially in developing countries with a high rural population, poorly served by doctors. About a century ago, Albert Calmette showed that it was possible to immunize an animal against snake venom and prepared the first antivenom serum, showing that the immunized animal's serum could save a second animal bitten by the same snake. This study was the starting point of modern antivenom serotherapy, which is still the way snake bites are treated.

At first glance, the best strategy in antivenom serotherapy consists of preparing a specific serum against all venomous snakes. Since there are over 400 species of such snakes, many of which live in the same region, it is often difficult to identify the biter. A polyvalent serum, efficient against all the species of a certain region, is thus much more useful than a series of monovalent serums. But the complexity of these venoms causes the serum to lose potency and efficiency with each additional species it is purportedly effective against. So a compromise must be made between polyvalence and protective efficiency, and it is sometimes necessary to prepare a number of polyvalent serums to "cover" a single region.

Choosing an antivenom serum is relatively simple in Europe, where most of them are prepared with venom from the asp viper (*Vipera aspis*), the European adder (*Vipera berus*), and the long-nosed viper (*Vipera ammodytes*). The situation is not always so simple, especially when the venomous herpetofauna's distribution is more complex, as is the case in central Africa, Central America, and southeast Asia.

In central Africa, some polyvalent serums are directed towards venomous savannah snakes—the puff adder (*Bitis arietans*), the black-necked cobra (*Naja nigricollis*), the black-and-white cobra (*Naja melanoleuca*), the spitting cobra (*Naja mossambica*), the pyramid viper (*Echis pyramidum*), and sometimes the Gaboon viper (*Bitis gabonica*), black mambas (*Dendroaspis polylepis*), green mambas (*D. viridis, D. jamesoni, D. augisticeps*). More complete polyvalent serums, targeted towards forest and savannah species, exist, but their effect is milder. Finally, since most bites in the African savannah come from the various *Echis* species, monovalent serums exist, but their efficiency is strictly limited to these species.

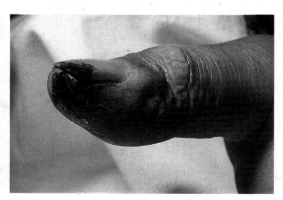

◁ FAR LEFT: *Palestinian viper (Daboia palestinae)*

◁ NEAR LEFT: *Bite by a Palestinian viper. The necrosis is clearly visible on the fingertip.*

▷ RIGHT: *Butantan Institute, São Paulo, Brazil*

In another area, new molecular biology techniques (cellular and protein engineering) that allow for the isolation of the protein-coding gene and, after genetic recombination, have this protein produced by a microorganism or by cultured cells, should now let us study rare proteins in venom and/or analyze the venom constituents that are difficult to obtain in sufficient quantities, as is the case in certain aglyphous and opistoglyphous snakes.

From another point of view, important progress may be made to improve the protective power of present-day antivenom serums. The animal serum now used for antivenom serums contains a majority of antibodies for proteins other than those in the venom, even when these animals are hyperimmunized. It is possible to significantly increase the protective power of an antivenom serum by purifying the antibodies which specifically recognize the venom's protein.

▽ BELOW: *Instituto Vital (Niteroi, Brazil); room with individual cages*

LATOXAN, A VENOM "FACTORY"

Yannick Vasse, *after Rudy Fourmy*

LATOXAN, a laboratory for the production of animal toxins, was created in 1982 in Rosans, in the French Alps, and is still there. Started at first in a renovated mill—now the home of many scorpions—since 1986 it occupies larger quarters, with an auditorium, a boiler room, a laboratory, a hymenopter room, and various areas for raising animals.

The 1000 to 1200 venomous snakes are stored in small low plastic boxes that pile up like drawers and that are usually translucent except for the boxes holding the shyer species. There is one snake per box. The larger boxes measure $15 \times 24 \times 6$ in. ($40 \times 60 \times 15$ cm); the smaller ones (around 12 in. [30 cm]) are for snakes measuring less than 3 ft. (1 m), although these snakes obviously lack exercise.

Species held are chosen according to client demand and influenced by competition. Most snakes are from Africa and the Middle East, especially *Echis, Dendrosapis,* and *Naja,* and there are few *Crotalus* (U.S. operations are extremely competitive) or *Bothrops* (raised by Pentapharm in Brazil).

The snakes are usually bought from indigenous hunters or hunted by Latoxan employees when the need is particularly great. Laboratories occasionally exchange snakes with each other.

Upon arrival, the animals' various characteristics are recorded (species, weight, sex, eating habits, etc.). They are quarantined, and any parasites, internal and external, are eliminated, followed by an antibiotic therapy. Once they are in satisfactory condition, they are taken to the breeding area.

No one is allowed to visit this area—only a few rare clients are allowed into an exhibit room. Showers are mandatory for those who enter the breeding areas. Employees wear a special outfit and boots, which are changed twice a day and must be rinsed from room to room.

For sanitary reasons, rooms must be entered in a prescribed order, and this order may not be departed from.

Strict hygiene and competence account for a large part of the good working order and success of such an operation. Employees must control temperatures, clean, inspect the snakes' food, water, and heating, and take daily care of mouse- and rat-breeding.

The snakes are fed every two to four with dead prey (chicks, mice, rats), but live prey is substituted if the former aren't accepted.

Drinking troughs are available one day per week, with acidified water (pH 4) to inhibit the development of bacteria such as the bacilla *Pseudomas aeruginosa,* responsible for many reptilian infections, such as the buccal canker.

Litter and boxes are disinfected entirely every two weeks.

Reproduction is sometimes sought, especially in the Egyptian cobra (*Naja haje*), the long-nosed viper (*Vipera ammodytes*), and the fer-de-lance (*Bothrops atrox*). One room is devoted to eggs and babies. If the young refuse to feed, they are fed with egg-dipped baby mice.

Venom is only sampled once the snakes are two years old. There are different methods, according to the fangs' morphology. It is usually done manually in Elapidae (gland compression and massage), electrically in Viperidae and mambas (gland compression is obtained by the use of two electrodes), and collected in small cannulas for opistoglyphs and small-fanged Elapidae; the latter method yields only a small amount of venom.

The venom is frozen at $-58°F$ ($-50°C$), lyophilized, and ground into a powder. It is kept at $-58°F$ ($-50°C$), away from light, and packed.

Price varies as to the amount of venom produced and the species. Snakes bred in this manner produce more venom than do those in nature; they are bigger, and their glands are more developed, since the snakes are handled so often.

△ *ABOVE: Catching a rattlesnake (*Crotalus durissus*), in Brazil*

The interval between venom samplings depends on the laboratory. At Pentapharm (Brazil), it is 28 days, which allows for a 60% reconstitution of the glands' initial contents; at Latoxan, it is usually adapted to the species and may be as short as 14 days, but the yield seems to be higher. At the Pasteur Institute in Casablanca it is daily, but the snake's life is shortened. This frequency is habitual in developing countries.

Venom quality imposes certain guarantees, and the Latoxan label fulfills three criteria: authenticity (which implies knowledge of the species), purity (obtained by a sampling method adapted to the species in question), and biological activity (which is preserved by low temperature).

Buying laboratories usually get crude venom. It is lyophilized and contains a multitude of different proteins. In fact, the integral venom is rarely necessary; rather it is a single protein with a particular action, which is usually isolated from the Latoxan

venom, sequenced and synthesized. Pure toxins, such as neurotoxins isolated from the *Naja nigricollis* venom, are also sold, but their production costs are high. Venom, or fractions thereof, have a number of uses: antivenom serum, pharmaceuticals, and for fundamental and applied research.

This highly specialized production, which subjects snakes to high concentrations of individuals, faces a number of pathological risks. These reptiles are highly sensitive to infections and there are germs of many origins.

Ultraviolet rays are often used to decontaminate water, utensils, and the atmosphere, but their yield is low. While they do limit germ transport, they do not sterilize. Many other measures (treating the animals, quarantine for the newly arrived, acidifying the water, rigorous precautions taken by the handlers, stringent cleaning of the cages) help to limit these risks.

To avoid eventual disease proliferation,

symptomatic animals are isolated or killed if they threaten the health of other snakes.

This strict hygiene also has some drawbacks: loss of time, cost, natural immunity inhibition, genetic mutations of germs that become resistant to antibiotics.

Employees must perform high-risk handlings daily. Although everything is done to facilitate such operations, employees aren't totally protected from accidents, although these are rare. Security measures are automatic for the handlers, who know that there is no room for error in this profession. The accident's severity depends on the speed and quality of the care administered.

In the long run, fumes from the disinfection products and techniques may lead to human respiratory trouble. The venom microparticles that are suspended in the air are harmful and can lead to hypersensitivity; the employee would then have allergic-type reactions to respiratory or cutaneous contact with venom.

▽ BELOW: *Dehydrated snake venom in flasks*

BITTEN BY *BOTHROPS MOOJENI*

Patrick David

WHEN READ FROM a medical point of view, this story of the dramatic consequences of a Viperidae bite on a young Brazilian and of his lengthy hospitalization shows us how dangerous the consequences of snakebite can be.

In 1963, in southeast Brazil, a 10-year-old boy was walking on some grass when he was bitten. The snake was killed and identified as *Bothrops moojeni*, locally known as "caissaca."

It was a subadult snake measuring 31½ in. (80 cm). The bite was located on the external side of the boy's right leg, a little above the ankle, and the envenomization was by both fangs.

During the seconds following the bite, the child felt a great pain and a burning sensation where he had been bitten. Blood erupted from both fang holes, but the bleeding stopped spontaneously after a few minutes. At the same time, a purple bruise (indicating that blood was spreading subcutaneously) appeared around the bite, while edema (swelling of the tissues due to the infiltration of bodily liquid) started developing.

About five minutes after the bite, the victim felt unwell, had vision trouble, and fainted. He came to a few minutes later, had cold sweats, nausea, and dizziness (these symptoms were probably accompanied by modifications in the arterial pressure, which was not measured due to a lack of equipment). Reclining and surrounded by the villagers, the young boy remained nauseated and vomiting.

Half an hour after the bite, the bruise had spread to about 4 in. (10 cm). An erythema (red cutaneous congestion) appeared around the bruise and over a large part of the leg. The bite's immediate region, which was rigid and extremely painful, turned blue. The edema had now reached the foot and the calf.

The victim was visited by a doctor about 15 minutes later. The wound was disinfected and a camphor-based cardiotonic administered. The dizzy spells stopped and the child was fully conscious, but he had a fever and strong abdominal pains. Arterial pressure was quite low, around 8. The pain was intense and the child was on the verge of fainting a number of times. His heartbeat reached 130/minute. The doctor put a tight bandage over the entire leg but no tourniquet.

An hour after the bite, the edema felt hard under shiny skin and had reached the knee. The leg had virtually doubled in volume. The bandage, which would by then have acted as a tourniquet, was removed, and the doctor decided to hospitalize the child. During the trip, the child became nauseated and dizzy again. His temperature rose to over 103°F (39.5°C).

After a four-hour car trip, the patient reached the hospital. He was immediately given a perfusion of glucosed saline, and penicillin was administered.

By the sixth hour, the edema had reached the middle of the thigh, and the purple bruise spread to a large part of the leg's external side (see picture). Analgesics were administered and a serotherapy begun, using 50 ml of "Antibotropico" serum from Instituto Butantan (São Paulo); the correct serum, administered by slow perfusion, remains the most active treatment in severe cases.

By the ninth hour the boy's general state seemed slightly improved, although fever and abdominal pains persisted.

After 20 hours an abundant nosebleed, stopped by local compression, appeared, as did some less drastic hemorrhages around the gums.

Blood analyses showed a Disseminated Intravascular Coagulation syndrome (DIVC) with fibrogen consumption, lowered plasma level, lowered platelet count, and increased bleeding time. The boy was given sedatives.

After 21 hours, hypertension, probably due to pain, appeared. The fever persisted.

During the night, 30 ml more of serum was administered and well tolerated by the patient. While the bruise spread, 5 phlyctens (large cutaneous vesicles filled with blood and serum), two of which reached ¾ in. (2 cm) in diameter, formed above the envenomization site.

◁ *LEFT:* Bothrops moojeni

The edema reached its maximal extension about 20 hours after the bite. The entire limb remained quite painful, quite hot, and very hard. The bitten area turned a brownish purple with a diameter of 2 in. (5 cm) soon after. Once the patient had spent a relatively calm night, the phlyctenes were lanced, emptied, and disinfected. The fever decreased somewhat by the second morning. The edema was still present, but the skin was not stretched so tight.

During the second day the perilesional area, brownish-purple, spread over about 4 in. (10 cm), and the patient's gums bled. Fever and abdominal pain persisted. Antibiotic treatments were continued.

By the evening of the third day, the perilesional area turned browner. Local disinfection was started. A cutaneous erosion appeared, followed by lymphatic oozing and finally necrosis, the destruction of superficial and deeper tissues, which turned brown and smelled putrid. The necrosis continued for the following six days despite regular antibiotic applications. The fever stabilized at 101.3°F (38.5°C), and the other symptoms (dizzy spells, cold sweats) disappeared.

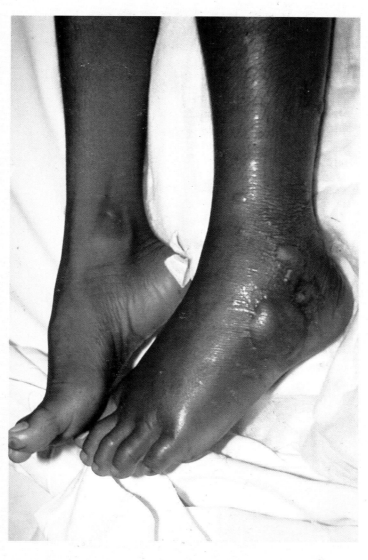

◁ LEFT: *Leg, six hours after* Bothrops moojeni *bite*

No surgical abscission of the necrotic tissues was attempted. Nor did the doctor perform a discharge fasciotomy. This operation, which consists of a longitudinal incision in the conjunctive tissues of the affected muscles may limit necrosis, but the risk of infection and hemorrhage was too great.

By the eighth day, the boy's general state improved despite a low and constant fever. The blood coagulation parameters were virtually normal. The extensive local edema decreased although the necrosis was still spreading, both in area and in depth.

This necrosis was only circumscribed after about ten days. By then it had spread over a large part of the leg's postero-external area. The fasciotomy was now possible. The operation is dangerous for healthy tissues when healthy and unhealthy tissue cannot be totally differentiated, since any alteration of healthy tissue must be avoided.

The operation was carried out on the twelfth day and revealed extensive depth. The ankle articulation was not cankered, but was severely inflamed due to the venom.

Local care was taken—antibiotic therapy to prevent gangrene—until the eighteenth day after the bite, although the edema was completely resorbed by the fifteenth day. A skin graft was decided on and successfully carried out in the fourth week.

The child left the hospital after forty-eight days and had a large and deep scar, an atrophy with weakness of the involved muscles, and a rigidity of the ankle. He will keep a pronounced limp and partial infirmity.

A description of this bite necessitates some comments.

This is a relatively old case ('60s) and it occurred in an area with little medical care, although the victim was very intensively taken care of.

The serum dose, which is the only truly efficient treatment in case of a dangerous bite, must depend on the amount of venom injected. This child only received 80 ml, which is little, considering the severe and early responses to the envenomization (hypotension, edema extension, coagulation trouble). Furthermore, children, by virtue of being small, often have worse snakebite syndromes, since the venom is only diluted in a small volume of blood.

Finally, this envenomization should not be taken as typical of *Bothrops*. Within a single genus, the composition of venom can vary from species to species. All *Bothrops* species have a venom that acts on coagulation, leading to a DIVC, which is more or less typical, depending on the dose and composition of the venom, and causing serious local necrosis.

Within a single species, the snake's age, size, and physical condition can make a difference. The venom of many *Bothrops* species has clearly hemolytic actions beyond proteolytic and cytolytic ones already discussed. This is true of *Bothrops atrox*, from South America.

PRINCIPAL ACTIONS OF VENOMS & THEIR SYMPTOMS

Patrick David

THE COMPLEXITY OF SNAKE venoms makes a precise, species-by-species description of each venom's action and symptoms difficult.

Yet these actions can be classified in four areas:
inflammatory;
attacks on cells and tissues;
attacks on the nervous system;
attacks on blood circulation.

Venoms are a complex mix of toxins and enzymes, with numerous targets. To further complicate matters, a venom's composition varies qualitatively and, especially, quantitatively, within a same species, according to populations or individuals, as well as the animal's size and age. Other factors influencing the effect of the poison on man include the amount of venom injected, as well as the victim's age and general health.

A specific venom always has a number of effects and thus leads to simultaneous symptoms of varying intensity.

The main genera or species generally, but not always, are responsible for the symptoms described below. The same taxon will be mentioned a number of times due to the venoms' multiple effects.

This four-part classification can only be considered a simplified, nonexhaustive summary of venom's clinical effects.

I. Inflammatory symptoms

▷ *Principal causes*
component increasing vascular walls' permeability to plasma;
a component which directly induces inflammation;
autoinflammatory reaction of the tissues.

▷ *Consequences*
sharp local pain;
appearance of an edema where the person was bitten that may extend over the bitten limb and to the trunk;
shock (hypotension) and collapse; ultimately followed by cardiac arrest.

▷ *Taxons involved:*
Practically every species in the Viperidae family (Viperinae and Crotalinae), as well as some Elapidae (*Naja atra, Naja mossambica, Pseudechis* sp).

▷ *Remarks:* The edema is often the first symptom noticed, after pain, when a person is bitten by a Viperidae. The edema may be large (*Daboia* sp., *Causus* sp., *Cro-*

talus sp., *Bothrops* sp., for example), or relatively small (for populations belonging to the genus *Echis*).

II. Effects on cells and tissues (cytotoxicity)

A. Hemmorrhagic symptoms

▷ *Principal causes:* Cytotoxins altering or destroying blood vessels walls. Of course, the intensity of the hemorrhage depends on the coagulation problems described in paragraph IV.

▷ *Consequences:*
sharp local pain;
local hemmorrhages: bruises, blisters, or hemorrhagic vesicles, unstoppable bleeding from the fang holes;
internal-organ hemorrhages. Depending on the intensity of coagulation problems described in paragraph IV, these may lead to hemorrhagic shock.

▷ *Taxons responsible: Vipera* sp., *Daboia* sp., *Bitis* sp., *Cerastes* sp., *Echis* sp., *Crotalus* sp., *Bothrops* sp., *Calloselasma rhodostoma, Deinagkistrodon acutus, Trimeresurus* sp., etc.

B. Attack on cutaneous, muscular and conjunctive tissues

1) *Tissue destruction (cytolysis)*
▷ *Principal causes:*
certain myotoxins;
proteolytic enzymes in particular.
▷ *Consequences:*
extreme, often unbearable pain;
destruction of tissues, leading to necrosis, whether deep or superficial, dry or putrid, small or extensive;
myoglobinuria.

▷ *Taxons responsible: Daboia* sp., *Bitis* sp., *Cerastes* sp., *Echis* sp., *Agkistrodon* sp., *Bothrops* sp., *Calloselasma rhodostoma, Trimeresurus flavoviridis, Naja pallida, Naja mossambica, Naja atra, Naja kaouthia* (*Naja naja* more or less frequently), *Pseudechis* sp.

2) *Alteration of the skeletal muscles*
▷ *Principal causes:* Various types of myotoxins which alter cell walls.
▷ *Consequences:*
violent muscle pain;
muscular degeneration;
myoglobinuria, kidney failure;
paralysis due to muscular failure.
▷ *Taxons responsible: Notechis* sp., *Oxyruanus* sp., *Hydrophis* sp., *Enhydrina*

schistosa, Daboia russelli, Bothrops sp., *Crotalus durissus, Crotalus scutatus.*

▷ *Consequences:* These muscular alterations generally do not involve necroses, and their causes and mechanics are different from those responsible for tissue destruction. This myotoxicity (rhabdomyolysis) is characteristic of Hydrophinae (marine snake) bites.

C. Alteration of cardiac cells (cardiotoxicity)

▷ *Main causes:* Various cardiotoxins alter the cell walls of the cardiac muscle.

▷ *Consequences:* Arhythmia, tachycardia, violent contractions of the heart, cardiac arrest;
vasoconstrictions, cardiac arrest.

▷ *Taxons responsible: Naja nigricollis, Pseudechis* sp., *Atractaspis* sp.

▷ *Remarks:* These are characteristic effects of *Atractaspis* bites.

D. Alteration of blood cells (hemotoxicity)

▷ *Main causes:* Cytotoxins alter red blood cells' membrane.

▷ *Consequences:*
alteration of the red blood cells;
circulatory shock, postponed collapses, anemia;
kidney failure.

▷ *Taxons responsible: Rhabdophis tigrinus, Daboia russelli, Demansia* sp., *Pseudechis* sp., *Crotalus* sp. (especially *C. durissus*), *Bothrops* sp., (*B. atrox* in particular).

III. Actions on the nervous system (neurotoxicity)

A. Blocking the nerve impulse

▷ **Main cause 1:**
Presynaptic toxins, which inhibit the emission of neurotransmitters.

Responsible taxons: Bungarus multicinctus, Micrurus sp., *Notechis* sp., *Oxyuranus scutellatus, Pseudonaja* sp., *Laticauda* sp., *Bitis gabonica* (certain populations), *Crotalus durissus, Crotalus scutalatus.*

▷ **Main cause 2:** Postsynaptic toxins, which inhibit the fixing of neurotransmitters.

▷ *Taxons responsible: Naja haje, Naja naja, Naja nigricollis, Bungarus* sp., *Acanthophis* sp., *Notechis* sp., *Hydrophis* sp.,

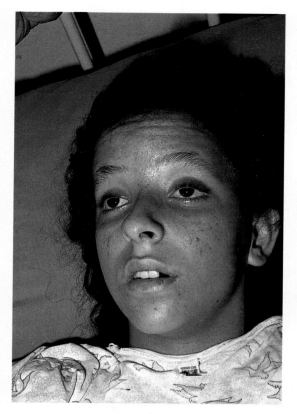

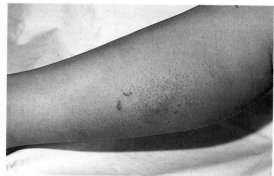

◁ LEFT: This 15-year-old Brazilian girl was bitten on the cheek (two hours before this photo was taken) by a tropical snake (Crotalus durissus terrificus). Note the bilateral ptosis (drooping eyelids), quite noticeable here, since the patient was trying to follow her doctor's hand (above and to the left of the photo). Also note the wrinkling of the eyebrows (due to contraction of the frontal muscle), due to the effort by the girl to raise her paralyzed eyelids. Finally, note the facial paralysis (cranial nerve VII), and the girl's inability to close her mouth. This girl was treated with a species-specific antivenin serum less than one hour after having been bitten. Twenty-one hours after the bite, the ptosis remained, along with myoglobinuria, resulting in a generalized rhabdomyolysis. Four days later, her ptosis and the "myopathic" appearance of her face had completely disappeared.

◁ LEFT: The area of the bite two hours after the accident described above. On the right can be seen the fangs' puncture marks, oozing blood. On the left, numerous bites made by the snake's mandibular teeth. There is a slight erythema, but almost no inflammation.

Lapernis sp., Enhydrina schistosa, Laticauda sp.

▷ Consequences: In both cases, there is a progressive paralysis of the skeletal muscles and face, leading to death by asphyxiation. The pain may be moderate.

▷ Remarks: Neurotoxic actions are characteristic of Elapidae, Hydrophinae and Crotalus durissus terrificus.

B. Stimulation of the nerve impulse

▷ Main causes: Neurotoxins enhance the emission of neurotransmitters.

▷ Consequences:
muscular tetany, spasms, excessive salivation.
paralysis due to the contraction of skeletal muscles, death by asphyxiation.

▷ Taxons responsible: All Dendroaspis species, the mambas.

▷ Remarks: These symptoms are characteristic of mamba bites.

IV. Actions on blood circulation (coagulopathies)

▷ Main causes: A number of components, toxins and enzymes, with pro-coagulant and anticoagulant actions, which alter the coagulation chain according to complex processes, depending on the amount of venom injected, the area of injection (subcutaneous, intramuscular, intravenous) and other factors.

A single venom often contains antagonistic elements, both pro- and anti-coagulants, but the result is generally a reduced, sometimes nonexistent coagulation factor.

▷ Consequences: Varied effects on blood coagulation, from pure fibrinolysis and total incoagulability, to thrombosis (rare), and DIVC syndrome (disseminated intravascular coagulation) whence:
formation of blood clots, leading to necrosis by obstructing vessels (local thromboses) or to embolisms; and:
more-or-less pronounced blood incoagulability, with local hemorrhaging (with symptoms like those described in paragraph II.A), or general hemorrhaging, leading to the formation of bruises far from the area bitten, and internal hemorrhaging, especially in the cerebral area.

▷ Responsible taxons: Disphodilus typus, Rhabdophis tigrinus, Vipera sp., Daboia sp., Bitis sp., Cerastes sp., Echis sp., Crotalus sp., Agkistrodon sp., Bothrops sp., Calloselasma rhodostoma, Deinagkistrodon Notechis sp., Oxyuranus scutellatus.

acutus, Trimeresurus sp., Pseudechis sp.,

▷ Remarks: Due to the complexity of the coagulopathic symptoms, and to their variability, the precise actions and symptoms cannot be detailed by genera and species.

The coagulation chain is more or less altered, and all combinations between incoagulability and thrombosis, whether local or global, are possible.

Some bites from certain species can lead to profuse hemorrhaging (Distpholidus typus, Echis leucogaster), while dangerous thromboses have been noted from some Crotalus bites.

V. Various actions

Most bites are accompanied by symptoms such as fevers, nausea, headaches, vomiting, sweating, etc., with varying degrees of intensity. They may be due to the causes mentioned above, or to the organism's reactions, such as anxiety.

Secondary infections, which are common in Naja and Bothrops bites, can lead to major complications.

Finally, allergies to venom are one cause of anaphylactic shock and collapse, especially in individuals having been bitten by a number of snakes of the same species.

COMMERCE, LEGISLATION & PROTECTION

Jean Lescure

Habitat destruction is without a doubt the greatest threat to snake populations. Other factors include the use of chemical herbicides or polluting fertilizers, and the introduction of allogeneic species that disturb the ecological balance. And without mentioning the gratuitous massacres that still occur, sampling in the wild for commercial purposes also plays an important role in the decline of many species.

DISTURBED NATURAL ENVIRONMENTS

Starting in the 1950s, Western countries developed, cities grew, suburbs encroached on agricultural lands, highways cut into forests. Agriculture was modernized with pesticides and by the draining of marshes. A balance with nature that had been built over centuries was broken. Affected were the wild fauna and flora—particularly diverse in wooded areas—which had adapted to the human environment.

leads to overexploitation of natural resources, and the local need for food and fuel is quite threatening. Intensive conversion to pasture is dangerous to vegetation, especially in arid zones. Excessive water consumption leads to lower water tables. Gigantic deforestation areas in certain tropical countries lead to the annual disappearance of thousands of acres (hectares) of tropical rain forests (South America, Australia, Indonesia, Madagascar) and of the forests' fauna.

Snakes are usually sold for three purposes: as "domestic" animals (coming from breeding facilities or hobbyists), leather for tanneries, and venom for medical research.

Not only Western and other industrialized nations, but also third-world countries, have increased the exploitation of their natural resources. International commerce and tourism have grown as foreign travel becomes more and more common. Traffic in wild fauna increases dangerously. Thousands of skins from large snakes (pythons, anacondas, boas) have been sent to tanneries. The importation of exotic species has increased, and there has been no hesitation in travelling far to capture rare species.

COMMERCE

There is a huge demand for snakes: each year, tens of thousands of live snakes, millions of skins, and tens of millions of leather products cross borders.

The snakes sold either come from breederies, or have been caught in the wild (which is, according to the WWF, the case in over 95% of the snakes sold since 1985). Capture, breeding, intended use, and commerce are sometimes regulated.

▶ Live snakes
The development of tourism and commerce in the third world are closely linked, and the general result is an organized traffic that jeopardizes wildlife. Unscrupulous "aficionados" have gone so far as to take small endangered Boidae from Round Island (near Mauritius). Experts say that in 1980 traffickers took up to a thousand Schweizer's vipers (*Daboia schweizeri*) off the island of Milos in the Aegean Sea.

Live-snake trade accounts for a much smaller percentage of total trade (2% on average) than that in skins, but involves large numbers nonetheless. In 1985, the United States imported 160,000 live snakes. Since then, having also recognized the hobbyist's predilection for rattlesnakes and other indigenous species, eight American snakes have been placed on the endangered list, which makes both their sale as domestic animals and their export illegal.

Among the 246,000 snakes imported into the United States between 1977 and 1983, most were *Boa constrictors*—over 80% of this species found on the market is destined to the U.S. Others were reticulated pythons (*Python reticulatus*) and rock pythons (*Python molarus*).

▽ BELOW: *The asp viper (*Vipera aspis*) occupies an area in France whose northern limit runs from the mouth of the Loire (the Atlantic) east to Lorraine.*

Some of the snakes sold in the United States were born in captivity, but most were taken in the wild. The live boas came primarily from the forests of Central America, Colombia, and Surinam, but this tendency has now been reversed, as many are born in captivity. Many aficionados are also interested in anacondas as pets.

We lack exact quantitative data on the trade of snakes that are not listed in the Washington Convention. It is well known, however, that African, South American, and Asian countries are the major exporters, while Western Europe, Japan, and the United States do most of the importing.

▶ Data on traffic

The snakes sold usually belong to rare, very localized, or particularly beautiful species. In the U.S., again, reptile traffic once emphasized Mexican species, but many of them now reproduce in captivity, and are thus legally available. There does exist an illegal luxury market for rare Mexican snakes such as the rosy boa (*Lichanura trivirgata roseofusca*). The Australian species *Acantophis pyrrhus*, the Indian rock python (*Python molurus molurus*), Willard's snake (*Crotalus willardi*), the gopher snake (*Drymarchon corais couperi*), and a subspecies of the garter snake (*Thamnophis sirtalis tetrataenia*) in the United States are all trafficked as well.

This trade is not surprising, considering the great profits that can be gained from it. Some confiscated rock pythons must have brought their sellers $500 each on the North American market and would have been sold for up to $2000 each to Japanese and European collectors. Since snakes are "cold-blooded," they travel relatively well, unlike birds and mammals, which die in large quantities under similar transport conditions.

Another problem is what to do with the live captured animals, since most countries lack appropriate storage facilities.

▶ Snake skins & manufactured products

Snake skins, whether untreated or tanned, usually come from Africa, South Asia, and America and are sent to leatherwork manufacturers on the East Coast of the U.S. or in western Europe. This trade may entail crossing numerous borders. Importing countries turn these skins into purses, handbags, shoes, and other goods. Boas, pythons, and the Oriental rat snake (*Ptyas mucosus*) and Acrochordidae are among those sold most often. Over 19,000 rat-snake skins or products made therefrom were imported into the United States in 1984. This species and the careened snake (*Elaphe carinata*), as well as *Cerberus rhynchops*, were the most prevalent on the market in 1985, accounting for 75% of snakeskin imports.

About 100,000 boa-constrictor skins are sold each year, although these snakes are listed in the Second Annex to the Washington Convention.

Among anacondas, the giant *Eunectes murinus* and the yellow anaconda, *Eunectes notaeus*, are also part of a thriving market. In 1985, 14,000 yellow-anaconda skins entered the U.S., coming from Argentina, Bolivia, Panama, and Peru. Many of these snakes were probably illicitly imported from Brazil.

Between 1980 and 1984, some 300,000 reticulated-python skins were exported from Indonesia and Thailand. They went to the U.S. via Singapore, and the U.S. also imported skins directly (50,000 in 1983). France, with its worldwide reputation for leather goods, imported 3600 anaconda (*Eunectes murinus, E. notaeus*) and 63,400 python skins the same year (numbers given to us by the European TRAFFIC bureau).

As is the case with most wildlife trade, the most expensive species are targeted, but, as they are usually protected or extinct, often related and cheaper species take their place. Many small pythons and boas, like the Asian blood python (*Python curtus*), are now pressured by the market: 950 of its skins were sold in 1980, and 58,500 in 1985. This snake is now seriously endangered by overexploitation.

Rock-python (*Python molurus*) trade has also led to various problems. One of its two subspecies, the Indian python (*P. m. molurus*), is listed in the First Annex to the Washington Convention, and thus cannot be sold. The other subspecies (*P. m. bivittatus*), found in southeast Asia, is listed in the Second Annex of the same convention and can only be sold with special authorization.

Very little is known about the African market, although species from there are appreciated by both hobbyists and leather workers. The rock python (*Python sebae*) has been heavily hunted for its skin, probably throughout its distribution area.

Some countries have instituted measures to control snake exports. India, which sold over three million skins between 1976 and 1979, has now outlawed most exports, allowing only for the sale of finished products, and these under government regulation. Sri Lanka has also stopped trade.

Countries that consume snake products still import protected species with the help of traffickers, who are always devising new strategies to transport skins, sometimes going so far as to counterfeit customs documents. Some species, like the rock python, have subspecies that resemble them and cannot be differentiated once the former have been turned into leather products. These animals often enjoy a different status under the Washington Convention, which allows the less scrupulous to avoid certain interdictions.

▶ Aquatic & marine snakes

The worldwide leather industry also slaughters millions of Asiatic aquatic snakes each year. In 1984, Indonesia exported two million Javanese Acrochordidae skins (*Acrochordus javanicus*). In 1985, the U.S. imported $1.4 million worth of karung, the name given to this animal's skin, which is particularly sturdy thanks to its non-covering scales. Another marine snake, *A. granulatus*, which is locally known as calabab, is also affected by this trade. The same year, close to 250,000 worked skins entered the U.S. There is also traffic in marine snakes (Hydrophinae) caught in great quantities in the Philippines for shoes and other accessories and then sold to the U.S. and Europe. In 1974, Philippine divers were catching 450,000 of these snakes a month in the areas surrounding Gato island, leading to the decline of local populations.

Nowadays, divers concentrate on populations surrounding the Celebes. These snakes, which are quite venomous, rarely attack unless provoked, and the divers catch them with their bare hands. The snakes are sold to local tanneries, often for a ridiculously low sum.

The Australian government allows for the sale of snakes caught in fishermen's nets "so as not to waste an otherwise lost resource," but does not allow for the export of these snakes' skins or of products made therefrom.

REGULATIONS: INTERNATIONAL
CONVENTIONS & NATIONAL LEGISLATION

Faced with stronger and stronger pressures on the world's wild flora and fauna, and thus on snakes, international organizations (United Nations Environmental Program, International Union for Nature Conservation), governments, scientists, and a variety of associations have become aware of the problem and have drafted international conventions to combat these pressures, or, at the very least, to save what can still be saved.

▶ *Washington Convention (CITES)*

This convention attempts to protect animal and vegetal species by regulating their international trade. It applies to the movement of live or dead animals, and products derived therefrom, across international borders. The Convention was signed in Washington on March 3, 1973, and has been implemented in 103 countries since 1990, including those of the EEC, which has established regulations for Community enforcement, known as

Annex C2. Protected species are grouped in three categories, known as Annexes, according to the degree of threat facing them.

Annex I

This group's species are threatened with extinction and absolutely cannot be traded. Only imports with a scientific purpose are allowed, and then only within a very specific framework. An import authorization is delivered by the appropriate national administrative bodies upon the advice of scientists. The country of origin then delivers an export authorization. Some snakes are listed in Annex I, like the Indian python, as well as endemic boa species threatened by the destruction of their biotope and native hobbyists' demands: Round Island (*Bolyeria multocarineta, Casarea dussumeria*), Puerto Rico (*Epicrates mununatus*), Jamaica (*E. subflavus*), and Madagascar (*Acrantophis dumerilii, A. madagascariensis, Sanzinia madagascariensis*).

Some of these snakes are part of an approved and regulated breeding program in the Jersey (U.K.) Zoo, where active breeding of threatened species is carried out in the hopes of reintroducing them to their original territories. Some species are contracted out to reliable hobbyists. Raising animals in various locations ensures that no epidemic will lead to the extinction of a threatened species.

Annex II

The species listed here are considered less endangered than those from Annex I. They may be traded across borders only when the country of origin has delivered an export permit, and the receiving country has issued an import permit.

▷ *RIGHT: This particular species of the garter snake,* Thamnophis sirtalis tetrataenia, *is superbly colored and is protected in its San Francisco area habitat.*

PROTECTION

The most efficient protection method for endangered snake species is still the creation of parks and refuges encompassing biotopes. Poland and the Czech Republic have preserved a river valley for the tessellated snake. Smooth snake (*Coronella austriaca*) stations are included in British refuges. In France, a "biotope decree," which is a measure adapted to small areas, has been promulgated to protect the Orsini's snake population in the Ventoux Mountains. The same should be done to help protect *Liophis cursos* in Martinique. All of these laws will be useless if snakes are still pursued and killed with atavistic hatred. Instead of disappearing, these practices are exacerbated by the news of viper "hunts," in which snakes are captured in one country and then flown by helicopter to a neighboring one.

The fear of snakes is very real for a rural society that is itself threatened with extinction. Meanwhile, urban dwellers want their country home to be in an "antiseptic" nature, from which all threats, such as snakes and other animals, have been eliminated. Unfortunately, changing mentalities is an arduous and long-term task, much more so than writing a law and attempting to apply it.

Wild fauna is increasingly threatened all over our planet, and no region is spared. Man *goes* everywhere, and *is* everywhere, directly or indi-

rectly. Acid rain, pollution, and fires are destroying snake habitats. What can be done for snakes' survival, even if they are less loved than pandas, dolphins, turtles, and whales?

The few numbers we have cited show that there is no common measure between the number of live snakes that are bought and raised by hobbyists and that of snake skins sold to leather workers. The worldwide and systematic destruction of any snake found in man's way is even more quantitatively important, but its impact touches on all species. The regulation of international trade by the Washington Convention must be applied in every country and adapted to market fluctuations.

The trade and exchange of captive-born snakes (which are healthier than those found in nature), should be sufficient to provide hobbyists with what they need. Adequately controlled reproduction centers could exist in many more countries.

Snake collecting by hobbyists poses some dangers to snakes—in its search for spectacular, rare species that are difficult to breed in captivity. The increasing rarity of Orsini's viper in certain parts of France is largely due to illegal captures. This traffic must be stopped and hobbyists must understand that threatened snakes may no longer be bought or sold, unless they're certifiably born in captivity.

BIBLIOGRAPHY

BELLAIRS, A. 1971. *Les Reptiles* (2nd part). La Grande Encyclopédie de la Nature, vol. X. Bordas, Paris-Montréal. 378 pp.

BODSON, L. 1984. Living reptiles in captivity: a historical survey from the origins to the end of the XVIIIth century. Pp. 15–32 *in:* BELS, V. & Van den SANDE, A.P., Eds. Maintenance and Reproduction of Reptiles in Captivity. Volume 1. *Acta Zoologica et Pathologica Antverpiensia* No. 78.

BON, C. 1991. Venins de serpents et sérums antivenimeux. *Bull. Soc. Herpét. Fr.*, 57: 1–18.

BRANCH, W.R. 1988. *Field guide to the snakes and other reptiles of southern Africa.* New Holland Publishers, London. 328 pp. 96 pls.

BUREAU OF MEDICINE AND SURGERY, U.S. DEPARTMENT OF THE NAVY (1979)—Anti-venin Sources. *in: Poisonous Snakes of the World,* pp. 169–180, United States Government Printing Office, Washington, D.C.

CAMBELL, J.A. & BRODIE, E.D. Jr., Eds. 1992. *Biology of the Pitvipers.* Selva, Tyler, TX. viii + 467 pp.

CAMPBELL, J.A. & LAMAR, W.W. 1989. *The Venomous Reptiles of Latin America.* Cornell University Press, Ithaca, NY. xii + 425 pp.

CEI, J.M. 1986. *Reptiles del centro, centro-oeste y sur de la Argentina. Herpetofauna de las zonas áridas y semiáridas.* Monografie IV, Museo Regionale di Scienze Naturali, Turin. 527 pp.

CHIPPAUX, J.P. 1986. *Les Serpents de la Guyane Française.* Faune Tropicale XXVII. ORSTOM, Paris. 165 pp.

CHIPPAUX, J.P. & GOYFFON, M. 1983. Producers of antivenoms sera. *Toxicon,* 21: 739–752.

CHRISTENSEN, P.A. 1979. Production and standardization of antivenin. Pp. 825–846. *In:* LEE, C.V., Ed., Snake Venoms. Handbook of Experimental Pharmacology, Vol. 52. Springer-Verlag, Berlin. 1130 p.

COBORN, J. *The Atlas of the Snakes of the World.* T.F.H. Publ., Neptune, NJ. 591 pp.

COGGER, H.G. 1992. *Reptiles and Amphibians of Australia.* 5th ed. Reed Books, Chatswood, NSW, Australia. 775 pp.

CORBETT, K. 1989. *The Conservation of European Reptiles and Amphibians.* C. Helm, London. 274 pp.

COX, M.J. 1991. *The Snakes of Thailand and Their Husbandry.* Krieger Publ. Co., Malabar, FL. xxxviii + 526 pp.

CREWS, D. & GARRICK, L.D. 1980. Methods of Inducing Reproduction in Captive Reptiles. Pp. 49–70 *in:* MURPHY, J.B. & COLLINS, J.T., Eds. *Reproductive Biology and Diseases of Captive Reptiles.* Contrib. Herpetol. No. 1, Society for the Study of Amphibians and Reptiles, Athens, OH.

DEMANGEOT, J. 1990. *Les milieux "naturels" du globe.* 3rd ed. Masson, Paris. 277 pp.

DUNSON, W.A. 1975. *The Biology of Sea Snakes.* University Park Press, Baltimore, MD. 530 p.

ECHTERNACHT, A. 1978. *Ainsi vivent les amphibiens et les reptiles.* Elsevier-Séquoia, Paris-Brussels. 142 pp.

ERNST, C.H. & BARBOUR, R.W. 1989. *Snakes of Eastern North America.* George Mason University Press, Fairfax, VA. vii + 282 pp.

FERGUSON, M.W.J. Ed. 1984. *The Structure, Development and Evolution of Reptiles.* Academic Press, London, 683 pp.

FITCH, H.S. 1970. Reproductive Cycles in Lizards and Snakes. *Univ. Kansas Mus. Nat. Hist. Misc. Publ.,* 52: 1–247.

FRYE, F. 1991. *Reptile Care. An Atlas of Diseases and Treatments.* Vol. I & Vol. II. T.F.H. Publishing Co., Neptune, NJ. 325 & 311 pp.

GANS, C. 1985. Limbless locomotion. A current overview. Pp. 13–22 *in:* Duncker, H.R. & Fleischer, G. *Functional Morphology of Vertebrates.* Eds. Gustav Fischer Verlag, Stuttgart-New York.

GANS, C. & TINKLE, D.W. 1977. *Biology of the Reptilia.* Vol. 7. *Ecology and behaviour.* A. Academic Press, London. xiii + 720 p.

GANS, C. & DAWSON, W.R. Eds. 1976. *Biology of the Reptilia.* Vol. 5. *Physiology A.* Academic Press, London. xv + 556 pp.

GANS, C. & GANS, K.A. Eds., 1978. *Biology of the Reptilia.* Vol. 8. *Physiology B.* Academic Press, London. xiii + 782 pp.

GANS, C. & POUGH, F.H. Eds. 1982. *Biology of the Reptilia.* Vol. 12. *Physiology C.* Academic Press, London. xv + 536 pp.

GANS, C. & POUGH, F.H. Eds., 1982. *Biology of the Reptilia.* Vol. 13. *Physiology D.* Academic Press, London. xiii + 345 pp.

GANS, C. & HUEY, R.B. Eds. 1988. *Biology of the Reptilia.* Vol. 16. *Defense and Life History.* Alan R. Liss Inc., New York. xi + 659 pp.

GASC, J.P. 1989. L'appareil de la morsure chez les serpents. *In: Serpents, venins, envenimations.* Soc. Herpétol. France, Ed. Marcel Mérieux: 75–87.

GREENE, H.W. & McDIARMID, W.F. 1981. Coral snake mimicry: does it occur? *Science,* 213: 1207–1212.

GRUBER, U. 1992. *Guide des Serpents d'Europe, d'Afrique du Nord et du Moyen-Orient.* Delachaux & Niestlé, Neuchâtel. 248 pp.

GRZIMEK, B. Ed. 1974. *Le Monde Animal.* Tome VI. *Reptiles.* Stauffacher S.A., Zurich. 585 p.

HALLIDAY, T.R. & ADLER, K. 1986. *The Encyclopedia of Reptiles and Amphibians.* Facts-on-File Inc., New York. 144 pp.

KORDONG, K.V. 1980. Evolutionary patterns in advanced snakes. *Amer. Zool.,* 20: 269–282.

KOCHVA, E. 1987. The origin of snakes and evolution of the venom apparatus. *Toxicon,* 25: 65–106.

LE GARFF, B. 1991. *Les Amphibiens et les Reptiles dans leur milieu.* Collection "Ecoguides," Bordas, Paris. 256 pp.

LELOUP, P. 1984. Differents aspects of the breeding of venomous snakes in large scale. Pp. 177–197 *in:* BELS, V. & Van den SANDE, A.P., Eds. *Maintenance and Reproduction of Reptiles in Captivity.* Volume I. Acta Zoologica et Pathologica Antverpiensia No. 78.

LILLYWHITE, H.B. 1987. Temperature, Energetics and Physiological Ecology. Pp. 422–477 *in:* SEIGEL, R.A., COLLINS, J.T. & NOVAK, S.S., Eds. *Snakes. Ecology and Evolutionary Biology.* Macmillan Publ. Co., New York-Turin-London.

LUXMOORE, R., GROOMBRIDGE, B. & BROADS, S. Eds., 1988. *Significant Trade in Wildlife: a Review of Selected Species in CITES Appendix II.* Volume 2: *Reptiles and Invertebrates.* I.U.C.N., Cambridge. xxi + 306 pp.

MARKEL, R.G. 1990. *Kingsnakes and Milk Snakes.* T.F.H., Neptune, NJ. 144 pp.

MATTISON, C. 1986. *Snakes of the World.* Blandford Press, Poole, Dorset. 190 pp.

MATZ, G. 1984. La réproduction des reptiles et les facteurs de son induction. Pp. 33–68 *in:* BELS, V. & Van den SANDE, A.P., Eds. *Maintenance and Reproduction of Reptiles in Captivity.* Volume I. Acta Zoologica et Pathologica Antverpiensia No. 78.

McDOWELL, S.B. 1987. Systematics. Pp. 3–50 *in:* SEIGEL, R.A., COLLINS, J.T. & NOVAK, S.S., Eds. *Snakes. Ecology and Evolutionary Biology.* Macmillan Publ. Co., New York-Turin-London.

MEHRTENS, J. 1987. *Living Snakes of the World in Color.* Sterling Publ. Co., New York. 480 pp.

MURPHY, J.B. & CAMPBELL, J.A. 1987. Captive Maintenance. Pp. 165–181 *in:* SEIGEL, R.A., COLLINS, J.T. & NOVAK, S.S., *Snakes. Ecology and Evolutionary Biology.* Macmillan Publ. Co., New York-Turin-London.

NAULLEAU, G. 1984. Les Serpents de France. *Rev. fr. Aquariol. Herpét.,* 11 (3–4): 1–56.

OBST, F.J., RICHTER, K. & JACOB, U. 1988. *The Completely Illustrated Atlas of Reptiles and Amphibians for the Terrarium.* T.F.H. Pub. Co., Neptune, NJ. 831 pp.

PARKER, H.W. & BELLAIRS, A. 1971. *Les Amphibiens. Les Reptiles* (1st part). La grande Encyclopédie de la Nature, vol. IX. Bordas, Paris-Montréal. 383 pp.

PARKER, H.W. & GRANDISON, A.G.C. 1977. *Snakes: a natural history.* 2nd ed. British Museum of Natural History, London, and Cornell Univ. Press, Ithaca, NY. iv + 108 pp.

PITMAN, C.R.S. 1974. *A Guide to the Snakes of Uganda.* Rev. Ed. Wheldon & Wesley, Codicote. 290 pp.

POPE, C.H. 1935. The Reptiles of China. *Natural History of Central Asia,* X. American Museum of Natural History, New York. LII + 604 pp.

POUGH, F.H. & GROVES, J.D. 1983. Specializations of the body form and food habits of snakes. *Amer. Zool.,* 23: 443–454.

RAGE, J.C. 1984. *Serpentes.* Encyclopedia of paleoherpetology, part 11. Eds. Gustav Fischer Verlag, Stuttgart-New York, xii + 80 pp.

ROSS, R.A. & MARZEC, G. 1990. *The Reproductive Husbandry of Pythons and Boas.* Institute for Herpetological Research, Stanford, CA. 270 pp.

SAINT-GIRONS, H. 1972. Les Serpents du Cambodge. *Mem. Mus. natn. Hist. nat.,* sér. A, Zoologie, 74: 1–170, 42 pls.

SEEGERS, W.H. & OUYANG, C. 1979. Snake venoms and blood coagulation. Pp. 684-749 *in:* LEE, C.V., Ed. *Snake venoms.* Handbook of Experimental Pharmacology, Vol. 52. Springer-Verlag, Berlin. 1130 pp.

STOCKER, K.F. 1990. Composition of snake venoms. Pp. 33–56. *in:* Stocker, K.F., Ed. *Medical Use of Snake Venoms Proteins.* CRC Press, Boca Raton, FL. 272 pp.

UNDERWOOD, G. 1967. *A contribution to the classification of snakes.* Trustees of the British Museum, London. 179 pp.

UNDERWOOD, G. & STIMSON, A.F. 1990. A classification of pythons (Serpentes: Pythoninae). *J. Zool. London,* 221: 565–603.

VILLIERS, A. 1975. *Les Serpents de l'Ouest Africain.* 3rd ed. Initiations et Études Africaines No. 11. Les Nouvelles Éditions Africaines, Dakar, Senegal. 195 pp.

VITT, L.J. 1987. Communities. Pp. 335–365 *in:* SEIGEL, R.A., COLLINS, J.T. & NOVAK, S.S., Eds. *Snake. Ecology and Evolutionary Biology.* Macmillan Publ. Co., New York-Turin-London.

ZINGALI, R. & BON, C. 1992. Les protéines de venin de serpent agissant sur les plaquettes sanguines. *Annales de l'Institut Pasteur. Actualités,* 2: 267–276.

ZUG, G.R. 1993. *Herpetology. An introductory biology of Amphibians and Reptiles.* Academic Press, San Diego, CA. xv + 527 pp.

INDEX TO SCIENTIFIC & COMMON NAMES

The light-face numbers refer to the text, **bold-face** numbers refer to illustrations. Scientific names are in *italics*.
When a name is cited several times over several pages, a range is given, e.g. 157–160.